THE GIRL
in the
TICKET OFFICE WINDOW

BOOK 1
of the Zara timeslip series

Patricia M Osborne

White Wings

Books

Copyright © Patricia M Osborne 2025

All rights reserved.
Published 2025 in Great Britain

by White Wings Books

ISBN978-0-9957107-7-1

No part of this publication may be reproduced, stored in a retrieval system, or transmitted in any form or by any means, electronic, mechanical, photocopy, recording or otherwise, without prior written permission of the copyright owners. Nor can it be circulated in any form of binding or cover other than that in which it is published and without similar condition including this condition being imposed on a subsequent purchaser.

The story, all names, characters, and incidents portrayed in this production are fictitious. No identification with actual persons (living or deceased), places, buildings, and products is intended or should be inferred.

No generative artificial intelligence (AI) was used in the writing of this work.

British Cataloguing Publication data:
A catalogue record of this book is available from the British Library

This book is also available as an ebook

In Memory of

my dearest mum,

Lila (1932-2014)

and

sister,

Heather (1956-2009)

Two courageous and inspiring women

A light went out in my heart when you both left this world

Girl misses train – catches a ride backwards in time

Chapter One

Strobe after strobe of blinding light seared through my eyelids then shattered into a thousand stars. I thought my head would burst. Stunned, I forced myself to reopen my eyes. *What the...?* My jeans and trench coat had gone. Instead, I was dressed in an emerald velvet gown to my ankles. Commuters carrying laptops had disappeared. In their place a few gentlemen in dark suits and bowler hats sauntered over to the platform, swinging large brollies at their sides. I stared up at the unfamiliar glass ceiling. What the hell had just happened?

I moved over to the ticket office window and peered at my reflection. A straw hat topped with flowers and cream feathers in a matching colour to the lace bodice was positioned on my piled-up hair. No sign of the wheeled suitcase either. It was like I'd stepped inside someone's dream. My pulse pounded. There had to be some kind of scientific explanation. I headed back out of the station hoping everything would be as usual but all was far from normal.

The road was empty with not a car in sight. I inhaled clean air. My stomach churned so I covered my mouth to stop throwing up. This couldn't be real. My eyes shot to a little girl in a white smock dress and straw boater perched on a fence. She appeared mesmerised by two young lads in a scuffle. They wore grey tweed flat caps just like my great grandfather had owned. I was losing myself in a history book. I blinked back salty tears. If this was real, supposing I never got back to my own time? Mum and Dad couldn't lose another child. And what would become of Chloe? My sister needed me.

The bridge ahead was blemish free and surrounded by greenery. As if in an early twentieth century movie, a gentleman in Edwardian dress promenaded out of The Fox Inn. His eyes lit up with recognition as he approached. 'Good morning, Lady Rebecca.' He doffed his bowler hat.

Lady Rebecca? Who the hell was I? My name was Zara. Once he'd passed me by I whispered, 'Please God, if there is a god' – I sobbed – 'please help me.'

After stepping off the pavement I witnessed another blinding flash. Disoriented, I stepped back and tripped. A blue Volkswagen almost hit me. The woman driver hooted her horn and raised her fist shouting abuse. The pedestrian man changed to green. As I hurried across the road my ankle boots felt huge on my feet; the court shoes had gone and so had the dress. I was wearing my own twenty-first century clothes and the suitcase rattled on wheels. The bridge was covered in grime and graffiti. The Fox Inn had disappeared and The Fox Revived had returned. Thank goodness I was back in 2023. I gave a sigh of relief. Had I gone through some kind of portal and then back out again?

My heart pulsated as I turned towards Bridge View Station. Avoiding the main entrance in case it sent me back, I slipped in through the side doorway.

Chloe tipped the tea into the cups. 'Here you go, Zara, just as you like it.' She passed me the bone china cup. 'Thanks for bringing my stuff over. I'll unpack shortly so you can take Mum's suitcase back.'

'Thanks, sis.' I glanced around staring into space.

'You okay?'

'Sure.' I took a sip of the drink and screwed up my nose. Chloe may be all domesticated but she'd never learnt to make a good brew. 'You seem happy?' I said.

'I am.' She beamed. 'You don't though. You look miserable. Have you had a row with what's-his-name?'

'Scott. No.'

'What's wrong with you then? I thought the idea of you visiting was to keep me company. With a gob like that you might as well've stayed at home.'

'Sorry.' I peered across at the open window and caught the sound of rushing waves. 'You're so lucky with this place. I'd love to live by the sea.'

'Yeah, we're fortunate that Matt's nan left it to him in her will. We'd never have been able to afford it otherwise. Not on Matt's money.'

I nodded unable to shake off my mood. 'Something weird happened on my way up to you today.'

'Something weird is always happening to you. Look, I asked you here for a reason. Don't make this visit all about you.'

'I wasn't.'

'Sounded like you were and anyway, I've something to tell you.'

'You're not getting a divorce are you?'

'After six months? Course not, silly. Getting married last September was the best thing I'd ever done in my life.'

'But eighteen was so young.'

Chloe frowned. 'Same age as Mum was. But it's not about that, is it? You've never liked Matt.'

'I never liked the idea of him making you give up work to keep house for him, if that's what you mean.'

'He didn't make me. It was my decision. I never had ambitions like you. Just because you're a top editor for a woman's magazine doesn't mean everyone else has to be.'

'I'm not a top editor. But never mind that. We're talking about you. You were brainy at school.'

'Not like you. It didn't interest me. This' – she waved her hands around the room – 'this is all I ever wanted.'

I got up and headed over to the window. 'Fancy a walk along the beach? It looks idyllic out there with the sun on the waves.'

'Only if you promise to get off your high horse.'

'I'll try.'

She picked up the cups and saucers. 'I'll just wash these and then we'll go.'

I walked across and took her arm. 'Leave them. We won't be long.'

'No, I'd rather do them. I like to come back to a clean place.'

'You mean in case he comes home and doesn't like it?'

'Will you stop it?' She rinsed the crockery under the tap. 'Never mind something weird happened to you earlier, you're acting awfully weird right now.'

⁓

We ambled along the pebbled beach. The waves swelled and bashed the rocks before heading back out to sea. I inhaled the salt air. It reminded me about the clean air at Bridge View earlier. Had I imagined it all?

'Let's sit down over there.' Chloe pointed. 'Like I said, there's something I want to talk to you about.'

I lowered myself onto the bench and Chloe took a seat next to me. A seagull flew down, perched on the wooden arm, and glared at us with its near-black eyes.

Chloe laughed. 'Do you reckon he's looking for food?'

'Probably. He's going to be disappointed though as we've got nothing for him.'

Her blue eyes sparkled. 'You know I said I had something to tell you?'

'Yes. What is it?'

'You're going to be an aunty.'

'What?'

The seagull stretched its wings wide and within seconds it was in the air and back down again on the pebbles about ten metres away.

Chloe's smiled dropped. 'Please be happy for me.'

'I am. Of course I am. Congratulations. Does Matt know?'

'Not yet. I only did the test a couple of hours ago. I wanted you to be the first person I told.'

I tried to smile. 'That's lovely. Will Matt be surprised?'

'Yeah, but it'll be a nice surprise. It's what we both want.'

'Then I'm really pleased for you.'

She took me into a hug. 'Thank you. I'm so happy. I can't wait to be a mum. I want about six...'

Supposing what happened to me earlier happened again, only the next time I might not come back. How would Chloe cope without me here to look out for her? I was sure it had really happened but the more I thought about it the more idiotic it seemed.

'...so anyway, I'll have lots to occupy me once this little one's born. Zara?'

'Sorry.'

Chloe tutted. 'I said, once this little one's born I'll have lots to occupy me.'

'When's it due?'

'November? December? I'm sure the midwife will confirm dates.'

'But you won't even be nineteen.'

'I know. Good isn't it? Means I'll be a nice young mum like our mum was when she had you. How do you think she'll feel about being a grandma when she's only forty-three?'

'I don't know.'

'Let's get an ice cream. It might perk you up a bit.'

'Okay.'

Chloe grabbed my hand like when she was a kid and hurried me across to the kiosk. 'What do you fancy? A Magnum?'

'All right but I'll get them.' I took my purse from my bag.

'You sure?'

'Yes.' I pulled a fiver out of the wallet. 'Two Magnums please.'

The curly haired lad passed a lolly to each of us and handed me fifty pence change.

'Cheers.' I strolled away with my sister. 'Keep it close,' I said, 'unless you want that seagull to snatch it out of your hand.'

'Ha ha. No way is that bird getting mine.' She licked the chocolate. 'Mmm. Yummy. I've had a real craving for one of these all morning.'

I smiled.

'Zara, you're still in that faraway place.' She patted my arm. 'Go on then, I'll let you tell me about the weird thing that happened to you.'

I sucked the ice cream. 'All right. Look, this is going to sound a bit far-fetched but...'

'Go on?'

'When I first went into the station at Bridge View...'

'Don't keep me in suspense.'

'Let's sit down.' I guided her over to another bench.

Once we were both seated I said, 'Promise not to laugh.'

'Course I won't.'

'When I headed into the station I somehow travelled back in time. I think I became someone else because although I looked like me, it wasn't me.'

Chloe rolled her eyes. 'What the hell do you mean it wasn't you?'

'I know it sounds implausible but it's true. These clothes' – I pulled at my trousers and top – 'had gone and I was wearing an Edwardian gown.'

She roared with laughter. 'Mum always said you had an overactive imagination. Perhaps instead of being an editor at that magazine you should write for it instead.'

'You promised not to laugh.'

'Sorry, it's just...'

'I'm telling you, it happened. Everywhere was different. Clean. Even the air. And a gentleman smiled at me, doffed his bowler hat, and called me Lady Rebecca. I was scared so I said a prayer and within seconds I was back in our time.'

'Sorry, sis, but you're totally mad. You saying a prayer. You don't even believe in God. Get yourself a decent life instead of inventing one.'

The door slammed as I stabbed a potato with a fork.

'Hey, what's that spud ever done to you.' My flatmate, Holly, hung her red parka on the back of the kitchen chair.

'Don't ask.'

'Come on, I can see you're itching to say something. Getting it off your chest might calm you down a bit.' She drew water from the tap into the kettle and flicked the switch. 'Coffee?'

'Go on then.'

She spooned Nescafé into two mugs. A bone china one for me from a set of two I got at Christmas from Mum and Dad. They were rather gorgeous. Pastel pink with an image of a wild flower.

'That bloody Matt.'

'Your sister's husband again? Here you go.'

'Cheers.' I took the cup. 'Not only did he get her to give up work but now he's got her bloody pregnant.' I picked up another potato. 'Fancy a jacket?'

'Sounds good, thanks.'

I pricked the second potato and put both in the microwave setting the heat for ten minutes on high.

'But that's what your Chloe wanted, wasn't it? I remember her telling me at her hen do that she hoped to get pregnant quickly. Here.' Holly handed me a plastic carton of fruit. 'While we wait for the spuds to cook.'

'Thanks.' I bit into a cube of Galia melon. 'Mmm. I never tire of this. It's my favourite.'

'I know. That's why I picked it up from the supermarket. What's really rattled you?'

There was no way I could tell Holly what was really bothering me. Not after Chloe had made fun of me like that. 'Oh I don't know. Can you believe she wouldn't come for a walk on the beach until she'd washed up two cups. Two cups for god's sake. Didn't want to come back to a mess. I'm not kidding you, the place was immaculate. Like a showhouse even.' I shook my head.

'There's nothing wrong with being houseproud, Zara.' She glanced around at our clutter. 'Not everyone likes to live like this.'

'This is homely, that's all.'

She shrugged. 'Whatever. All I'm saying is that you and Chloe are like chalk and cheese. Your mum keeps a nice tidy home.'

'Yeah, she does, but she's not a teenager, is she?'

'Even so. Look, is there something else worrying you? Have you had a row with Scott?'

'No. Why do people keep asking me that? It's just Chloe. There goes her life. Knee deep in nappies and she won't even be nineteen.'

Holly rested her hand on the back of mine. 'It's not what you'd want but it's obviously what she wants. You have to let her live her life.'

I took a deep breath. 'I suppose so. Good job our Michael isn't around. He'd have had something to say about that, for sure.'

'You still miss him, don't you?'

I squeezed my eyelids. 'Yeah, I do. He was far too young. Bloody drunk driver.' I sipped my drink. 'There's no way Mum and Dad would've let our Chloe marry that Matt if they hadn't been grieving.'

'Didn't you say Matt told your Dad that Chloe was pregnant before they got married?'

'Yes. Bloody liar. Although maybe they thought she was. Who knows?' I took out two knives and forks from the cutlery drawer. Somehow I had to shift this mood. 'Right, enough of this. Are you in tonight?'

'I am indeed.'

'Then how about we curl up in front of the tele and watch a girlie film?'

'Sounds like a plan.'

'I'll miss you once you move out?'

'Move out? What are you talking about?'

'You and Adam, I thought...'

She dashed her hand into the air. 'Don't worry. I've no intention of settling down until I'm at least thirty.'

'Phew.' Yes, it was the right thing not to tell Holly. I needed to sort this out in my own head first. Tomorrow I'd get up early and go back to the station before work. I had to satisfy myself that I wasn't going mad.

Chapter Two

By six o'clock I was up, showered, and managed to grab a quick cup of tea before leaving the flat. I had a meeting at eight so there wasn't much time to make a diversion to the train station. My heart skipped a beat. Did I really want to do this? I had to. How else would I know? I picked up my pace and dashed towards my destination. The sun was blazing although there was a crisp chill in the air. Getting up early had meant I'd been treated to a gorgeous tangerine sky.

The outside of Bridge View station was quiet; another half hour and I was sure it would be full of commuters. Tracing the same steps as yesterday I made for the foyer. Daffodils in large pots bobbed their heads in the breeze. Everything looked normal but supposing it changed again? My heart thumped. No, I couldn't do it. I checked my watch. There wasn't time now anyway if I was to make that meeting at eight. I'd try again tomorrow.

'Nice of you to join us, Miss Wiseman.' Annabel, the editor-in-chief, poured out coffee and shoved a cup in front of me as I sat down. I loved how she dressed in nineteen-seventies fashion. Today she wore a layered gypsy skirt in flowery material, a pink peasant top with puffed sleeves, and despite being fifty-five she was still young looking with a gorgeous figure and blonde wavy hair hanging past her shoulders.

'Thanks. Sorry, Annabel, my tummy was playing up this morning.'

'Are you all right to work? You haven't got a bug, have you? We don't want the whole magazine team down with norovirus or something worse.'

'No, it's nothing like that. Just my nervous tummy.'

'Good. Right, let's get to discussing the content for this month's issue. Scott?'

He winked at me before opening his laptop. Scott was gorgeous and could have any girl he wanted. Smartly dressed, fair hair cut close to his scalp, and an immaculately groomed beard. Why wasn't I ready to commit? It wasn't like I was a teenager like Chloe. I'd be twenty-five in June.

Scott read from the screen. 'I've got three reviews ready. *A French Tragedy* shown at Bluebell Theatre last night, one for *Planet Terror* released last week at the cinema, and finally one for the new local girl band, Aurora.' He closed the lid of his laptop and leaned back in the executive chair.

'Well done, Scott. How about you, Zara?'

'Um.'

'Never mind, we'll come back to you.' Annabel turned to Josh. 'How are you doing on advertising space?'

Josh, a young ginger-haired guy with freckles, fresh from uni, rested back with a smug look. 'Filled for the next three months.' He grinned.

'Well done, Josh. Looks like someone will get his bonus in June. Now' – Annabel glanced around the table – 'we need something new. Something that will bring in more readers. See if we can claim some of the younger market. Ideas anyone?'

The team chatted but my mind was wandering back to the station. I shouldn't have backed out of going in. Now I still didn't know whether it was real or in my mind. And if it was real, would it have been so bad? Exciting surely? I was supposed to be an adventurer so why didn't I embrace the experience instead of running away like a chicken? Tomorrow, I'd try again.

Annabel popped the lid on her fountain pen. 'Well if no one else has anything else to add, we'll leave it at that.'

The clatter of chairs and chatter filled the room as the team dispersed. I stood up to leave but before I'd even got away from the table, Annabel said, 'Not so quick, young lady. Sit back down.'

'Sorry?'

'I said, sit down.'

Scott glanced at Annabel. 'Would you like me to stay?'

'Yes please.' She smiled at him.

I looked to Scott and Annabel before pulling the chair out and slumping back into the seat. 'Look, I said I was sorry for being late.'

'It's not that, Zara. We're concerned about you. Is there something going on that we should know?'

'No, why?'

'Well let's face it, you were hardly with us in the meeting and Scott said you seemed to have been in another world. Are you worried about something?'

I chewed my lip. 'No. My tummy's just been playing up a little, like I said.'

'Well as long as that's all it is. You know my door is always open, don't you? And if you don't want to confide in me, talk to Scott.'

Scott nodded. 'That's right,' he said. 'You know I'm always here for you, babe.'

'I will. Thanks, both of you.'

Annabel rose from her seat, gathered up the pile of papers from the table, and popped her iPhone into her bag. She glared at me. 'Can I at least rely on you to get the edits for this month's issue to me by end of play today?'

'Of course.' I waited for my boss to leave before getting up.

Scott was at my side. He put his arms around me. 'You sure you're okay, darling?'

'I'm sure.'

He dropped his arms. 'Am I seeing you tonight?'

'Can we see how today goes? To be honest I'm feeling pretty drained.'

'As long as you're not going off me.' He picked up his laptop briefcase, swung it across his shoulder and followed me out of the room.

⚜

Holly was already in Double Dee's coffee shop when I arrived.

I flopped into the brown leather sofa. 'Sorry I'm late. Annabel collared me as I was leaving.'

'No worries. I've ordered us each a cheese and pickle sarnie.'

'Coffee too, I hope.'

'Of course. Here comes Dave now. God, any woman would die for hair like his.'

'Shh,' I said, 'he'll hear you.'

'Afternoon, ladies. How are you two today?'

'Good thanks, Dave. How are you?'

Dave and his husband Dan ran the coffee shop. I liked that it was independent rather than one of the big chains as that meant we got personal service, luxurious sofas with scatter cushions, homemade food, and the most delicious coffee. It was the only one like it in Bridge View.

Dave brushed his blond curly locks away from his forehead. 'Can't complain, you know?' His rich blue eyes sparkled. He was gorgeous. Shame he was married and gay as I swear I could've fallen for him. His partner Dan wasn't much of a looker but he had the most gentle manner. They both did really.

Dave popped the tray down onto the table. 'Bon appetit, girls.'

'Cheers,' we answered almost in unison.

'You left early this morning?' Holly took a bite of her sandwich.

'I had a meeting.'

'Ah. Wondered if that might be the case. Go okay?'

'Depends how you define okay. I was late this morning and Annabel didn't seem that happy with me.'

'How come? Did you go somewhere else first?' Holly licked her lips. 'This bread's yummy. I love how they make it themselves.'

'Yeah, me too. I popped into the station as I'd misplaced my purse and thought someone may have handed it in.'

'And had they?'

'No.' I gave a small laugh. 'Would you believe I found it in my handbag when I was asking the woman behind the glass? So embarrassing.'

Holly nudged me. 'What are you like? Hey guess who I saw the other day?'

'No idea. Who?'

'Emma, our course leader from the MA. When we were chatting she seemed surprised that you weren't writing for the magazine. Said she'd been checking the mag for stories by you.'

'Why?'

'Because you're such a good writer.'

'No better than you and you're not writing.'

'Our degree results said otherwise. For me it was more of a hobby but you have real talent, Zara. You should speak to your boss. See what she says.'

'Nah. I'm happy as I am.'

'What do you reckon then, sweetheart?' Scott brushed his lips against mine. 'Are we on for tonight?'

'Actually, hun, do you mind if we leave it? I didn't sleep that well last night and all I feel like doing is going home for a bath and crashing early.'

'You do remember I've got that conference Wednesday for three nights?'

'I'd forgotten about that.'

'So we're on for tonight?'

'Sorry.'

'You're not blowing me off, are you?'

'No, it's nothing like that.' I reached across and kissed him. 'I've just a lot going on in my head right now.'

'All right, as long as it's not me. I'll go out for a pint with the lads then and when I get back from the conference we'll set up a time to go for a meal at that new Italian in town. I've been itching to try it out plus Annabel's asked me to review it.'

'It's a date.'

Chapter Three

It had been days since I was last at the station and I needed to get back there to check out whether what had happened was real or in my imagination. I was careful to take the exact route I'd taken before. As I reached Bridge View village my heart gave a little hammer. Would I be brave enough to go into the station when I got there? I was filled with trepidation, the adventurer in me telling me to go for it while the chicken was backing me away. I saw the headlines. *First Woman to Time Travel* or *Woman Sectioned for Thinking she could Time Travel*. Chloe was wrong, I was sure of it. It wasn't my vivid imagination. It had happened.

I took my time sauntering through the bridge trying to avoid the dirt and graffiti that plastered the dark stonework. When I reached the traffic lights the road was quiet. The red man turned green and I wandered across the crossing and into the station foyer where it was business as usual with a few early commuters checking their mobiles but not busy enough that I couldn't move about freely. I hung around waiting. Nothing happened. I headed for Platform 2. Still nothing. So it had been in my imagination. I'd just breathed a sigh of relief when once again I was blinded by a bright light. I held the sides of my head to stop the pressure until eventually the flash burst into tiny clusters and I was able to reopen my eyes.

Bloody hell, it had happened again. I was dressed in a gold ruffled silk gown. Why had I put myself in this situation? I tried to breathe slowly in order to stop the panic. Last time I'd returned to my own time so there was no reason why I shouldn't again. Maybe I'd even get to delve a little further whilst I was here. Going by the dress I was wearing, I was obviously well off. I hurried over to the ticket office sash window to check my reflection. Today I wore a different hat. A wide brim with a gold ribbon matching the gown. With my legs turning to jelly, I made towards the exit as I'd done before.

Straight ahead was The Fox Inn where I crossed the road. The same little girl I'd seen the other day was sitting by the picket fence scraping mud from the ground with her fingers. She wiped the dirt across her face making her look like a right little urchin. I wondered whose daughter she was.

Panic hit me as heavy footsteps approached behind me.

'Rebecca. Wait.'

I turned around and came face to face with a handsome gentleman most likely in his late twenties dressed in a dark checked suit. The jacket was long and the shirt had a high collar boasting a bow tie. Blond hair curled across his brow, wispy sideburns peeped from under a bowler hat, and a cute little tache made his lips appear thicker. I offered a nervous smile.

'Sister dear. I was on my way to find you. We will walk together.' He hooked his arm in mine.

My heart drummed faster as we stopped at a high, arched metal gate with Bridge View Hall etched in gold. The gentleman pushed the gate open revealing a massive house ahead. He guided me along a path with flower beds either side where red and yellow tulips swayed. 'An acquaintance of mine is coming down from London this afternoon especially to meet you.'

I frowned. The house was in clear view now. It had church-like tall windows with decorative corbels, a curved doorway, several chimneys, and patterned bricks around the eaves.

'I know, I know,' he continued, 'you keep saying you don't need a husband but sister dear, you've been widowed now for more than two years and the villagers expect you to remarry.' The gentleman knocked on the heavy wooden door.

My pulse pounded. I clenched my fists. There was no way I wanted to go through that door. The idea filled me with dread. If I went in there I wasn't sure I'd come back out again.

I wanted to run but my feet were stuck. Instead I blinked, the familiar light flashed and swam for a moment before shattering, and when I re-opened my eyes I was back in my own clothes standing outside a derelict mansion. I peered up at the roof with its missing tiles. Its chimneys were smashed and the windows were empty of glass. With my heart still hammering I tried to make sense of it all. There was no way I'd imagined what had just happened. The guy said he was my brother. I peered down at my clothes again to reassure myself. Yes, I was wearing my own skirt, blouse, and high heeled shoes. I shook my head. No, I hadn't imagined it. I had to go back again but wasn't sure when. Was this some kind of devilry? What would Mum and Dad, regular churchgoers, make of this? I reasoned with myself that this was a scientific experiment. If only I had someone I could trust to share this with. Someone who wouldn't think I should be sectioned. After all, would I have acted any differently if Chloe or Holly had told me my story? I feared not.

Relieved to be back in my own time, I wondered why this former magnificent building had been left to rot like this. Lady Rebecca. Was she an ancestor of mine? We looked identical and her brother had mistaken me as her. So many questions I didn't have answers for.

The traffic was building up. Horns hooted and tyres screeched as I made my way to work wondering how I was going to get through the day.

After pressing *send* I closed down my computer and headed to my boss's office. I knocked on the door.

'Come.'

'Afternoon, Annabel. Just to let you know that I've emailed you the edits on the new guy's article. It's good. I think you'll like it.'

'Thanks, Zara.' She took off her square reading glasses. The dark frames contrasted with her blonde waves. 'Thanks for getting that done so quickly. How are you finding working with Jack Simmons?'

'All right. His work barely had any errors, and he's easy to get on with.'

'I thought he'd fit in well with the team. Scott will have to watch himself with the standard Jack's showing.' She glanced up at me. 'Better not let on to Scott what I just said.'

'I won't, don't worry.' I chuckled.

Annabel tapped the desk. 'Have you got five minutes?'

'Er. Yes.'

'Good. Before you sit down, pour us both a coffee.'

I headed to the coffee pot on the cupboard by the window, and tipped the jug into two mugs trying to avoid spilling the contents. Annabel had hers black with no sugar like me so there was no need to worry about milk. I carried the drinks over. 'What is it you'd like to speak to me about?' I sank into the soft chair opposite my boss. My legs trembled as I wondered why she wanted to talk to me.

'Nothing really. Just a catch-up. Anything planned for this weekend?'

'Mum and Dad have invited me over to tea on Sunday.'

'Scott too?'

'Yeah, as far as I know. He's back from the conference late this evening.'

'How are things going with you two?'

I squinted, confused why she was asking that. 'Same old. You know?'

'We won't be hearing wedding bells anytime soon then?'

'No way.'

'I see.' She pressed her lips tightly together. 'You've been together for a while now.'

'Almost three years.'

'This isn't going to get messy now, is it?'

I frowned. 'Why would it?'

'Well it's obvious to one and all that Scott has strong feelings for you.'

I shook my head. 'No he doesn't,' I lied, 'we're casual. He knows that.'

'Just be careful. I don't want to lose either of you from the firm. You're both my top team members.' She took a deep breath. 'This is why I discourage employees from dating each other.'

I rose from my seat and leaned forward on the desk. 'Honestly, Annabel, you're worrying unnecessarily. I promise.'

She rested back in the chair. 'Well I hope so. Have a good weekend and make sure you give that man of yours some quality time.'

Scott pulled up outside in his red Porsche. I slammed the flat door closed and hurried downstairs to meet him. He stretched across the passenger seat to click open the door.

'How was the conference?' I asked as I sank into the luxurious black bucket seat.

'Good. Shame you didn't come. The hotel room was to die for. You and me could've had some interesting nights' – he winked – 'if you know what I mean.'

I laughed. 'None of that talk in front of my mum and dad if you don't mind.'

'You know me, babe' – he planted a kiss on my lips before driving away – 'always on my best behaviour.'

'Hmm, yes, I do know you. That's what I'm worried about.'

Scott pressed a button on the dashboard and Miley Cyrus blasted from the speaker. He took the corner far too quickly causing the tyres to screech.

'Oi. Slow down, will you? I'd like to arrive at my parents' house in one piece.'

He relaxed the accelerator pedal, put his foot on the brake, and parked up by the kerb. 'Sorry. I got carried away. Look, Zara, are we okay?'

'Yes, why?'

He glared at me with his big brown eyes. 'You've been kind of distant lately.'

I playfully slapped his hand. 'Nothing to do with you, babe. It's just me. Like I said there's a lot going on. Worried about my kid sister too.'

'Chloe? Why?'

'She's pregnant.'

'Good god. She's still a kid herself.'

'I know. Don't say anything though as I'm sworn to secrecy although I've a feeling they could be making an announcement today at tea.' I checked my watch. 'We should go. You know how my mum hates me to be late. She'll be getting anxious in case anything's happened to me.'

'Sorry. I'll drive more carefully.' He pressed the ignition and drove away smoothly.

Scott pulled up outside my parents' detached house. They really should've downsized now there was just the two of them but they wouldn't leave. Said it held too many memories. They'd been planning on selling up before Michael's death two years ago but afterwards refused to sell. My brother's room was done out like a shrine. It was too sad. Twenty-one and full of hopes and all gone because of one drunk driver.

I turned the key in the lock. The clatter of dishes greeted us as we entered the hallway. 'Hiya,' I called.

Mum rushed to the door quickly, removing her apron, and twinkling her eyes at Scott.

'Good afternoon, Mrs Wiseman,' he said, 'how's my favourite lady?'

Mum hunched her shoulders almost up to her chin. 'Get off with you. Now why would you be interested in an old biddy like me with a gorgeous girl on your arm like our Zara? Come on in. You too, darling.' She kissed me on the cheek. 'Chloe's already here with Matthew. They've got some big news to announce.'

I smiled. 'I can't wait.'

'Can you pass the salad, please, Zara?' Matt glared at me.

I pushed the large wooden bowl towards him. Using the tongs, he served himself a large helping of iceberg lettuce, sliced tomatoes, cucumber and radishes. Mum certainly knew how to make a nice salad and it went perfectly with the stuffed couscous peppers. Our parents had brought us all up as vegetarians. That worked well with Scott too although Matt was a meat eater. Not today though at Mum's table. I smiled to myself. There was no way Mum would have meat, or fish for that matter, in her house. I wondered if Matt had tried converting Chloe to become a carnivore. My stomach turned as I thought about last time we all went out to a restaurant and the piece of steak he'd ordered arrived oozing with blood on the plate. Yuk.

'Zara' – Mum stood up from the table and stacked the plates – 'are you all right, love?'

'Yes, sorry. Just a new project I'm working on taking over my mind.'

'Well, while you're here, darling,' Dad said, 'can you stay with us, please? Your mother's worked hard to make today a nice family day.' He turned to Chloe. 'Anyway your sister has an announcement.' His eyes sparkled as he gazed at Mum. 'Put the dishes down, love, and let our daughter tell us what we're here for.'

Mum retook her seat, grinning. 'Chloe?'

Chloe turned to Matt. He took her hand. 'Go on, babe,' he prompted.

'Mum, Dad, you're going to be a grannie and grandad.'

A tear fell to Mum's cheek. Wiping away the droplet, she sobbed. 'I knew it. Oh darling, thank you. This is just what your father and I need.' She looked across at Dad. 'We can turn one of the bedrooms into a nursery. We're happy to be babysitters, aren't we, Tim?'

Good god, I couldn't believe my ears. They were all over being grandparents. Couldn't they see that Chloe was still a child?

'If only our Michael were here to see his little sister become a mother.' Mum sniffled. 'He'd have been a great uncle.'

'Yes, he would have,' Dad said.

'If only we hadn't given him the money to buy that motorbike for his twenty-first.' Mum blew her nose. 'If only we could change things.'

'Mum' – I got up from the table and put my arm around her shoulders – 'it wasn't your fault. The only person to blame was the bastard driving the car under the influence of alcohol. Michael had a right to ride a motorbike if that's what he wanted. That despicable human being, however, had no right to do what he did. I hope to god he rots in jail.'

'Now, now, Zara.' Dad pulled me away from Mum. 'Your mother doesn't need to hear all that now. This is a celebration. You're going to be an aunty. This is good news.'

Matt was smoking on a bench by the fish pond. He glanced up as I headed over. 'Hiya there.'

'Hi.' I took a seat next to him. 'Those Koi carp are gorgeous, aren't they?'

'They are.' He flicked his ash.

'Oi, careful not to flick that into the fish. Anyway, you'll have to give the fags up now with a baby coming along.'

'Yeah, I will. Not going to be easy though.'

'Nevertheless if my sister can give up having a drink and go through nine months of pregnancy the least you can do is stop smoking.'

His eyes narrowed. 'What is it with you? You really don't like me, do you?'

I gave a small laugh. 'You've noticed.'

'Why? What the hell have I ever done to you to make you dislike me so much? Or is it that you're jealous?'

'Jealous. You've got to be kidding me.'

'Then what?' He stubbed the cigarette out into the metal lid.

'I don't like the way you control my sister.'

'Control? What are you talking about?'

I took a deep breath. 'Making her give up work once you were married for starters.'

He slammed his hand down on the bench. 'You don't know what the feckin hell you're talking about. I didn't make her give up work. It was her choice.'

'And of course you don't like her being at home at your beck and call.'

'Yes, I like her being at home, because that's what she wants, but not at my beck and call.'

I clenched my fists. 'Then how come you won't let her help with your accounts?'

'Because she doesn't know how to do them. And what am I supposed to say to the woman who's been doing them since the business started. You expect me to sack her?'

'Course not. But what about Chloe being too frightened to leave two dirty mugs on the draining board in case you think she's keeping a bad house.'

He shook his head. 'I'm not sitting here listening to any more of this drivel.' He twisted his index finger into the side of his head. 'You're in cloud cuckoo land, girl. I think losing your brother must've turned your brain.'

Chapter Four

One result popped up on the screen when I typed Bridge View Hall into the search engine. The property was up for auction next month. I tapped my lip. Surely there should be something more. Something to explain why it had been allowed to get into its derelict state.

Someone touched the back of my chair. I spun around. 'Bloody Hell, Scott. You made me jump.'

'Sorry. I didn't mean to give you a fright.'

'That's what happens when you creep up behind someone.' I closed the tabs on the internet browser.

'You seemed engrossed. What you up to?'

'Nothing much.' I took a deep breath. 'Actually, you know that big old house in Bridge View opposite the train station?'

He squinted. 'Big house?'

'The rundown one.'

'Oh you mean Bridge View Hall? The building with barely a roof?'

'Yes, that's the one. What do you know about it?'

'Not a lot. Only that it's been in that state for as long as I can remember. Why the interest?'

'It's going up for auction.'

'About time they did something with it.' He chuckled. 'You thinking of making a bid?'

'Maybe,' I joked. 'No, of course not, but I wouldn't mind a nosey around the site. Fancy coming with me?'

'Why would you want to explore a load of old rubble?'

'It's more than that and you know it. It's still beautiful, and I reckon there's likely to be a lot of historical facts around it.'

'I suppose I was being a little harsh there. It was likely a stunning structure in its time and if it makes my girl happy then sure, of course I'll come with you. I take it they're offering viewings ahead of the sale?'

'That's what the post on the search engine said.' I clicked the start button on the screen and closed down the PC.

Scott rubbed his beard. 'When did you want to go?'

'This evening?'

'Aren't we already going out to dinner with Holly and Adam?'

'Yes, but we could do this first.'

He rolled his eyes. 'If that's what you'd like to do.'

'Well if you'd rather not, I can easily go on my own, and meet you all at the restaurant.'

Scott put his arm around me. 'Hey, what gives, Zara? I said I'll come. It just seemed a strange request, that's all.'

'Sorry. I suppose it is but you know how I've always been interested in old buildings and seeing this up for auction, well, I'm just curious.'

'You know what curiosity did, don't you?'

'Fine. I'll go by myself if you're going to be like that.'

'Hey' – he rubbed his fingers across the top of my arm – 'I'm just jesting. Okay?'

'Okay.'

He bent his head and kissed me on the lips prickling my chin. 'It's time to knock off now anyway.'

'I know. That's why I closed down my computer.' I rose from the chair.

'I'd better go and do the same. Tell you what, I'll see you outside in' – he peered up at the clock on the wall – 'fifteen mins?'

'Brilliant.' I wrapped my arms around his neck. 'You're the best.'

'I know. And don't you forget it.' He winked.

'I won't. See you shortly.'

Scott headed out of the door and I packed away the files on my desk. At first I'd been irritated with him interrupting me but viewing the house was a much better idea. Hopefully I'd get some answers. Something which would confirm I wasn't going mad.

※

Scott pulled up outside Bridge View Hall. I got out of the car and peered over the crooked iron gates.

He followed me. 'Are you sure someone's here today?'

'Well, no. But the post gave this address for viewings and enquiries. And look' – I pointed to the overgrown grass – 'they've made a footpath. That's new. Therefore it must be okay.'

'Not necessarily.' He pushed open the creaking gate, took my hand and led me along the trail.

I thought back to that other time when I'd wandered arm in arm with Rebecca's brother. He seemed a nice gentleman. I wondered what his name was. As Scott and I treaded up the pathway there were no flowerbeds with nodding tulips or any other bloom for that matter. The trees were still there but taller. Branches bashed the derelict structure.

On reaching the front entrance Scott tapped the oak wood door. 'At least this is still intact.' He peered up at the glassless windows. 'Wonder what the new owners will do with this place.'

'They need to get a buyer first. Do you think they will?'

'Someone will buy it. A builder, or maybe a young, urban professional from London.'

'I imagine it must be listed. What do you think?'

'Looking at those decorative corbels, I'd say so.'

'At least that means they can't demolish it. Maybe they'll turn it into an executive apartment complex with a gym and swimming pool for the residents.'

Scott raised his eyebrows. 'Maybe.'

'Or possibly a spa hotel. That would be nice, wouldn't it?'

'Make for a nice wedding venue.' He grinned.

'I'm sure it would but even better for a girlie spa day.'

'Whatever they do, I reckon they'll have their work cut out with a conversion. I mean, look at the state of it. And I wasn't wrong in my comment about it being absent a roof.'

'I wonder why they let it get to this condition. Such a shame.' I peered up at the church like windows. Even without glass they still held their beauty. That was it. I made up my mind to try to get back through the portal so I could see what the house had been like inside. It must've been magnificent in its day. My heart quickened at the thought of travelling again through time. But I knew I must. 'Be an adventurer, Zara,' I whispered.

'What's that, babe?'

'Nothing. Just thinking aloud.'

'Oh right. Well let's have a nosey around the back and see if we can find someone.' Scott headed along the cleared path, his feet crunching on the newly placed gravel.

I followed him. 'Wow. Check out that purple.'

Before Scott could comment about the mass of dog-violet in front of us, footsteps squeaked from behind. We turned around to a stocky man in a navy vintage suit.

'We were just coming to find you,' Scott said.

'Good evening.' He studied the screen on his iPad before making eye contact with Scott. 'You must be Mike. I'm Bob from the agency.'

'No, actually, I'm not. We heard this place was open for viewing so thought we'd pop down on the off chance.'

Bob rubbed his bald head. 'I'm sorry but you can't just turn up without an appointment. You'll have to phone the office and book a time.' His gaze moved towards the side fence as a grey car pulled up. 'Looks like that's my viewer now' – he held an arm out to his side – 'so if you don't mind.'

'Sure.' Scott took my hand. 'Come on love.'

I let him lead me out of the grounds in silence. As we reached the Porsche and climbed in, Scott said, 'Well that wasn't like you. What happened there? You never said a word.'

'Well considering that big guy blanked me, I didn't really get the chance. Rude or what.'

'I'm sure that wasn't the case.'

'It absolutely was. I reckon he's a right stuck up chauvinist in his nineteen-sixties or seventies suit and squeaky black shoes. I mean who wears a getup like that these days?'

'Not worth getting upset over, sweetheart. Anyway, if you want to view we'd better make sure we book first. We'll need to think up a plan though as they're not going to want to be showing around time wasters. Perhaps I could say I'm doing an article for the magazine.' Scott pushed the ignition button on the dashboard and drove us away from Bridge View Hall.

The new Italian restaurant, Filippos, was the only lit up shopfront in the precinct. Holly and Adam waved from an inside window.

'Oh look' – I pointed – 'they're here.'

Scott glanced at his iPhone. 'Well, at least we're not late. Although how we've managed to get here on time is beyond me.'

'Are you angry with me?'

'What makes you think that?'

'The way you just spoke.'

'Nope, I'm hungry, that's all. What with skipping lunch because I had a meeting and then going straight to the site from work, I've not eaten since this morning.'

'Sorry, hun. I hadn't realised.' I pushed open the door and headed in. 'Cool.' Rectangular dining tables covered in white cloths contrasted with black-cushioned chairs. Ambient lighting offered a relaxing venue. 'Looks posh.'

A young woman peered up from the podium. 'Good evening. Do you have a booking?' Her dark brown eyes sparkled. Not only did she have stunning eyes but eyebrows set just right, a cute nose, and plump lips with the corners turned up. Her diamond drop earrings reflected the light.

'Yes,' I answered, 'in the name of Wiseman but I see our friends' – I signalled across to Holly and Adam – 'are already here. Is it okay if we go through?'

'Of course. I'll give you these and be over shortly to take your order.' She passed us each a menu.

'Cheers.' Scott followed me.

'Hi, guys.' I slipped into the seat opposite Holly. 'Isn't that waitress gorgeous?'

'You noticed too?' Holly laughed. 'Adam couldn't keep his eyes off her.'

'Oi.' Adam nudged Holly. 'That's not true.'

'Yes, it is. Not that I blame you. The girl's dynamite. Wish I looked like that.'

'Scott made sure he got an eyeful too.'

'No, I didn't.' He sank into the seat next to me. 'You know I only have eyes for you.'

Holly put a hand to her mouth. 'Someone pass me the sick bucket quick.'

Scott tutted. 'You girls. Sometimes...' He buried his head in the menu. 'Let's sort out what we want to order.'

Holly rolled her eyes. 'Get him, grumpy or what?'

'Leave him alone.' I rubbed Scott's arm. 'He's not eaten all day because he's been helping me out.'

'Oh aye?' Holly tittered.

I tapped her hand. 'Not like that.'

Adam picked up the menu. 'I'm pretty hungry too. I think I'll have a marguerita.'

Holly leaned closer to him. 'Shall we share, babe?'

'Sorry, angel, but I'm famished. If you can't eat a whole one you can always ask the girl to put the remainder in a box to take home.'

'Yeah, suppose so. Unless...' She glared at me.

'Not unless you fancy sharing a diavola?'

She shook her head. 'No thanks, that's the spicy one with hot peppers, isn't it?'

'Yep.' I laughed. 'My favourite.'

'I'll have a diavola too.' Scott put the menu down. 'Wine, ladies?'

I studied the wine list. 'A rosé would be nice. What do you think, Holl?'

'That suits me.'

'And I'll have a beer.' Scott passed the drinks list to Adam.

'You're okay, dude. I'll have a beer too.'

The waitress headed our way. The red uniform contrasted with her black hair. 'You folks ready to order?' She smiled.

'Yes, thanks.' I glanced up at her name badge. 'A diavola for me, but can you make it vegetarian please, Francesca?'

'We can do that.' She tapped into her iPad.

'Can you make that two vegetarian diavolas, please?' Scott asked.

'And two margheritas?' Holly said.

The waitress continued to tap our drinks order into the iPad. 'Okay,' she said, 'your meals won't be long but in the meantime I'll bring over the drinks.' She sashayed towards the kitchen.

'Oi.' Holly nudged Adam. 'Stop looking.'

'Ow. That hurt. Stop nudging me or I'll nudge you back.'

'Now now, children.' Scott drummed his fingertips on the table. 'Zara, are you going to tell these two what we've been up to?'

'Could do, I suppose. Not sure they'll find it that interesting though.' I found myself thinking about the mansion and how I longed to be inside. I wished I could go back this minute while I was feeling strong. Scott staying over this weekend meant there'd be no opportunity until after work on Monday.

❧

Holly struggled to get the key in the lock.

'Here, let me.' I turned the key and leaned on the door to open it. Holly and Adam pushed past and staggered into the hallway. They'd both had far too much to drink. Scott and I followed them in.

'We're heading straight to bed.' Holly took Adam's hand and pulled him along the corridor to her room. The door slammed as we reached the kitchen.

'Coffee.' I filled the kettle.

Scott twisted me around, placed his arms around my neck, and pressed his lips hard on mine. 'Or we could skip coffee and go straight to bed.'

'If you don't want coffee I might as well forget this.' I flicked the kettle switch off.

'Coffee will keep you awake all night. Apart from the fact' – he smothered my neck with kisses – 'isn't this what you want too? It's been ages since we had some proper time together.'

The scent from his aftershave made me feel sexy. 'Sure, why not.' I let him lead me into the bedroom and we dropped onto my bed. Scott smothered my neck and shoulders with kisses. I unbuttoned his shirt, threw off my top and slipped off my skirt.

'This is what I've been waiting to do all day.' He moved his lips down my naked body.

After making love, I snuggled into Scott's chest feeling his heartbeat. What was wrong with me? He was every girl's dream. Not only handsome, but attentive, romantic, and loyal. Although I'd accused him of looking at that glamorous waitress in the restaurant, I knew quite well that he'd barely glanced at her, so why couldn't I say those three magic words he wanted to hear? What was lacking in our relationship? I couldn't have a more considerate lover. Was he too safe and I needed danger? Was that why I longed to be inside that house?

'Don't you love me even a teeny bit?' Scott kissed the top of my arm.

I curled up facing the window so he could cuddle up to me. 'I love us.'

'I don't mind waiting but you will tell me if I'm wasting my time?' He ran his fingers through my hair.

'I will.'

'Think I'll try and get some kip. You should too. It's been a long day.'

'Okay. Night, darling.'

He flipped over, facing away from me. 'Sleep well, baby,' he mumbled.

In what seemed only minutes his body rose up and down under the covers in a slow rhythm as he snored. After a while and unable to sleep, I slid out of bed, put on my dressing gown, and headed over to the window. A full moon and stars broke the blackness of the sky. I mulled over Scott's words. If I told him he was wasting his time he'd be gone. How would I feel without him in my life? The thought made my stomach churn. I didn't want to lose him. Did that mean I loved him but didn't know what love was? Maybe after my adventure I'd be ready to commit. That was it. I'd definitely go back to the house after work on Monday.

Chapter Five

At last the day was over. I trudged out of the office into the warm air. Scott made me jump when he suddenly appeared. 'You've got to stop doing that.' I laughed.

'Oops, I do apologise. I never meant to creep up on you. I just wanted to check that I definitely can't tempt you to spend the evening with me?'

'Sorry, darling, but I need some quiet time in front of the tele.'

'I can be quiet.'

'I need time on my own. Sorry.'

'Okay. I give in, but only if you're still up for tomorrow.'

'Tomorrow?'

He sighed. 'You've forgotten, haven't you? You said you'd come to watch that band, Dark Chaos.'

'Oh yes, I had forgotten but no, that's fine, I'll come with you. Aren't they those old codgers from the seventies?'

Scott laughed. 'Yeah. They're reuniting for a tour.'

'Hobbling across the stage no doubt.'

'Possibly.' Scott stroked my cheek. 'Let's do dinner straight from here and then on to the theatre.'

'Sounds good.'

'Great. It's a date then.'

'It's a date.' I put my arms around him and gave him a long passionate kiss. 'See you in the morning.'

He dangled his keys. 'Sure I can't tempt you with a lift home?'

'No thanks. I need the exercise.'

'Okey dokes.' He headed across the car park.

Commuters huddled out of the station and climbed into cars. Hopefully that was the rush hour finished. As I moved forward to the entrance, a lad on one of those e-scooters almost knocked me over. I shook my head. 'Watch where you're going.'

He turned around and stuck two fingers up at me.

'Rude sod,' I muttered under my breath and headed inside the foyer. Luckily it was almost empty. I paced backwards and forwards but nothing happened. I sighed. It must've been in my imagination. But then why had it happened twice? No, it must've been real. I moved towards Platform 2 and the next moment there was the flash. The pressure hit me, taking me a few seconds to gain my balance. Where was I? This wasn't the railway station.

Confused I glanced around. I was in the back garden of Bridge View Hall. I recognised it from when Scott and I had visited the site. Green velvet fabric brushed my ankles. I peered down at my gown. At least I was dressed, unlike Audrey Niffenegger's Henry DeTamble who arrived naked when he time travelled. I touched my head to try and work out what kind of hat I was wearing. A wide brim. Maybe flowers on top.

Shuffling footsteps came from behind disturbing my thoughts.

'There you are, sister.' Rebecca's brother twisted me around to face him. 'The garden is beautiful this time of year, is it not? Shall we stroll?'

I looked up at him, smiled and answered, hoping I sounded like Rebecca. 'Yes, brother, that's a lovely idea. I'd like that.'

'Excellent.' He took my arm and guided me down the lawn pathway, halting at a bed of peonies in bloom boasting a variety of colours, pink, red, orange, yellow and white. The red was a brilliant crimson like the one Mum and Dad had in their garden. 'What do you think of this spread, sister? Our gardener has done us proud, has he not?'

'They're beautiful.' I bent down to sniff a flower. 'It's delightful,' I said, hoping I answered the way Rebecca would. 'This one has a hint of lemon.'

He took a sniff. 'It does indeed. Come, let us sit for a while.' He took my arm again and continued along the path. This time it was me who stopped when we reached a mass of small mid-blue flowers on tall stems. 'These are wonderful.' A hint of an earthy smell reached my nose.

'You always say that. I swear the cornflower is your favourite. Come. Let's rest. I need to speak to you.'

As he continued to lead me to the bench a rush of running water caught my ear. I twisted around to a large stone three tiered cascading water fountain.

'The gardener fixed it earlier today. It's as good as new now, is it not?' Rebecca's brother led me to a fancy metal seat with curvy arms.

I took the seat next to him. 'It's wonderful.'

'You haven't forgotten Sir Richard's coming this evening?'

Sir Richard. He was the gentleman that was mentioned before. The suitable husband. Was this another visit or had time stayed still here? 'No, brother. I haven't forgotten. I'm looking forward to our meeting.'

He rested his fingertips on the back of my hand. 'It's important you make a good impression.'

I wanted to ask why but instead just smiled. 'I will.'

'Good.' He gazed up at the grey clouds. 'It looks like rain. We should hurry inside as you do not wish to get a chill. Come, Mary's waiting to help you dress. It's vital you look your best.' He retook my arm and led me past the cornflowers, past the peonies, and past a striking magenta rhododendron bush close to the front of the mansion. He tapped the large brass knocker on the immaculate oak door. Butterflies danced in my stomach. I was finally going to see what the house was like inside.

Before the door opened a flash caused me to blink and when I reopened my eyes I found myself back in the station foyer struggling to stand upright.

A porter came over and touched my arm. 'Are you all right, miss?'

I managed to say, 'I'm not sure. I'm feeling rather...'

He led me to a seat. 'Sit here for a while.' He disappeared but in a moment was back with a paper cup, the type used in vending machines. 'Drink this. It will help.'

'Thank you' – I sipped the sweet tea – 'you're very kind.'

'Have you eaten?'

'No.'

'Wait one moment.' He charged off again and this time returned with a chocolate bar. 'Eat this.' He passed me a KitKat. 'I hope you're not one of those young women always on a diet.'

'No.' I gave a small laugh as I unwrapped the chocolate biscuit and took a bite hoping it would stop me feeling jittery.

'Would you like me to call someone for you?'

'No thanks. I'm sure I'll be fine in a minute. I'm probably just hungry as I skipped lunch.'

'You young ladies.' He shook his head. 'You must look after yourself. If you're sure you're okay, I'd better get back as the six-fifteen's due in five minutes.'

'I'm fine, thank you.' I continued to nibble on the chocolate as the porter headed to the platform.

It wasn't fair. I hadn't panicked so why had I been sent back? Maybe there was a time limit on how long I could stay there for. Would I ever get to see inside the house? I'd try to make it happen again but not today as I was too drained. I leaned back on the bench mulling things over as the station foyer emptied.

The porter re-appeared. 'You still here, dear? You sure you don't want me to call someone for you?'

'No. I'm going now.' I staggered up from the seat. 'Thank you for your help and kindness.'

'No worries. I've got a daughter and I'd hope if she were ever in trouble that some kind soul would help her. You take care now.'

'Thanks.' I wandered out of the side door and headed home with my legs still wobbly. Why did I feel this way? Were the timeslips weakening me?

Holly opened the door as I reached the flat. 'I saw you coming from the window. What happened? You look dreadful.'

I stumbled into the hallway. 'I don't know. Think it must be some kind of bug. I'll go straight to bed if you don't mind.'

'No, of course. Want me to bring you something?'

'No, ta. Just want to sleep.' I made for my room, flopped on the bed and closed my eyes.

※

My stomach rumbled. I turned over and flicked on the bedside lamp. 20:45 glowed green on the digital clock. I shivered, stepped off the bed, grabbed my fluffy white robe from the wardrobe and staggered out of the room, into the kitchen.

'Is that you, Zara?' Holly called from the lounge.

'Yes, only me.'

Holly hurried into the kitchen. 'You gave me a bit of a fright.'

'Sorry, I didn't mean to scare you. I must've gone straight to sleep the moment my head hit the pillow and now I've woken up starving. Apart from a KitKat, I've not eaten anything all day.'

'No wonder you looked like death earlier. Told you not to skip breakfast.' She took a plate of pasta from the fridge and stuck it into the microwave. 'I saved you some dinner. Take a seat at the table. Want a cuppa?'

'Cheers, Holl.' I sank into the leather cushioned oak chair. One of Mum and Dad's castoffs when they'd bought a new dining suite.

Holly shook the kettle to check the water level before hitting the switch. The microwave peeped. She took out the steaming tomato pasta.

'Smells yummy.' My stomach gurgled in anticipation.

'Here.' She put the meal in front of me. 'Want some parmesan or grated cheddar?'

'No, ta.' I picked up the cutlery and scooped a forkful of pasta into my mouth. 'Mmm. Lovely.'

'Zara' – Holly frowned – 'are you pregnant?'

I almost choked on the food. 'What?'

'You can tell me.'

'Of course I'm not.'

'You sure? Maybe you need to do a test?'

'I don't need to do a bloody test. I know I'm not pregnant.'

'Then you should probably book an appointment with the GP. You look rough.'

'I'm just tired. Probably been overdoing it and like you said I shouldn't have starved myself today. Nothing that a good feed won't sort out. Don't worry, hun.' I filled my fork again. 'How come you didn't see Adam this evening? Thought you and he were supposed to be going out.'

'We were, but to be honest, I was worried about you, so texted him and told him I was needed here.'

I pushed pasta into my mouth. 'This is really tasty. You shouldn't have cancelled your plans but I appreciate the thought.'

She sat down beside me. 'That's what friends do.'

'Thanks.' My mobile bleeped.

'Before you get that' – Holly stroked my arm – 'don't be cross but I messaged Scott to let him know you weren't well. That's probably him now.'

I tutted, picking up the phone. 'Yep it's him. He's asking if he can pop round. That's the last thing I need.' I sighed. 'Look, Holl, I don't have the energy to text him back. Will you do it for me? Tell him I'm sleeping.'

'You want me to lie?'

'It's only a white lie. Honestly, I'm exhausted. I don't have the strength to deal with him right now. Once I've finished this' – I signalled to my dinner – 'I'll have a quick shower and go back to bed.' I slid the iPhone across the table.

Holly picked it up. 'So should I say you won't be in to work tomorrow?'

'No,' I answered abruptly, 'don't say that. Of course I'm going to work. Say I'm feeling better but have gone to bed for an early night.'

She tapped into the screen. 'There' – she pushed the mobile back to me – 'the deed is done.'

Chapter Six

At five o'clock, I hurried into the Ladies to change. I pulled my new designer dress from the carrier and offered it up. It was gorgeous. I stripped down to my bra and pants, gave myself a quick spray of deodorant and stepped into the burgundy velvet dress. Scott was going to love it. The flattering high waist and long lace sleeves gave it a luxurious look. I gazed in the mirror and twirled. It was perfect. I was chuffed at only paying half price in the sale. I stepped into my black faux suede boots and zipped up the sides. This frock was at least ten centimetres above my knee.

A touch up of make-up, a ruffle of my hair, a spray of Black Opium and I was ready. I stuffed my day clothes into the carrier bag and went in search of Scott.

He whistled at me in reception. 'Wow. You look amazing. You trying to give those old guys in the band a heart attack?'

I laughed. 'Don't be daft.' I kissed him on the lips.

He shook his head. 'Seriously, Zara, you look hot. Makes me want to rip your clothes off right now.'

'Well you can't.' I giggled. 'You reckon I'll do then?'

'You know damn well you will. You more than do. I'm definitely punching.'

The theatre was packed. I peered around at the audience. Most of them looked older than Mum and Dad. I didn't think there was a single person under fifty besides Scott and me. We took our seat in the middle of the fourth row next to a couple in their sixties.

The woman smiled. 'You two are a bit young to remember this band, aren't you?'

I laughed. 'Yeah, but my boyfriend's doing a review for Bridge View Feminine Smile.'

'A good magazine. My daughter has a subscription and I've skimmed through it a few times. You never know' – she turned towards Scott – 'you may even get the youngsters interested in seeing Dark Chaos if you write a good review.'

'Maybe,' Scott said. 'I'll have to see what we think once they've performed.' The lights went down low. 'It looks like we're about to find out.'

A bald-headed guy with a slight paunch swaggered onto the stage. Everyone clapped.

'Thank you. It's good to be back with our fans. Hopefully most of you will recognise me as Paul, the band's manager. I know' – he chuckled – 'I've aged well. Maybe I've transported myself back in time.'

The audience roared.

Paul held up his hands. 'Thank you.' He coughed to clear his throat. 'Before the curtain's pulled back I have some bad news. Unfortunately Greg's unable to be with us this evening as he's taken to his bed with that dreaded virus, but don't worry, he's up to date with his jabs so I'm sure he'll be up and about in no time.'

The curtain opened. 'And on drums, we have your favourite heartthrob, Steve.' A spotlight hovered over the drummer.

The women clapped and screamed. Mind you, who could blame them? He was still a good looking bloke with long dark hair. He must've dyed it though.

'On guitar we have Ray, our lead singer.'

The spotlight settled on the guitarist. Everyone clapped but he didn't get the same response as Steve. Ray was stocky with receding white hair touching his shoulders.

'John on keyboard.' A lanky six-footer with purple spikey hair stood up and bowed.

'And then we have our bass guitarist. Please give an extra applause for Vic who's stood in last minute to replace Greg.'

The audience applauded.

'And now, I'll get off the stage and leave you to hear what you've all come for. Dark Chaos everyone.'

Viewers clapped and screamed stopping only once the lights were lowered. Ray strummed a few chords and the band joined in with 'Hot Love' from the seventies.

The woman next to me whispered, 'I loved Marc Bolan from T-Rex. I expect you're too young to remember him.'

I smiled.

Dark Chaos continued with songs from The Sweet, Bee Gees, Eagles and Rod Stewart.

Ray backed off to the side of the stage as the drummer strutted down to the front. Steve spoke into the microphone. 'I'd now like to sing my very own composition which reached number one in nineteen seventy-seven.' With the group as backing he sang, 'My world was full but then you left, leaving me in the cold darkness, you broke my heart...'

When he'd finished the audience clapped and screamed. 'I've got this record,' the woman next to me said.

I smiled. 'It's nice. I like it.' And I did. They weren't bad for old codgers. Scott appeared to be enjoying them too. I reckoned they were going to get a great review.

Paul climbed back up on the stage. 'The band will now play their final number, a brand new piece which Ray and Steve have composed between them. 'Rising from the Floorboards.' Paul jumped off the platform and the group started playing with Ray and Steve singing into the microphone.

'When skeletons rise from the floorboards...'

What on earth was that about? I glared at Scott. He shrugged. It was a nice tune though. Like a ballad.

The show was finally over. I was glad to get up from my seat after almost three hours with the exception of a fifteen minute interval.

The woman next to me patted my hand. 'Something to tell your children. Nice to meet you both. I hope he gives Dark Chaos a good review. I'll look out for it in the magazine.'

'I'm sure he will.' I smiled.

⊱⊰

The station was in sight. I'd taken a day's holiday to try to get back to the mansion. I hurried into the empty foyer and hoped the nice porter wasn't there in case he started asking questions. I made my way straight to Platform 2 and within no time the flash stopped me in my tracks. Feeling dizzy and sick I closed my eyes and when I opened them I was standing next to Rebecca's brother outside the front of Bridge View Hall. Hadn't time moved? I grabbed his arm to steady myself.

'What is it, sister? You've gone a deathly white. I hope you're not sickening for something.'

'I fear I'm hungry as I missed breakfast.'

He shook his head. 'You need to look after yourself. Our future is banking on you. I will arrange for Cook to make you a sandwich.'

The front door opened. My stomach churned. I was finally going to see inside. A young housemaid in a white pinafore over a black frock to her ankles smiled. 'Sir Edward. Lady Rebecca.' She curtsied and stood aside. Golden blonde strands peeped from the white mobcap.

'Thank you, Ruby.' Rebecca's brother led me into the extensive hallway.

Straight ahead a wide stairway with a mahogany banister and decorative spindles winded into a curve either side. Four dish like shades beamed from a gilded ornate lamp sitting on top of the banister post. Adjacent to the staircase was a small table with a single light adorning a gold tasselled teal lampshade. It was like stepping back into history. A picture of a young red-headed woman at a desk hung on the wall in a gilt frame.

I couldn't believe I was finally inside the house.

'Rebecca, Mary is waiting for you.' He signalled to the stairs. 'I will arrange for Ruby to bring you some sustenance.'

I made my way upstairs and hoped there'd be a clue as to where my room was. However, I needn't have concerned myself because as I reached the last step a woman appeared in a uniform like Ruby's.

'There you are, Lady Rebecca, Sir Edward has been frantic. Still you're here now. Come quickly, I have your gown ready.' The maid made her way along the landing stopping at a room with a double door. I followed her in. A large four-poster with lime green furnishings dominated the room. I strolled over to the dressing table in front of the wide bay window and looked out into the garden.

Mary held up a powder blue gown in embroidered lace with lots of ruffles. 'I thought this.' She hung the dress on a clothes rail and rushed to the side of the wardrobe, returning with a folding oak flowery screen for my decency. She undressed me down to a pink satin steel-boned corset before picking up the frock.

Once I was fully robed she signalled for me to sit at the dressing table where she brushed my long dark hair, pinned it up and added a silver headband. I stared in the glass wondering what Scott would make of me now.

'Rebecca.' There was a tap on the door. 'Are you ready? Sir Richard has arrived.'

'Coming, Edward.' I rose from the draylon stool, my pulse pounding. What was this gentleman going to be like? And was it my first meeting with him? Before I had my answer the flash came forcing me to clutch my temples, praying for the pressure to release before darkness hit me.

'Miss. Miss.' Someone helped me from the ground and guided me to a bench.

I looked up to see the porter who'd helped me last time.

'This is becoming a bit of a habit.' He offered a bottle of water. 'Sip.'

'Thank you.' I swayed, feeling faint.

'Have you skipped lunch again?'

I frowned. 'No, I've eaten. What happened?'

'You fainted. You're lucky I was passing. I'm about to go on shift.' He handed me a sandwich. 'I hope you like cheese.'

'Thank you.' I nibbled at the wholemeal bread.

'Red Leicester, my favourite.' He chuckled.

'Sorry, I shouldn't be eating your dinner.'

'It's all right, dear. Me missus gives me plenty.' He patted his stomach. 'Too much in fact. You sit there for a while. I need to whip into work and see if someone will cover me for a bit. Don't move.'

'I won't.'

He hurried over to the station and I glanced around me. The derelict mansion was just behind. Don't move, he'd said. Chance would be a fine thing. I felt so weak. Was Holly right? Could I be pregnant? Surely not though. Scott and I were always careful. I shook my head. No, there was no way I could be. But why was I feeling so drained and dizzy. Perhaps I was anaemic. Maybe I should see a doctor. I thought back to what had happened before being sent back. I'd managed to get inside the house. It had been wonderful in its day. I ran my fingers down my T-shirt and jeans imagining I was still wearing that powder blue gown. Such luxury. And that bedroom. I imagined sleeping in that bed. Maybe next time I'd get to meet Sir Richard. I went to stand up but my legs wouldn't hold me so grabbed the seat and sat down again. This was worse than the last time I'd timeslipped. Either I was ill or this time travel was weakening me. I had to go back though. No way could I stop now. I needed to know why I was sent there. There had to be a reason.

The porter rushed back. 'How are you doing, lovey? Want me to phone someone?'

'Could you call me a cab?'

'There's a couple outside on the rank. I'll run over and get one to come over.' He rushed back across the road and within seconds a black taxi drove up by the side of me with the porter running behind.

'Lean on me,' the porter said.

I rose from the bench, did as he asked, and let him help me into the back seat of the vehicle.

Chapter Seven

Scott strode into my office. 'Good to have you back. We missed you. How you feeling now?'

I peered up from the computer screen. 'Much better, thanks.'

'You sure?'

'Yes, and the doctor must think so too, otherwise he wouldn't have said I could return to work, now would he? Two weeks off is enough for anybody.' I smiled. 'Thanks for caring though.'

'Always, you know that.' He put his arm around my shoulders.

'Sorry, but I need to catch up with these emails so I can get going on the paperwork.'

'Hmm, I'm afraid that'll have to wait a little longer as Annabel's asked to see you.'

'Oh?' She didn't normally ask to see me without a time booked in advance. Had she had enough of me taking time off work? 'She's not going to fire me, is she?'

'Don't be daft, course she isn't. I expect she wants to check where you're at.'

'Right.' I locked my screen. My stomach churned. 'I'd better go and see what she wants then.'

I rose from the desk, picked up my handbag, and made my way out of the door with Scott at my side. 'New outfit?' he asked as we walked, commenting on my white linen trousers and sage green polyester tunic.

'Newish, but I don't think you've seen me in it. Bought it back in March. You like?'

'I love, although' – he clasped his hand in mine – 'have you lost weight?'

'Maybe a little, and before you start, it's nothing to worry about. I've had that bug, remember?'

'Suppose so.'

We headed down the corridor and stopped at his office. 'Good luck.' He pecked me on the cheek. 'Make sure you pop in once you're finished and let me know how it went.'

'Will do.' I wandered up the corridor a few feet more. We were lucky to have such lovely offices to work in. Annabel had inherited the building from her grandfather who'd run a newspaper but she wasn't interested in continuing anything big. She wanted something intimate for women. Something to make them feel good. She was a fair boss too. Never raised her voice but always managed to motivate the team to get things done. Hopefully she'd be fair with me now.

The door was open. I hovered outside staring in at Annabel's spacious office with the spotless desk. How did she do it? It wasn't like she didn't work hard, she did, yet she always managed to give that laid-back appearance. She looked gorgeous as always, her blonde hair curled loosely and clipped behind the ears showing off drop earrings with coloured gems that matched her rainbow blouse.

' Zara' – Annabel waved me in – 'don't stand out there. Come and sit down.'

'Thanks.' I had palpitations. I'd bet Annabel never had this problem.

'Don't look so worried. It's good to have you back' She poured two cups of coffee from the pot and pushed one towards me as I sank into the deep-cushioned moulded seat. 'Now,' she said, 'how are you feeling?'

'Good, thanks.'

'You're looking a little peaky. Are you sure you're well enough to be here?'

'Yes, absolutely.' I picked up the cup and took a sip.

'What did the doctor say?'

'Well, like you know, he signed me off for two weeks. Told me to rest, which I did, but now I'm back and raring to go.'

'Did he do any investigations?'

'Lots of blood tests. He thought I might've been anaemic but everything came back normal. Nothing wrong with me. He thinks I was suffering from exhaustion but I've no idea why I should've been. Anyway, I'm fine now.' I gave a small laugh.

'If you're sure. Now, I don't want to put any pressure on you, but when do you think you'll have the latest edits ready?'

I cleared my throat. 'By the end of today, if that's not too late.'

'Good girl. That's perfect.'

I went to stand up.

'No, stay' – her black gypsy skirt swayed as she stepped away from the desk and came around the other side – 'finish your coffee.'

'Thanks.'

She leaned on the back of my seat. 'What did you think of that band you went to see with Scott?'

'I liked them.'

'Scott's given them a wonderful review so I'm planning on sending a member of the team to do an interview.'

I lowered my shoulders, relaxing a little. 'That's a brilliant idea. I think the magazine readers will love that.' I drank back the rest of my drink. 'Well, if I'm going to get those edits finished by five' – I rose – 'I'd better get on.'

'Okay, but, Zara...'

I stopped in the doorway. 'Yes?'

'If you're not feeling well... please come and talk to me.'

I smiled. 'I will.' I headed out of the office, down the corridor and past Scott's office.

'Hey,' he called after me. 'I thought you were popping in to let me know how you got on?'

'Sorry' – I brushed a stray lock of hair behind my ear – 'I forgot.'

He cuddled me. 'What are you like?'

'Yeah, I know. Look, I'd better get back to my desk only I've promised Annabel she'll have the latest edits by end of day.'

'Why on earth did you do that?'

'Because I want to get back on top of things.'

'Okey dokes, but look after yourself. By the way, is it all right if I come around this evening?' He gave me that pleading smile.

Bridge View Hall held my thoughts. I ought to get back there but then I was still feeling drained even though I'd given Annabel the impression I was fine. Maybe I should wait a few more days. It would be nice to curl up and chill with Scott. We hadn't done that for a while and he was such a good boyfriend. 'All right. What time?'

'Why don't I come home with you straight from work? We can ring for pizza. That way you won't have to worry about cooking and I'll know you're eating.'

And considerate too. 'If you like.'

He lowered his lips to mine. 'I do like. See you later, gorgeous.'

⤝

After finishing off the edits I attached the file to Annabel's email address and pressed send. There, done. I glanced up at the clock. Just enough time to whip to the Ladies before meeting Scott. I needed to work out my next station visit even if I was playing with my health, the craving to fulfil my purpose was too strong.

⤝

The front doorbell rang.

Scott rose from the sofa. 'I'll get it. Probably the pizza.'

'Ta. I'll put the kettle on. Unless you'd rather have wine?'

'Wine would be good.' He made his way down the hallway and I headed into the kitchen. On autopilot I selected a bottle of Pinot Grigio from the fridge and placed it on the table along with glasses and plates.

Scott dropped the large pizza box between our two table settings. 'Smells yummy. I'm famished.'

'Help yourself.' I poured the wine into two glasses before sitting opposite him. My mind drifted off to the house. The four-poster bed, the gorgeous powder blue gown, Edward and then there was Richard whom I was yet to meet. Or should I say Rebecca had to meet?

'Hey, where've you gone?' Scott waved his hand in front of my eyes.

'Sorry?'

'I said cheers. You were miles away.'

'Sorry, cheers.' I raised my glass.

He selected a huge slice of veggie pizza and took a bite. 'Bloody Hell.' He shot from his chair, grabbed a tumbler from the side and filled it with water from the tap. 'That's bloody hot. I think I must've bitten into a jalapeño. Shall I get you a glass of water while I'm up?'

'Please.' I should've said *no* to him coming around. I didn't feel like conversation or anything else. All I could think of was getting back to the house. Why was I so tired though? Maybe I was eating too much junk food? This pizza for one. I needed to think healthier.

After dinner, Scott said, 'Tell you what, Zara, why don't we take our wine into the lounge and cuddle up on the couch to watch TV?'

'If you like.'

He sighed. 'Would you rather I wasn't here? I'm not feeling very wanted right now.'

'Sorry.'

'Sorry, but?'

I took a deep breath. 'Do you mind if we call it a night? I know I said I was back to normal but...'

'But what?'

I shrugged. 'I'm not really sure. Just feeling drained. Probably after being back at work, and rushing those edits to Annabel. Do you mind?'

'I can stay though?'

I wanted him to go but... 'How much wine have you had?'

'Not a lot' – he lifted the bottle – 'as you can see. Not even a glass.'

'So you can drive?'

He huffed before smiling. 'If that's what you want?'

I wished I could tell him it wasn't but I needed him to go. He was such a lovely, kind man, and I felt mean treating him like this, but wanted to be left to my own thoughts. 'It is.'

'Long as you're not going off me.'

I reached for his hand across the table. 'I promise I'm not.'

Chapter Eight

Scott dropped me at the flat after work. 'You sure you wouldn't like me to come in for a while?'

'Positive.'

'It is Friday.'

'Exactly. It's been a tough week.' I got out of the Porsche and closed the passenger door.

He stepped from the car. 'Oi, don't think you're leaving me without a goodbye kiss.'

'As if I would.' I put my arms around him and inhaled the gorgeous amber scent of aftershave. He smelt good, but no... he had to go home. I'd made up my mind that I was off to the station first thing.

'Are you sure I can't stay?' He raised his eyebrows and I nearly gave into the plea in his gorgeous hazel eyes.

'Sorry, darling, but I need an early night.'

'We can have an early night.' He smothered my neck in playful kisses.

I pushed him away. 'An early night to sleep. Now go.' I laughed.

He drooped his shoulders. 'Okay, if I must.'

'Yes, you must. Anyway, I'll see you Sunday because don't forget Chloe's invited us down to hers for tea. I need you for moral support. Mum and Dad are coming too.'

'I look forward to it, babe.' He pecked me on the lips, climbed back into the car and drove off.

It wasn't even eight o'clock in the morning when I reached the station at Bridge View and already the sun was warm. I'd arrived early to try and avoid the crowds with families off to Brighton for the day. Holly had stayed out all night at Adam's so I didn't have to explain where I was going.

I munched on a cereal bar, a precaution to find a way through this time travel without fainting. Once finished, I screwed up the wrapper, popped it in the bin, and made my way inside the almost empty foyer. I headed towards the platform but before getting very far I was blinded by light. My head screamed with immense pain forcing me to close my eyes.

When I opened them again I was back in the room with the four-poster bed and wearing the powder blue gown, standing by the draylon stool. Mary, Rebecca's lady's maid, was behind me and Edward in front. Time seemed to have stood still again since my last visit. Weird.

'Come along, Rebecca.' Edward took my arm, led me downstairs and along the hallway. He stopped outside a room. 'Now remember, it's important you impress him.'

'Why?'

'We've spoken about this. It's your duty to ensure this marriage goes ahead.'

'But why?'

'Sister, we are almost penniless. Now do as I ask unless you want us to be ruined.' He opened the double doors into a spacious drawing room furnished with mahogany bookcases, small round tables, and heavy pink floral drapes hung either side of the large picture window. A man with a full head of hair, dressed in a dark suit, peered out into the garden. Was that Richard?

Edward coughed. 'Sir Richard, please accept my apologies for the delay. May I present my sister, Lady Rebecca.'

Richard spun around. Gosh, he reminded me of Colin Firth when he played Mr Darcy in Pride and Prejudice. My parents had bought me the special edition on DVD one Christmas. I loved watching it over and over again. The ruffle of lace on Richard's shirt was almost the exact same as the one worn by Mr Darcy on the disc cover.

'Forgive me, Lady Rebecca, I did not hear you enter.' Richard made his way towards me.

My stomach curdled. Edward's words rang in my head. *Almost penniless*. He was selling Rebecca. There was no other way to put it. I couldn't let this happen. This must've been why I was sent here. Why should Rebecca be forced to marry someone for money? She wouldn't be able to stand up to her brother but I could. I was a twenty-first century woman and no man, gentleman or otherwise, would get away with pushing me around.

Edward whispered. 'Remember, be nice.' He nudged me closer.

'My dear, lady' – Richard smiled – 'please, sit with me.'

He might be handsome but I couldn't allow Rebecca to be sold like a prostitute. I hurried out of the room. On leaving I overheard Edward apologising on my behalf. I had to stand my ground. Rebecca didn't deserve this. I'd got half way upstairs when Edward grabbed me, squeezing my wrist. 'What do you think you're doing? We've been through this. Richard is the answer to our prayers. You should be thankful he wants to marry you.'

'Thankful?' I shouted. 'You think I should be thankful that you want to sell me like a whore?'

He tugged at my arm. 'Mind your language, woman. How dare you speak to me like that? Know your place.'

I struggled from his grip. 'Know my place. Go to hell.'

Edward slapped my face. 'Wayward woman. You will be obedient. Do you understand?' His eyes narrowed.

To think I thought Edward appeared kind. He was anything but. My cheek stung. 'No. No, I won't, and you can't force me to marry Richard or anyone else.'

Edward pressed his fingertips into my neck. Oh my god, he was going to strangle me. 'Can't I?' he said. 'We'll see about that.' He seized my arm again and dragged me back downstairs, along the hallway and pushed me into the drawing room. 'I'm sorry about that, Sir Richard. My sister lost her senses for a while but she's fine now. Isn't that right, sister?'

I frowned. How was I going to get out of this one? He was far too strong for me. I blinked. Nothing happened. I blinked again. Why wasn't I being sent back? I couldn't deal with this now.

Richard smiled and came towards me. 'Do not fear me, Lady Rebecca. I mean you no harm. Edward, please, if your sister is to be my betrothed, please allow us some time on our own?'

Edward clenched his fists. 'I'm not sure.'

Richard gave Edward a nod.

'Very well. I'll have Ruby organise tea.'

Why did Richard want me on his own? What was he going to do? If he tried anything I was ready to knee him where it hurt.

Edward closed the door behind him and Richard reached for my hand.

I jerked away.

'Lady Rebecca,' he whispered, 'please, I mean you no harm,' he repeated. 'Trust me. Please sit with me.'

I followed him to the mahogany framed couch but remained standing, taking in his appearance. His hair was similar to Mr Darcy's, although Richard's was probably an inch or two longer, but with the same soft waves, and a lock of curls fell across his forehead. 'He can't force me to marry you.'

'Shh, and listen.' His reddish-brown eyes sparkled. 'I'm on your side.'

He seemed genuine. 'What do you mean?'

'Are you aware your brother mortgaged Bridge View Hall?'

I shook my head.

'Well he has, and by doing so he's committed fraud.'

'Fraud?'

'Yes, fraud. The house belongs to you.'

'To me?' Not Edward or Rebecca's late husband.

'Yes, my dear. Admittedly when Sir Samuel, your late husband, married you, he paid the debt to unmortgage it, but the house was kept in your name. Did you sign any paperwork agreeing to the mortgage?'

I shook my head again, assuming Rebecca wouldn't be aware.

'I can see this has shaken you. I asked you to trust me, and that's what I need you to do.' He cleared his throat. 'What your brother doesn't know is that Samuel was my childhood friend, we grew up together, like brothers, and I fear his death was not accidental.'

That didn't sound right. Surely if he was Rebecca's husband's best friend, Edward would know him and Rebecca too? Was Richard up to something? 'I don't understand,' I said, 'if that's so, surely either my brother or myself would have met you before.'

'Unfortunately, dear lady, I never got that pleasure as I've been working in France until six months ago. I was introduced to Edward in London by a mutual acquaintance who mentioned a beautiful widow looking for a husband.'

That still didn't sound right. Wouldn't Samuel have mentioned Richard in conversation, and if that were the case, while I was ignorant because I wasn't Rebecca, surely Edward would know of him?

'Of course, I see you are confused, my childhood name was different, I was known as Alfred at school.' He peered into my eyes looking for some recognition.

Assuming he was being honest I kept it vague and said, 'Oh yes, I do recall Samuel telling me stories about an Alfred.'

Richard nodded. 'I imagine he told many, with me not always shown in the best light.' He chuckled.

I smiled, ready to accept his explanation, at least for now, and lowered myself on the seat next to him. My heart beat faster sitting so close to this gorgeous man. He was a complete contrast to Scott. Dark hair against fair. A mass of hair against Scott's almost crew cut. Clean shaven except for the sideburns.

'Your brother was with Samuel at the time of his accident. Yes?'

'Yes,' I agreed although I'd no idea.

'And there were no other witnesses?'

I shook my head.

'Firstly, I don't understand why they were even at Beachy Head as Samuel didn't like heights.'

I shrugged.

'And secondly, I'm sure he didn't fall, but was pushed.'

I gasped. Surely Edward wasn't capable of murder? But then he had put his hands around my throat. 'But why would Edward do that?' I asked. 'He's my brother.'

'Because, my dear lady, your brother is not who he seems. He's a gambler, a cheat, and he spends most of his time in illicit houses with sinful women. And I've no intention of letting him get hold of my inheritance to squander. Even more so, I value my life. I do not trust him. He has committed murder once, which I'm unable to prove, but between us, you and me, we could build enough evidence to support a case and have him convicted for fraud and illegal activities to put him away for a very long time. Will you help me?'

Now I understood why I was here. It wasn't to save Rebecca from Richard but to save her from Edward. 'Yes' – I nodded – 'I'll help you but...' A light flashed up in front of my eyes causing me to blink and the next thing I was back in the station in my own clothes. My head whirled. I hurried to the Ladies just in time to throw up.

I unlocked the door and almost fell into the flat.

Holly rushed towards me. 'What the... You look like death. Where've you been?'

'I'll be okay in a minute. I think I just need something to eat.'

'Sit down and I'll get you a coffee and some toast.' Holding me up, she guided me into our small lounge where I slumped onto the sofa and closed my eyes.

'Is the light too bright for you?'

'I feel nauseous.'

'I'll drop the blinds. That blazing sun coming in won't help. You could have a migraine. Would you like me to get some paracetamol?'

'You're okay. Expect it's hunger,' I whispered before she left the room. Hunger or was it the time travelling making me ill?

I couldn't stop now though. I had to go back. Scary, but there was no other way. At least now I knew what my purpose was. Could Edward really be a murderer like Richard had suggested?

Holly put a mug of coffee down in front of me. 'Drink that. Your toast'll be ready in a sec, and then, Zara, you're going to tell me what's been going on. Right?'

I rubbed my eyes. 'Is that a new top?'

'Yeah. Got it in the sale from Next. Do you like it?'

'I think so but can't see it properly in this light. Open the blinds will you? I'm feeling a bit shivery anyway with the heat being blocked out.'

She strode over to the window and fiddled with the cord. 'Tell you what, I'll leave them down a bit and that way they'll shield us from the worst but we'll still get light into the room.' She sloped back towards me and twirled to show off her outfit. 'You like?'

'Yeah, I do, especially that lace top. The cobalt blue brings out the colour in your eyes and it's a good contrast with your blonde hair. And is that a dobby spot?'

'Yep. That's what drew me to it. Well that and the colour. It's so comfy too.'

'How much was it?'

'Should've been thirty-five but with the sale I got it for sixteen. Over fifty percent off.'

'And it goes perfectly with your jeans.'

'You can borrow it if you like.'

'Cheers.' We were both a size twelve so often wore each other's clothes.

'Anway, I'm going to sort that toast now, and then you and me are going to talk. Right?' she repeated.

'Right.' Could I trust her? There was that word again. Richard asked Rebecca to trust him. I needed to tell someone though. I took a deep breath before picking up the mug and sipping the beverage. My stomach appreciated the warm liquid as it went down.

Holly was back before I knew it. 'Here you go.' She passed me a plate with a couple of slices of toast.

'Thanks.' My tummy rumbled. I nibbled on the almost burnt bread. Maybe I was just hungry?

'So have you been at Scott's?'

'No, I went to the train station.'

She fiddled with the gold chunky chain around her neck. 'The station, why? Did you have a row with Scott and he refused to bring you home? I'll give him what for when I see him.'

'No, he went back to his place last night and I stayed here. This morning I went to the station. If I tell you why, do you promise to trust me?'

'Of course. You're not in any trouble though, are you, Zara?'

I shook my head. 'No. Not that kind of trouble anyway. Sit down and I'll try to explain.'

She took a seat next to me and squeezed my hand. 'I'm listening.'

'I'm not sure whether I should tell you. You probably won't believe me.'

'Try me.'

'Okay. Well I've been timeslipping.

'Don't be daft, Zara. Be serious.'

I looked her straight in the eye. 'I said you wouldn't believe me.'

'Stop messing about.'

'You think I'm lying?'

'No, sweetie, of course not. I think you've been dreaming. I said you should be writing rather than editing. Timeslip would make a great story. You should pitch the idea to Annabel.'

I remained straight-faced. 'Then you don't believe me?'

'If you're being serious. Then yes, of course, but...'

'But?'

'I don't understand. How?'

'The first time it happened by accident. Remember when I went down to Chloe's just after she'd moved in?'

'Yeah.'

'It was then. I was in the station about to make my way to the platform when there was all this flashing in front of me. I'd no idea what was going on and the next thing I was standing in the station back in Edwardian times. Wearing a gown and everything.'

'Sounds fascinating.'

'It is. Although at times also scary.'

Holly fiddled with her fingers. 'I bet.'

'You do trust me?'

'I said so, didn't I?'

'Right. Well, my purpose is to save this Lady Rebecca from her murderous brother. You should see Rebecca, Holl. She looks just like me. I can't help wondering if she's one of my ancestors. We're so alike.' I sighed. 'I wish I could take you with me and then you'd see for yourself.'

'Why can't you?'

'I'm not sure it would work.'

'We could try. We have to try.' She put her hands together like in prayer. 'Please, Zara. We've always done everything together. Let's do this. Let me join your adventure.'

Could I take her back with me? At least then I'd be showing her it was real. It would be lovely to have someone to share this with me and who better than my best friend?

'All right. Let's give it a try.'

'Great. Tell me how it happens. What do we do?'

'Like I said, normally as I approach the platform I get flashes in front of me. At first it was a lot worse, so it might be awful for you, whereas now, I'm finding it easier to transport but seem to have reactions once I'm back. I think it's draining me.'

'I'll take that chance. Take me with you.'

'All right but we need to wait a couple of days to allow me to recover a bit.'

'That's fine. Just tell me when and I'll make sure I'm free.'

Chapter Nine

I inhaled a whiff of sea air as I got out of the Porsche. 'Mmm, don't you just love that smell?' I gazed towards the water. 'Check out those waves. They're so still.'

Scott put his arm around me. 'Bliss. Hope we get a chance to come for a stroll before dark.'

'Me too. Far too nice to be inside. Look at the sky. Not a cloud in sight. I wish I lived here.'

He stroked my cheek. 'Marry me, darling, and I'll buy you a lovely house on the beach.'

I laughed. 'Scott, you know I'm not ready for marriage.'

He squeezed my waist. 'Can't blame a guy for trying. Come on, we'd better go and find the others.'

'Ooh, check this out.' I inspected the Ford parked outside my sister's. 'I wonder if this is Dad's? Mum said they were hoping to pick up the new car yesterday.'

Scott tapped the bonnet. 'Could be. It's rather tasty.'

'Tasty?' I laughed. 'Come on, let's go and find out.' We hurried along the path, past a rhododendron, and stopped at the porch. 'I love June, don't you? We get warmth, lighter nights and these gorgeous things.' I pointed to the fiery orange blooms.

'Gorgeous just like you.'

I laughed, nudging him. 'What are you like?' I pressed the bell.

Within seconds the door opened and Matt greeted us with a grin. 'Hi there, Zara. Scott.' He went to kiss me on the cheek but I backed away. 'Hope you're not going to try and cause trouble again,' he said to me.

Grr. I frowned. 'Pick on Zara, is it? Just because I didn't want a kiss.'

Scott nudged my elbow. 'Don't,' he whispered.

'I'm not.' I pushed through into the hallway. 'Chloe,' I called.

She came through. 'Hi, there, sis. Glad you could make it. Mum and Dad are in the lounge. Go through.'

'Ta.' I made my way into the large room. Dad was by the window gazing out at the sea and Mum was busy plumping up the teal linen scatter cushions. Didn't she ever stop?

I headed over to Dad. 'Is the blue Puma parked outside yours?'

He spun around. 'Zara, good to see you up and about. No Scott?'

'He's in the hall chatting to Matt.'

Dad stared at me. 'You're still looking peaky, my girl.' He patted my arm. 'Laura, what do you think?'

Mum hurried over. 'Your father's right. Your face is ashen. What did the doctor say?'

I sighed. 'I told you all this on the phone. He did lots of tests and found nothing wrong with me.'

Mum tutted. 'Well you haven't always looked like a vampire. Something must be wrong. Go back and ask for a second opinion.'

'Stop fussing. Both of you. Anyway, you didn't answer me. So is the Ford yours?'

'Yes, yes it is, love.' Dad beamed.

'Come on then. Tell me about it then.' I knew he wouldn't be able to resist talking about his new toy. 'Is it electric?'

'Hybrid. She's nice to drive too.'

I laughed. 'Why do men always call their cars she?'

'A term of endearment, my child. Your mother likes Harriet too.'

'Harriet?' I looked at Mum.

Mum chuckled. 'The name your father has given to the car. She's comfy to drive and not too hard to park.'

Chloe wandered in with Scott and Matt. 'What are you all chatting about?' she asked. 'Sit down and make yourselves comfy. Tea will be ready shortly.'

'How are you now,' I asked her.

'Good, thanks. The nausea seems to have passed. Just like Mum said it would,' Chloe answered smiling with a hand behind her back. 'We had our three month scan this week. Want to see?'

Mum's face beamed. 'Come on then. Let's have a peep.' She flopped down on the sofa.

Chloe perched next to Mum. 'Want to see, Zara?'

'Yeah.' I sat the other side of Mum, and Chloe passed the print to her.

'Oh, Chloe.' Mum dabbed her eyes with a tissue. 'This is marvellous. Our little girl becoming a mother.' She looked up at me. 'Are you sure you're not pregnant too, Zara? That's just how I looked when I was expecting you.'

'I'm sure.' I glanced across to Scott sitting back in an armchair. 'Tell them I'm not expecting.'

Everyone turned to Scott.

'She's not pregnant.' He fidgeted in the seat. 'Not that I'd mind if we were but I'd rather put a gold band on her finger first.'

Mum gave a wide grin. 'Does this mean you're engaged?' She hugged me. 'Congratulations, darling.'

'Stop it. Stop it, all of you.' I shot up from the sofa. 'For the last time, I'm not pregnant, Scott and me are not engaged, and I'm not blasted sick. Now can we get back to talking about Chloe's baby?'

'She's right.' Chloe tugged on Mum's arm. 'I've just shown you a picture of your grandchild and you're more interested in Zara.' Chloe leapt off the couch and ran from the room.

'Now look what you've done.' Dad glared at me.

'Well, it wasn't me,' I said. 'It's you lot. I'll go after her.'

'No' – Matt scowled – 'you've done enough. I'll go.'

Seething, I shook my head. 'It's not fair, I'm getting the blame when I didn't even do anything.'

Scott was at my side. 'Why don't we go for a walk on the beach while everyone calms down?'

'Good idea.' I let him lead me from the room, out of the house and towards the seafront. It was far too nice to be indoors on a day like this anyway. 'I wish we'd never bothered to come. I mean what the hell am I supposed to have done?'

'I don't know, darling. I think your mum and dad are just worried about you. They're right though.'

I clenched my fist. 'What do you mean?'

'About you still looking peaky. Maybe your mum's got a point about asking for a second opinion.'

'Don't you start. I'm fine,' I said as a black labrador darted past and into the sea. 'That's a good idea' – I slipped my feet from my sandals – 'let's stroll up there where it's quieter and go for a paddle.'

'You don't need to ask me twice.' He pulled off his shoes and socks. Once we reached a deserted part of the beach he said, 'Go on then. I'll race you.'

I charged towards the waves but it was Scott who got there first. He rolled up his trousers and held out a hand. 'Come on, then.'

I took his hand and we toddled into the warm water. 'This is perfect,' I said. 'The weather's gorgeous.'

'It sure is. Shame we didn't bring our swimming gear.'

The blazing sun prickled the back of my neck. 'Yeah, and some sun lotion. Hope I don't get burnt.'

'Relax, babe. We won't stay long.' He leaned over, dipped his hands into the sea and splashed me.

'Oi.' I giggled and flicked the warm water back at him.

After playing around for about ten minutes I said, 'You know we should be getting back. Seriously, I don't want to get the blame for ruining dinner.'

'They won't be angry, babe, because they'll be too busy laughing when they see us.'

'What do you mean?'

'Well, if I look anything like you...'

'What?'

'Your hair.'

I touched it. 'It's drenched. Right, Scott Edwards, you're for it.' I chased him towards the dune.

'You can't catch me.' He laughed, racing on ahead until he stopped suddenly, let me catch up, put his arms out and pulled me down with him onto the sand.

'Scott. We need to go.'

'Soon, just give me a few minutes.'

'Why?'

He stroked my shoulders. 'You know how I feel about you.'

I flicked a fly away from my nose. 'Flippin thing.'

'He's gone now. Concentrate. I'm trying to ask you something.'

Don't tell me he's going to ask the question again. 'Don't,' I whispered.

'You know how much I love you.'

'We've been through this.'

'I know we joked earlier, but' – he knelt on the sand – 'darling, will you marry me?'

I shook my head. 'No, Scott, I'm sorry but I won't. I don't want to think about marrying you or anyone else right now.'

'We don't have to rush to get married. Just engaged. Let me make you mine.'

I sat upright. 'I'm not a possession you know. Make you mine, for god's sake, Scott.'

'I didn't mean it like that.' He smothered my neck with kisses.

'Don't.' I pushed him away. 'You know I'm not ready to be tied down. I've never misled you. I told you this from the start.'

He rose from his knees in slow motion before flopping down next to me. 'I know, but maybe I'm done waiting.'

'Meaning?'

'Do you love me?'

I sighed. 'Not this again. I've told you before, I love us, I love being with you, and I'd hate to be without you. So I don't know, maybe that means I love you.'

'I won't stop trying, you know?'

'Maybe I don't want you to. But for now we need to get back to my sister's before they all start ganging up on me for ruining dinner.'

Scott clambered up and held out his hand to help me.

'Ta.'

'We okay?' He pecked me on the cheek.

'Sure,' I answered as we stepped on to the promenade.

We all gathered around the table. Chloe had put on a wonderful spread. A big bowl of chilli, jacket potatoes, boiled rice, salad, and French bread. She thrived on domesticity.

'Did your mother tell you we'll buy the pram?' Dad helped himself to a jacket potato, a couple of scoopfuls of chilli, and a serving of salad.

Chloe nodded. 'Yes, she mentioned it on the phone last week. We've chosen one, haven't we, Matt?'

'Yeah, but it isn't cheap, Mr Wiseman.'

'Dad, please, Matt. You're family. You too, Scott. I know you and Zara aren't married yet but we still see you as a son.'

'For goodness sake, Dad. Will you stop it?' That was all I needed after Scott's gesture on the beach.

'Sorry, sweetheart. I was just trying to make Scott feel part of the family.'

I shook my head. 'Please, don't.' I forced myself to chuckle. 'You'll frighten him off.'

'It's all right, Zara,' Scott said, 'I'm not going anywhere.'

'See. He's not going anywhere.' Dad turned back to Chloe. 'Don't worry about the money, love. It's not every day I become a grandad.' He looked over at me. 'And don't worry, Zara, we'll do the same for you.'

I laughed. 'I'm not worried. You'll have a long time to save up for me as I'm not in a rush to have kids.' I glanced at Scott.

He shrugged. 'Plenty of time for that, darling. I'm not in a rush to tie myself down with a family either.'

The conversation stayed on baby stuff. When was the next scan? What about the crib? Did they have a colour scheme for the nursery? But I was more concerned with why Dad had turned on me earlier. I could understand Matt as he'd use any excuse to make me the one in the wrong but it wasn't like Dad. Something wasn't right. 'I'll buy the crib,' I said.

The table went silent. 'You sure?' Chloe asked.

'I said so, didn't I? After all I will be Aunty Zara.'

'Thank you, sis. You're the best.'

'No worries.' Hopefully that would keep them all off my back. I could easily afford to buy the crib from my savings and it was the least I could do for my niece or nephew. I needed to get to the bottom of what was going on with Dad though.

Mum and Chloe cleared away the dishes. 'I don't mind helping,' I said.

'No, we're okay.' Mum ran the tap. 'Keep your father company as the boys have gone outside for a smoke.'

I stood in the door entrance. 'So Matt's not given up yet?'

'No' – Chloe tied an apron around her waist – 'and I don't expect him to either as long as he doesn't smoke inside. So' – she glared – 'if it doesn't matter to me, then it shouldn't matter to you. Okay?'

'Okay.' I shrugged. 'I was just looking out for you.'

'I know, sis, but honestly' – she picked up the tea towel and took a plate from the drainer – 'I don't need you to.'

'I'll go and find Dad then.' I headed out of the kitchen, into the lounge and found him staring out of the window.

I strolled up to him and hooked my arm in his. 'You all right, Dad?'

He spun around. 'Hello, Zara, love. Yes, I'm good.'

'What was that about earlier then?'

'Sorry?'

'You snapping at me?'

'I shouldn't have done that.' He turned back to the window.

'Look, I know there's something wrong. Are you ill? Or is it Mum?'

'I'm fine, sweetheart.' He led me to the sofa and I cuddled up to him. He coughed. 'I'm not sure that I should be telling you this but...' He glimpsed over at the doorway.

'What is it?'

'Your mother...'

'Is something wrong with her?'

'Nothing serious, love. Or at least we hope not. She's not been herself lately, and then with you looking poorly too, well it all got a little too much for me.' He patted my hand. 'Mum's had some tests.'

'What sort of tests?'

'Anaemia, thyroid, that sort of thing. It might not be anything but she's tired all the time. Don't let on that I've said anything.'

I stared into space.

'Zara. You've got to promise.'

'I promise but only if you keep me posted. When does she go back to the doctor?'

'Next week. Between you and me, she's still struggling with the loss of Michael so I think the doctor may refer her for counselling. I've been nagging at her since, but well you know how your mum likes to pretend everything's all right.'

Michael's accident had hit Mum badly but then it had hit Dad just as bad.

'Maybe you both need counselling?'

'I'm fine. It's harder for your mother because she's stuck in the house all day whereas I can forget for a while at the office.'

'If Mum's results come back negative and it's counselling she needs...'

'Yes?'

'Maybe we should encourage her to get a job?'

'I can provide for my family, Zara, without sending your mother out to work.'

'You're very old fashioned for a modern day husband.'

'That may be so but it was how I was brought up and I don't intend to change my ways now.'

'Mum could get something voluntary. Something to give her purpose. What do you think?'

'We'll see. I've a feeling once the baby comes along she'll be far too wrapped up in being a grandma to think of anything else.'

Footsteps headed towards the lounge.

'Shh, now. Not a word, remember.'

'Mum's the word,' I joked.

We got stuck in a traffic jam on the motorway. Scott sighed. 'This is all we needed.'

'There must've been an accident.'

'You're probably right. I knew I should've put the Sat Nav on. Set it up will you, love? It might offer us a diversion.'

I hit favourites on the screen and ticked my postcode. 'Done.'

'Cheers. Anyway, did you manage to find out what had got into your dad?'

'I did.'

'And.' Scott inched the car forward a couple of yards.

'Er.'

'You don't have to tell me if you'd rather not.' He glanced at the live traffic signs. 'Two hour delay.' He sighed.

'Hang on. Look, Sat Nav's showing to turn off at that junction.'

'Brill.' He crept the car a few feet more. 'Well?'

'Dad's worried about Mum.'

'Thought it might be something like that. Is she ill?'

'She's suffering from tiredness so had some tests. Dad thinks it's emotional exhaustion and to do with our Michael.'

'Could be. I can't help thinking that the same applies to you.'

'What? Is this all because I turned your marriage proposal down?'

'No. It's because I'm worried about you' – he cleared his throat – 'after all the doctor couldn't find anything wrong with you and there has to be a reason for your decline in health.'

'Well it's nothing to do with Michael.' Scott was really starting to irritate me. 'I can tell you that now.'

'If you say so.'

'I do. So just leave it.' I pushed the radio button and sang along in my head to Ed Sheeran.

Scott finally managed to pull off the motorway.

Chapter Ten

Edward was a murderer and needed to be punished. Richard had a plan but it was dangerous. Was I brave enough to go back and be part of it?' My stomach curdled. I had no choice. It was my mission. Justice had to happen. Therefore, I had to be brave and go back to the house.

I'd promised Holly she could come with me after work this evening, but supposing that didn't go to plan. If only I could go this morning but then that wouldn't go down well with Annabel if I took another day off work.

I turned over in bed and caught sight of the clock flashing 08.20am. *Bloody hell.* I was late for another meeting. Darting out of bed, I shot into the bathroom.

Puffing and panting I bustled into the conference room. Faces around the table glared at me.

'Sorry, Everyone.' I faced Annabel. 'Really sorry. I overslept.'

Annabel sighed. 'This is becoming a bit of a habit, Zara. Are you feeling well enough to be here?'

'Yes, I'm fine. Like I said, I just overslept.'

'Very well. Get yourself a drink before sitting down.'

'Thanks.' I headed over to the counter, poured coffee from the jug into a mug, and took a seat at the boardroom table next to Scott.

'Now as I said, we're still looking for something new for the magazine.' She turned to me. 'Zara, I don't suppose you've got any ideas?'

Remembering what Holly had said about my writing, I concluded that this was the perfect time to mention it and Annabel would see me as conscientious. 'Actually, I have.'

Annabel rolled her eyes. 'Hallelujah. It seems Zara is with us after all. So what's this idea then, girl?'

'I'm thinking a fictional serial.'

Annabel put her cup down. 'Details.'

I fiddled with my ballpoint pen. 'Supposing we have a woman, or a man, that accidentally slips through a portal and travels through time.'

Annabel nodded. 'Yes, that could bring us some young readership in. And who would we get to write this?'

'Me.'

'You?'

'Yes, me. Why not? I got a distinction in my MA creative writing degree.'

'That's right, you did. Only the other day your course tutor was asking me why I hadn't grabbed you for the writers' team.'

'And as it's my idea, surely I should be the one to write it.'

'Tell me more about the plot.'

'I was thinking maybe there could be two of her, or him. Both in this time era and two doppelgangers back in time.'

'No.' Annabel shook her head. 'We'll keep it to one character and make it a woman. I like the idea of a woman going back in time.'

'Great.' I put my pen down. 'So I can write it?'

Annabel glanced around the table. 'Let's see what the team think.'

I took a sip of coffee. Now I'd done it. Was I even up to it? Holly seemed to think I was, and Emma must've thought so too from what Annabel had just said.

'A show of hands,' Annabel continued, 'if you like the idea of the project and think that Zara's the woman for the job.'

I peered around the table. My pulse pounded as I watched the hands go up in turn.

'Eddie,' Annabel asked, 'you're a *no* then?'

'I don't think it'll work.'

'Why not?'

'It's a woman's magazine so I don't think the topic will interest them for starters, and secondly, Zara's an editor not a writer.'

'You're suggesting that women don't like time travel? That sounds like a stereotype. Perhaps working for Bridge View Feminine Smile isn't the right place for a man like you.'

He scrunched up his face. 'That's not what I meant. I just thought...'

'Hmm, well the show of hands suggest whatever you thought is wrong.' Annabel faced Scott. 'I noticed your hand didn't go up.'

He chewed the end of his biro. 'Nope. Not that I don't think it's an ace idea, but...'

Annabel continued to face him. 'But?'

'This sounds like a big project. If it's a serial rather than a one off story then I can't help wondering whether Zara as a new writer will be up to it.'

Annabel looked at me. 'He has a point.'

I glared at Scott. Out of everybody around the table I thought he'd have supported me. 'Everyone has to start somewhere, surely?'

'Yes' – Scott glared back at me – 'and normally a new writer would start with a one-off piece. What you're asking is to do is huge.'

Annabel turned to Scott. 'So what would your solution be to incorporate this idea?'

'We should look at having a team of writers on it. Each taking a turn.' Scott stared at me. 'Nothing personal, Zara, but you're already struggling, so how are you going to manage something new like this?'

'You're wrong, Scott.' I gulped. 'Maybe this is just what I need. Something different. I'm not asking to be a full-time writer and I'll still continue with my position as junior editor, but, please, Annabel. Give me a chance.'

'Zara's right. I understand where you're coming from Scott, but it is her idea and I think we should let her give it a go. If it doesn't look like it's working then we'll just pull it.' Annabel faced me. 'Zara, we'll run it for a trial period of three months and see how it goes. You'll write the instalments and I'll oversee before print.' She glanced around the table. 'Zara can do this. I have every confidence in her.'

I smiled. 'Thanks, Annabel.'

'Okay, people, get to your stations and let's see some action.' Annabel gathered up the files in front of her before rising from her seat. As I stood up to leave the boardroom, she came over to me. 'I was getting worried about you today but I see you had a brilliant plan plotting in your head all along.' She patted my shoulder. 'Well done, Zara,' she said before following the rest of the team out of the door leaving just Scott and me.

'That's a cool idea you've come up with, Zara,' he said. 'Who'd have thought it?'

'An idea you think I'm not up to.' I made my way to the doorway. 'Cheers, Scott.'

I was working through the edits on an article when Annabel headed into my office. 'Got a moment?' She leaned on the back of my chair.

'Sure.'

'Now I know in the meeting I said I had every confidence in you, and I do, but' – she cleared her throat – 'do you think you could put a synopsis together for the ideas you have?'

I thought about my experience so far in the house. 'Yes, I can do that.'

'Great.' She stood upright. 'Bring it to me by' – she turned her wrist to check the Rolex gold bracelet watch – 'shall we say four o'clock?'

'Sure. Would you like me to email it?'

'Yes, that would be good, but I'd still like to see you. Bring a hard copy so we can discuss it.'

'Okay.' I smiled. 'Er, should I carry on with these edits first?'

'No. Make the story your priority. I don't need those edits in a hurry as I've not made a decision yet whether to run that article this month or not.'

'All right. Thanks.' I grinned.

'Until later then.'

As she walked out of the office I clicked my computer back to life, opened up a Word document and typed *The Girl in the Ticket Office Window*. I had a title but where would I go from there? My fingers hovered over the keyboard. Where should I start? Ah, yes, probably best to start with when I first got into the house and what it was like inside. And that powder blue gown I found myself dressed in with all those ruffles and lace.

Yes. I typed quickly as I tried to recall everything I'd experienced to date and fabricated a little.

The machine clanked and clicked before whirring and whooshing as it dropped my printed pieces of paper into the tray. I retrieved the copies from the printer, scanning my eyes over the text before placing the papers in a buff file. Hopefully, Annabel would be happy with this. I made for her office and knocked on the door.

'Come.'

'Afternoon, Annabel.' I passed her the file and stood by her desk.

'Thank you. I'm looking forward to reading this.' She beamed. 'Do me a favour, Zara, and pour me a coffee. Help yourself to one too if you fancy.'

With my hand shaking, I tipped the coffee jug into two mugs trying to avoid spilling the contents and placed one cup next to Annabel and the other on the opposite side of the desk before taking a seat.

'Cheers, darling.' She scanned the pages. 'Hmm. Yes, I like that. Hmm, yes.' And she carried on like that until she came to the end of the last page.

'Well?'

'I like it. I love the title. And I love how it's a woman. We'll break the publications up into the different timeslips so we just give the reader enough to hook them ready for the next issue. Well done. I reckon you're on to a winner here. Why we've never used you as a writer before I don't know. I think that should change. Expect to see a small pay rise in your bank account next month.'

'Wow. Thanks, Annabel.'

'Shall we say exactly one week to get the first issue done? That way it will give me time to provide you with feedback for start of play a week Monday.'

'Great.' I picked up my cup and downed the coffee. 'I'm off home now if that's okay with you?'

'Zara' – she held her gaze – 'this is excellent. Keep it up. Don't let me down.'

The weatherman said we were in for a heatwave and he was right. Even at gone seven in the evening it was still warm. I quickly changed into a white sleeveless T-shirt and navy-print skater skirt. This would keep me cool. Had I done the right thing allowing Holly to come with me? It was too late now though as we were leaving any minute. But what would happen if it didn't work? Would she think I'd been lying?

I hurried downstairs and called, 'Are you ready, Holl?'

She rushed into the hallway in a skirt similar to mine except in pink, and her T-shirt had puffed sleeves. 'Will I do?'

'You'll do fine. If it works you won't be wearing that when you get there.'

She chuckled. 'As long as I'm wearing something.'

I slid a small rattan bag over my shoulder. 'Let's go.' Once we were both outside I banged the front door shut. 'Come on.' I hooked my arm in Holly's but she held back. 'What's up?'

She chewed her lip. 'Nothing. Just a little nervous, I suppose.'

'You sure you want to come?'

'Yes.'

'Let's get a move on then before it gets too late.' I almost dragged her along. As we ambled along the footpath towards Bridge View I wondered about Holly coming with me. I'd never seen anyone she resembled. Did that mean she wasn't meant to go back? Oh well, we'd soon find out.

A bell tinged nonstop behind us. I turned around to see a teenager on a bicycle pinging frantically to move us out of the way.

I gently pulled Holly over to one side, and glared at the lad. 'This is a footpath you know? You're not supposed to be cycling here.'

'Yeah, I am.' He sneered. 'For your information, it's for cyclists too. Check the sign if you don't believe me.' He stuck his fingers up as he rode past then rang the blasted bell again.

'Rude,' Holly said.

'That's the trouble coming out this time of the day.' I tutted. 'Let's hope the station's emptied by now.' I stopped as we reached the derelict mansion. 'This is where Rebecca lived, but honestly, Holl, it was gorgeous back then.' I thought back to Edward squeezing my neck and winced.

'Zara' – Holly nudged me – 'you okay?'

I touched my throat. 'Sorry, I was lost there for a moment. Last time I went back, Rebecca's brother almost throttled me.'

'What? Should you be doing this? I mean, do you think you'll be safe?'

'I hope so. I think it'll be fine though, because he needs me alive to marry Richard. Afterwards is a different matter but Richard has a plan to protect both Rebecca and himself.'

'If you're sure' – Holly frowned – 'but I don't like it.'

'Don't worry. Come on. Wait until you see inside the house. You're going to love it.'

She pushed the pedestrian button at the traffic lights and within seconds the green man blinked. We crossed over to the train station and stopped outside the entrance.

'At least it looks quiet.' I faced Holly. 'You ready?'

Her eyes widened. 'As I'll ever be.'

'Are you sure you want to do this?'

She nodded and followed me inside. 'What happens now?'

'Like I said, I make for the platform but don't get far usually before going through the portal.'

She moved towards the platform and halted abruptly.

'You okay?' I asked.

'I'm sorry' – she stuttered – 'I. I can't.' She rushed out of the foyer with me close behind. 'I'm sorry,' she repeated.

'Hey, it's okay.' I hugged her. 'You do believe me though?'

'Yes. No. I don't know. But if it is real then I don't want you to do it anymore. It's too dangerous. Please, Zara, say you'll stop.'

'I can't stop because Rebecca needs me. Besides I believe this is my purpose in life and I just never knew it before. Tell you what, let's go home, make some hot chocolate, and watch Colin Firth in *Pride and Prejudice*.'

'Again.' She forced a little laugh.

Chapter Eleven

Whispering came from inside the lounge.

I pushed the door open. 'What's going on?'

They both stayed silent so I glanced from Holly to Scott. 'Is someone going to tell me?'

Scott pulled at his beard. 'Darling' – he rose from the chair and put his arms around me – 'you have to stop this.'

'What?' I glared at Holly.

'Sorry, Zara, I had to tell him.'

'You promised. You said you believed me.'

Scott dropped his arms. 'Don't blame her. She does believe you. Well she thinks she does. Actually, she seems as confused as you.' He rolled his eyes. 'I mean what the hell's going on? Earlier today you pitch this same idea for a story and now you think it's real? For fuck's sake, babe. What cloud are you on?'

'Scott.' Holly's eyes narrowed. 'Now I wish I'd never told you.'

'Then why did you?' I shouted.

'Because she was trying to protect you' – Scott huffed – 'that's why. For some reason she doesn't want to disbelieve this nonsense in case any of it's true. Which is absolutely ludicrous. And she wants me' – he pressed a finger to his chest – 'she wants me to go back in time with you, if it's real, because she thinks you need protection.' He shook his head. 'Bloody hell, Zara. This has got to stop. I'm seriously worried about you. You need medical help.'

I sighed. 'Not this again. I keep telling everyone that I'm perfectly fine. How many more times do I have to say the same thing over and over again?'

He put his arms around me again. 'Calm down, darling.

'Me calm down. It's not me swearing at you, is it?'

'Sorry, darling, I shouldn't have exploded like that. I'm just worried. Your physical tests may have been fine but what about your mental health?'

'What about it?'

'I'm concerned. You're making up these far-fetched stories. You're delusional.'

I shoved his hands off me. 'I'm not delusional.' I gritted my teeth. 'I might have known you wouldn't understand.'

'No, I don't. So let me get this' – he took a deep breath – 'you, Zara Wiseman, just happened to slip through a time portal at the train station and go back to the old mansion, Bridge View Hall. Is that correct?'

'Yes.'

'And while you're there you decide that you've been sent to save some woman. Rebecca?'

'Yes. And Rebecca looks just like me. I think she might be an ancestor of mine.'

'Seriously?' He stared at me straight-faced. 'I'd laugh if it wasn't so worrying. I mean you really believe this?'

'You're just jealous it's happening to me and not you. I bet you'd love to do the story?'

'It's a great story. Yes. A story, Zara, and that's all it is. Wake up.'

'But it's more than that, Scott. If you really loved me you'd trust what I'm saying. It's really happening and I believe that's what's making me ill. But I can't stop. Not yet. I can't. Sir Richard, the gentleman Rebecca's brother wants her to marry, has come up with a plan to trick Edward and get him put into prison for a long time.'

'Darling, you're clearly confused. Your mind's playing tricks, most likely because you're still grieving from losing Michael.'

'I'm not confused. You're just not listening. Why don't you just leave before I end up saying something I'll regret? Go on, get out. Now.'

Scott held his hands up in front. 'Fine, I'm going, but you know where I am if you need my help.' He went to kiss me but I moved out of his reach.

⊱

The Puma was parked outside the flat when I got home. I rushed up the path and turned the key in the lock. Why was Dad here? Had something happened to Mum? There was no way he'd come all this way for nothing. I hurried along the hallway and into the lounge.

'Dad, what are you doing here?' I looked around. 'And who let you in?'

'Holly. She's gone for a walk to give us a chance to talk.'

'I'll put the kettle on.'

He took my hand. 'Leave that for now. I want to speak to you. Sit down.'

Was it Mum? I didn't know what I'd do if something had happened to her. First Michael and now... 'What's happened to Mum?'

'Your mum's fine. Well she's not fine, she's depressed, and the doctor's referred her for counselling.' He coughed to clear his throat. 'In fact, darling, there's a chance for us all to have family counselling.'

'Family counselling? What do you mean?'

'A chance for us all to sit down together and talk about our feelings.'

'I don't need to talk to anyone, but I'm glad you and Mum will be seeing someone. Thanks for thinking of me though.'

He scratched his head. 'Scott's worried about you.'

'I don't believe this.'

'Don't blame him. I'm concerned too.'

'There's no need.'

He squeezed my fingers. 'Listen, love. Have you looked at yourself in the mirror of late? You don't look well. And then this delusion business.'

'I've already told Scott I'm not delusional.'

He leaned closer. 'Time travelling, darling? Who do you think you are? Doctor Who?'

'No, I think I'm Zara Wiseman and I've a responsibility to help an Edwardian lady, who could be one of my ancestors, that's who I think I am.'

'It's worse than I feared. We need to get you help.' He held me in his arms. 'Oh darling. Come for counselling with your mother and me. Or individually if you prefer. Losing Michael's been tough on you too, and then with Chloe getting married, and now starting her own family, it probably feels like you're losing another sibling. The counsellor will be able to talk you through that.'

'Dad, stop it. This is outrageous. I don't need counselling and it's clear I can't trust anyone around here. I think you should leave.'

He patted me on the back of my hand before rising from the couch. 'Have a think, Zara. You don't have to make up your mind today.'

He strode out of the room. 'See you soon, love.' The front door slammed.

※

I hurried into the station foyer. Delusional. I'd show them. The platform was empty. Why wasn't I timeslipping? I wandered up and down. Glanced at my watch. Half past two, not that it should matter what time of the day it was. I was about to give up and go home when I was blinded by light and overcome with nausea. My head finally stopped spinning and, when I opened my eyes, I'd gone through the portal and was dressed in a high bodice royal blue pinstripe gown with the skirt hem brushing my ankles. Richard had his arm hooked in mine and I carried a blue parasol in my other hand.

'You look beautiful today, Lady Rebecca,' he said.

'Thank you.' A kaleidoscope of butterflies danced in my stomach. This man was gorgeous. I felt like Colin Firth's leading lady.

The sun was warm and I wondered whether it was June here too. There had to be a way for me to find out what date and year I was in. It wasn't like I could ask anyone. Maybe I could find a newspaper.

'You're quiet, my dear.' Richard led me to a larch loveseat under an arched trellis. 'This will offer us shade as the sun is strong today.'

'Thank you.' I closed up the parasol and leaned it against the wooden lattice. A spicy fragrance travelled from the deep-pink climbing roses reminding me of incense. I half expected to sneeze but strangely enough the scent didn't bother me. It was rather nice.

Richard faced me. 'I'd like to advise you how far I am with our plan.'

'Yes?' I gazed into Richard's mahogany eyes. I'd never seen eyes quite like them. The golden brown reminded me of cognac. Not that I drank it myself. I longed for Richard to take me into his arms and smother me in kisses. It was torture being so close to this handsome man and not being touched. Now I knew why I'd been holding back on Scott's proposal. He'd never made me feel like this. I managed to hold myself together enough to say, 'The plan, yes? Do we have sufficient evidence to get Edward sent to prison?'

He smiled, setting my heart racing again. 'Why don't we go for a wander around the village away from prying ears?'

Richard was right. The last thing we wanted was Edward getting wind of everything. Apart from that, it would be nice to get away from the mansion for a while. 'Yes, that sounds like a nice idea.'

'Good.' He rose from the seat and reached for my hand assisting me to stand. Such a gentleman.

I let him guide me out of the arched gate. People hurried to the train station while other couples strolled arm in arm like Richard and me. Being in close vicinity to the station made me nervous. I wasn't ready to go back.

Richard sensed my unease. 'What's wrong?'

'Nothing. I suppose I'm just a little worried about the plan.'

'There is no need, my dear. I believe we've gathered almost enough evidence to have him locked up for a very long time and you'll be free, or...'

'Or?'

'We can marry in six weeks as pre-arranged, but don't worry, I've initiated precautions to ensure your brother won't get anything from our estates under any circumstances, therefore there'll be no gain for him to cause either of us any harm.'

'Married?' Would Rebecca want to marry him? I hoped Richard wouldn't be able to detect my pounding pulse. If it were me sitting there as me, and not Rebecca, I'd marry him without hesitation, but I had to think about Rebecca and what she'd want. How was it possible for me to feel this way about Richard so quickly? Scott and I had been together for almost three years yet he'd never made me feel like this. Part of me wished I could become Rebecca forever and stay with Richard, but then what of my parents? They'd already lost Michael. It would break them to lose another child. And Chloe needed me too so there was no choice, I had to go back.

'I'm not going to force you into anything. Once your brother's locked up you'll be free to do whatever you choose but, I won't lie, Rebecca, I'd be honoured to become your husband. Do you think there's any hope we may have a future together?'

I smiled, sensing my eyes twinkling. 'I might be persuaded.'

'Very well, my dear. I shall woo you. And you may make your decision at any time. Even if that means rejecting me at the altar, but not before Edward has been arrested.'

'Oh look,' I said recognising the little girl squatting on the pavement next to two young boys sparring on the four-foot brick wall. 'That little girl would be so pretty if her face were clean.'

'Come on.' He led me closer to the children.

The boys scrambled down from the wall and the little girl jumped up. The taller lad held out a hand. 'Please, mister, have you a penny to spare?'

Richard leaned down to the little girl. 'What's your name?'

'Daisy, mister,' she answered in a quiet tone.

'And how old are you?'

She looked to the older boy.

'Daisy's four, mister. She's me sister. And this is me brother. He's five and I'm seven. Have you a penny to spare?'

Richard took a small leather pouch from his jacket. 'And what's your name?' he asked the lad.

'George, sir' – he pointed – 'and he's John.'

'George, like the new king?' Richard smiled.

'I dunno.'

Poor little things. Flesh barely covered their arms and legs. They'd probably never had a decent meal. Richard must've thought so too because he dug into the pouch and said to the children, 'Now here's the plan.'

The children's eyes widened. 'Yes, mister,' the older lad answered.

Richard held a coin close to the older boy. 'Buy a bar of chocolate to share with your brother and sister.' He pulled out another coin. 'And with this penny, you must buy a loaf of bread to take home to your mother.'

George held his hand up to take the coins. 'Ta, mister.'

'You understand now? The shopkeeper will tell me if you didn't buy the bread and then there'll be no more pennies.'

'Yes, mister,' George answered with a huge grin. Giggling, Daisy and John gathered close to George.

Richard straightened his back and re-linked his arm in mine. 'Shall we?'

'That was kind.'

'I can't abide seeing starving children. London's full of the little street urchins. I try to help where I can' – he shook his head – 'but there are so many. If only I could do more.'

Richard was such a kind, generous man. He'd make a good husband for Rebecca. That is, unless all this was a front. When we reached a tearoom, he stopped and asked, 'Shall we?'

A tearoom sounded fascinating. 'Thank you.'

With Richard's arm still linked in mine we entered the premises which was much larger on the inside than outside. Numerous square tables finished with lace cloths filled the outside area with the inner space clear for what looked like a dance floor.

'Come this way, sir, madam.' A waitress in a uniform similar to Ruby's, but with a starched cap, showed us to a table by the window. 'I'll be back shortly to take your order.'

I glanced around. Amber shades dangled from the terracotta ceiling with matching wall lamps positioned symmetrically around the walls. Small landscaped pictures livened up the flowery wallpaper.

Richard caught the attention of the waitress.

She hurried over. 'Yes, sir? Are you ready to order.'

He turned to me. 'Would you like to see the menu, Rebecca?'

'No, thank you. I'm happy for you to order.'

'In that case' – he looked back at the waitress – 'why don't you bring us your speciality?'

'Certainly, sir.' She headed over to the back of the room.

'Seems we're just in time.' Richard gazed upwards at the balcony. 'The orchestra's getting ready to play.'

I peered up at the musicians. At least that explained the empty space. I wondered if Richard knew about the tea dance when suggesting we come in here. The thought of him holding me close while we sashayed across the floor made my heart skip.

It wasn't long before the waitress reappeared with our order and transferred it from a trolley onto the table. Dainty sandwiches and a variety of small cakes were served on a silverware stand. A matching dish of bourbons was placed in the centre of the table along with a silverware teapot, milk jug and sugar basin. She poured each of us a cup of tea. 'Madam. Sir,' she said before leaving our table and making her way to the entrance to greet more customers.

The bone china reminded me of a set Mum and Dad had in a display cabinet. It had a design of pink roses and swags, just the same. Mum had inherited it from her mother, and she her mother before her. I supposed one day it would be mine.

Our waitress seated a young attractive lady and gentleman at the table in front of us. I imagined they must be courting as the gentleman couldn't keep his eyes off the woman. As she took her seat she smiled at me. The place was filling up. Couples dressed comparable to us were shown to their tables. I imagined they'd all come in for the tea dance which would begin shortly.

My stomach rumbled when I took a bite of the cheese and cucumber sandwich. I hadn't realised I was so hungry. Richard grinned. Oh my goodness, he'd heard it. I sensed my face flushing which he seemed to find even more amusing.

By the time we'd finished tea the musicians had started to play light classical music. 'Shall we?' Richard rose from his seat and passed me his hand.

'Thank you.' I let him lead me to the small dance floor where already three couples glided around the room. Richard put one hand behind my back and took mine in the other. As he guided me around the floor my feet knew exactly where to move. My pulse pounded. I was in love.

Oh no. Everything blurred. . I tried to resist but the flashes blinded me.

~

I'm moving. What's happening? Sirens screamed. My arms were trapped. A light shone into my eye. 'It's all right, miss. You're in an ambulance and I'm a paramedic. We're taking you to A&E.'

'What?' I tried to sit up. 'Stop the vehicle. I'm fine.'

'You need to be checked over. You were found unconscious at the train station.'

Unconscious. 'Let me out.' I tugged at the restraints and tried to unclip them but didn't have the strength. 'Let me out.' I screamed again.

'Calm down, miss. Let's get you to the hospital and have the doctors check you over. If they think you're fine they won't admit you and you can go home. Please, let me do my job.'

I sat upright on the trolley. 'I told you, there's nothing wrong with me. Can I go home now, please?'

'Just a couple more tests.' The doctor listened to my chest through his stethoscope. He wrinkled his nose. 'That all seems okay.' He picked up the chart. 'The CT scan was fine. Blood pressure all right. Blood tests okay. Your pulse is rather high but that doesn't explain what caused you to collapse. Has this happened before?'

'No. Maybe it was because I was upset?'

'That shouldn't have this effect on you. I'd like to admit you overnight for observation and if nothing untoward happens you can be discharged.'

'And if I want to discharge myself now?'

'That's your prerogative but I recommend you don't.'

'Well, I don't intend to stay here for a moment longer than necessary, so please, just bring me any relevant paperwork and I'll sign it.'

He shook his head. 'Very well. I must make it clear that you're discharging yourself against my medical advice. If you experience nausea, dizziness, confusion, change of behaviour, or a headache that persists following painkillers, please go to A&E. Is there anyone we can call for you?'

'No, thank you. I don't want anyone to know I'm here.'

Chapter Twelve

Someone tapped on my bedroom door. I rolled over in bed. The clock blinked 8:10am. What the hell? I forced myself up to a sitting position.

The tap came again but this time the door opened slightly and Holly peeped in from the doorway. 'Just checking you're okay. I'm off to work in a min but if you need me to stay?'

'I must've overslept.' My head whirled. 'To be honest, Holl, I'm not feeling so good.' I lay back down.

She stepped in and came towards the bed. 'You don't look well, Zara. Your face is ever so white. Have you been back in time again?'

'No,' I lied. 'It must be a bug.' I held a hand over my mouth. 'Think I'm going to...' I managed to scramble out of bed and make it to the bathroom just in time. What was wrong with me? Surely this couldn't all be to do with the time travel. Perhaps I should've listened to the doctor and stayed in for observation. Had I hit my head when transporting back and that's why I went unconscious? Supposing I had a concussion? So many questions. I flushed the loo. After washing my hands, and giving my face a quick splash, I staggered back to bed.

'Here.' Holly held out a glass of water.

'Ta.' I took a sip. 'Thanks.'

She perched on the edge of the bed and stroked my cheek. 'You know I only told Scott because I was worried about you.'

'I know.' I passed the glass back to her and rested my head on the pillow. 'Don't worry about it. It's not your fault he was being an arse.'

She felt my forehead. 'You don't feel hot. At least that's something. Would you like me to ring work for you?'

'No, but if you don't mind messaging Scott and asking him to speak to Annabel. I'll work at home later if this nausea passes.'

'Sure. I can do that. Text me if you need anything.'

'I will. I'll take things easy. Maybe catch up on a bit of TV.'

'Okay. See you later then.'

'See you later.' I snuggled back down under the cover.

The front door closed. I jumped. My heart skipped a beat. Who was in the flat?

'Only me.' The voice was Mum's. What the hell was she doing here? She wandered into the bedroom. 'Scott called me. He was worried. Said you were off work with a sickness bug.'

I pulled myself up. Mum was next to me plumping up my pillows. 'How are you feeling now? I see you're still wearing that vampire face.'

'Thirsty.' I gazed up at her. 'You're wet. Is it raining?'

'Just a little shower. I'll get you some water.' She left the bedroom door ajar. I heard the tap run, a door shut, and high heels click clacking on the parquet flooring as Mum walked back to my room. 'Here you are.' She passed me the glass.

'Thanks, Mum. You shouldn't have come all this way though. Are you in the Puma?' I sipped the water. 'My lips are so sore.' I rooted in my bedside drawer for a Lypsyl. 'Ah, there it is.' I ran the clear stick across my lips. 'That's better.'

'Yes, I'm in the car. I've brought you some soup which I'll heat up shortly.'

'Not sure I can eat anything.'

'You need to try. Nothing worse than vomiting on an empty stomach.'

I took another sip of water. 'I'll get up to have it then.'

'Good, I was hoping you'd say that because I've brought something else.'

'Something else?'

Mum dipped into her shopping bag. 'This.'

'A pregnancy test. What for?'

'It's all right you saying you're not, Zara, but you have the classic symptoms. Do it for me. Please.'

'It'll come up negative.'

'You don't know that. By the way, you upset your dad yesterday.'

'Sorry. I'll ring him and apologise.'

'See that you do. I'll get that soup sorted, and you can do the test before I go.'

'Can you hang off doing the soup for fifteen minutes or so while I take a quick shower?'

'Do you need me to help you in the shower?'

'No thanks, Mum. I'm not five.'

Mum put a bowl of steaming soup and a bread roll in front of me.

'Aren't you having any?'

'No, dear, I ate at lunchtime. Now eat up.'

I picked up the spoon and took sips of the hot tomato liquid. It was soothing as it sank down to my stomach. 'This is good, Mum.' I dipped the roll in. I hadn't even realised I was hungry. Before long I'd emptied the bowl and mopped the bap around the edges leaving it spotlessly clean.

Mum stared at me. 'That's better. You've a little colour flowing into your cheeks now.' She glanced up at the clock. 'Four o'clock. If I'm going to miss the peak traffic I'd better go in a few minutes.' She handed me the test. 'Will you do this now, please?'

'I'll do it later, Mum.'

'Please, Zara. I'd like to see the result.'

I huffed. 'Charming. You don't trust me.'

'Nothing to do with trust. Just do it for me.'

'Sure.' I snatched the wand, hurried into the bathroom and followed the instructions. This was ridiculous. There was no way I could be pregnant but it was useless arguing with Mum. At least once it was done she'd have to leave me alone and stop going on about it. I flushed the toilet, washed my hands, and wandered back into the kitchen with the test. 'Just the case of waiting three minutes.'

'Have you set a timer?'

'Not yet.' I tore a couple of sheets of paper towel from the roll and laid them across the table before placing the test down. Afterwards I set the timer on my mobile.

The alarm buzzed. Before I had a chance to check, Mum had the test in her fingers. 'It must be too early.'

'What?'

'It's negative but that doesn't mean a thing.'

I tutted. 'I told you, it's not possible for me to be pregnant.' Was she never going to stop going on? Just because Chloe was expecting Mum had got this notion that I must be, or should be more like.

'I still think you are.' Mum packed away the soup container into her bag.

I sighed.

'Don't give me that, Zara. When you become a mother, you'll understand.'

'Sorry, Mum. Thanks for caring.'

She patted me on the shoulder. 'Of course, I care love.' She kissed me on the cheek. 'I'll let myself out. You rest.'

Chapter Thirteen

My hands trembled as I sat across from Annabel in her office.

'It's good to have you back again, Zara, but I can't help wondering if you're returning too soon.'

'I'm fine.'

'That's what you said last time and then you were off again. The thing is I'm thinking that maybe I need to get a temp in to assist on the editing side of things.'

I shot up from the chair. 'You're sacking me?'

'Not at all. You're far too good a worker for that. Like I've always said, you and Scott are my top team members, but I have to think about the magazine. A little help won't hurt and it'll take the pressure off you. Also allows you more time to work on the serial. How's the next episode going?'

'Almost there. Like I said on the phone, I've been working from home.' I rested my hand on the desk. 'And you know, I can always take some of the editing stuff home?'

'No, I don't want you to do that. I want you to step back a bit and give your body time to recover. In all the years you've been here I've never known you to have a day off sick, yet these last three months or so I don't think we've had a month go by without you being off for at least one day.'

'I'm sorry. I'll try harder.'

'I'm not blaming you, Zara. You can't help your health but if it is...'

'What?'

'I can recommend a good counsellor.'

'Why?'

'You've been through a lot. What with losing your brother...'

'Has Scott said something?'

'Don't blame Scott, he's just looking out for you but he may have mentioned...'

'What?'

'That you believe you've been time travelling.'

I clenched my fists. 'He did what?'

'He cares about you. We all do.' Annabel kept her normal calm self and unlike me, didn't raise her voice. She tapped the keys on the computer keyboard. 'Ah, yes' – she checked the screen – 'here's my contact, Dr Craig Fields. I'll email you his details. I'd like you to make an appointment.'

'I don't need to see anyone.'

'Zara, it wasn't a request. If you want to keep working at Feminine Smile then you'll do as I ask.'

I took a deep breath. 'Fine.' I stood up. 'If that's it, I'd better get back to work.'

'That's it.' Annabel smiled. 'Let me know when your first appointment is. Craig's expecting your call and has promised to find you a slot in the next week.'

'Next week. You mean you've already spoken to him?'

'Yes, I have. Like I said, Zara, this isn't a request.'

Bloody hell. How was I going to get out of this one? Right at this moment I hated Scott and wanted to tell him he was dumped.

Curled up on the couch, I nibbled a handful of salted peanuts. 'Can you believe that Annabel's getting someone in to do my job?'

'I thought you said to help you.'

'Yes, that's what she said, but it's my job. I've worked bloody hard to get this far and I don't want to start losing responsibility now.'

'But she hasn't said that, has she?'

'Well no. But...' I took a deep breath. 'And she's insisting I see a doctor.'

Holly squinted. 'But you've seen one, or do you mean a company doctor? One of those that employers make you see when you've had too much time off work?'

'No, he's a psychiatrist, and she said I have to make an appointment to see him, like now.'

'Why would she do that?'

I glared at her. 'Why do you think?'

She shrugged. 'No idea.'

'Because Scott bloody told her about the time travel and now she thinks I'm mad too. When you know I'm not.' I downed a glass of Prosecco.

'I do. Although...' Holly picked up the remote and switched on the TV.

'Although what, Holl? You said you believed me.'

'Yeah, I do. I just don't think it'll hurt for you to talk to someone professional. Anyway you shouldn't get poorly again now that you've stopped.' She glared at me. 'You have stopped, haven't you?'

'What difference does it make? I can tell you don't believe me. Why did you pretend?'

'I didn't really pretend. I wanted to believe you and I got excited at the thought of an adventure.'

I scowled.

'Let's not fall out. Now shall we watch *Virgin River*? The women in work were raving about it.'

'You watch whatever you like.' I got up from the couch. 'I'm off to bed.'

'Zara, please. Don't be like that.'

Don't be like that. She was as bad as the rest of them. I slammed the lounge door wishing I was back at Bridge View Hall and curled up in Richard's arms.

Chapter Fourteen

Overhead branches from sycamore and oak almost concealed the narrow timber trail. Leaves brushed against my hand as I gripped the wooden handrail and climbed the garden sleepers. Vibrant pink-purple Fuchsia dangled their fairy blooms from giant flowerpots positioned either side of the path. Finally, I reached the top of the steps and ambled across to the lodge. Its cedar shade made me think of Richard's eyes. I wished I could be with him now instead of having to talk to some doctor about my feelings. Tomorrow was the weekend so I'd get the chance to visit Bridge View Hall then. The thought of spending time with Richard gave me a warm glow. Hopefully my next visit wouldn't land me in an ambulance like last time, although it hadn't taken me that long to recover, and I didn't have a concussion after all. My body would soon adjust to the timeslips, I was sure, or at least hoped. I couldn't stop. More to the point, I didn't want to. The idea of helping one of my ancestors gave me a buzz.

A brass plate displaying Dr Craig Fields BSc(Hons), MBBS(Hons), FRCPsych in a black fancy font was screwed to the slatted wall. I was about to knock when the part-glazed door opened and a dark-haired guy with bushy eyebrows stared at me through his tinted designer glasses.

He smiled. 'Good afternoon, you must be Zara.' He appeared far too young to be a psychiatrist. Seemed rather casual too in the short-sleeved maroon shirt with the top buttons open revealing his hairless chest. A trimmed beard, nothing like Scott's, accentuated the doctor's good looks.

'Yes, I'm Zara Wiseman. And you must be Dr Fields.'

'Craig, please. That is, if you feel comfortable with the informality.'

'Okay.' I yearned to run back down the steps.

'Come on in.' He opened the door wider.

'Thank you.' I stepped into the well-lit area and gazed around the room. Black picture frames in various sizes dominated the white-painted walls. A beech desk against one wall caught my attention. In particular, I was drawn to the large table lamp with an amber shade because the brass angel base seemed out of place. Two teal velour armchairs with contrasting orange-striped scatter cushions were positioned either side of the wide, single-paned window. I searched for a couch but there wasn't one.

Craig signalled me to sit on one of the chairs. 'Please.'

'Thanks.' I took a seat, expecting him to sit at his desk but he pulled up the matching armchair and sat opposite me.

'So, how are you, Zara?' he asked in a soft voice.

'Fine.'

'Are you able to expand on that?'

'Not really.'

'Why is that?'

'Why should I?'

'You seem a little angry,' he said in a monotonic voice.

I stared through the window thinking about Richard. He'd mentioned street children in London. Was it any different now? Everywhere I turned someone was homeless.

'Zara? Are you angry?'

I answered without turning back. 'Wouldn't you be?'

'If you explained why, then I might understand.'

I twisted round. 'Because my boss forced me to come here. Threatened to sack me if I didn't.'

'And you don't think that could be because Annabel, Ms Walsh, is concerned about your welfare?'

I shot up from the chair. 'You're on first-name basis with Annabel?'

'I am, but don't worry, everything you say to me is confidential. Please, sit back down.' His tone remained unchanged. 'Why don't you tell me what's bothering you?'

'Because there's nothing to tell.' I gulped. 'I'm really thirsty. Any chance of a drink? It was hard work trekking up those steps in this heat.'

'Sorry, I should've thought.' He got up and strode to the fridge.

I was back at the tea dance with Richard whirling me around the floor. Why did I have to get sent back home? Shivers of excitement ran down my spine at the thought of being in his arms.

'Water okay?'

'As long as it's wet and cold, I don't care.'

Craig took out a jug of water and filled a tall tumbler. 'Ice?'

'Thanks.'

The glass jingled when he dropped the cubes in. He put the jug back in the fridge before heading back and passing me the drink. 'Here you go.'

'Cheers.' I took a swig before turning back to the window. 'Did you grow that palm tree?'

'No, it was here when I bought the property. Do you like it?'

'Makes me feel like I'm in the Mediterranean.' I sipped the water. 'Are you sure you're qualified? I mean, you don't look old enough.'

'Thank you for the compliment. I can assure you that I'm fully qualified. Didn't you see the plate by the door?'

Showing off now, was he? I glanced around the room. 'Do you live here?'

'No, I have a small cottage half a mile away. This lodge came up for sale a couple of years back so I snapped it up. It's a perfect place for me to work and a calm space for my clients to relax.'

It was rather nice. I caught sight of the bookcase on the other side of the room. 'You've got a lot of books. Are they all about counselling?'

He chuckled. 'Good gracious, no. I read fiction too. What kind of books do you like to read?'

I could see what he was doing. He was trying to be my friend so I'd open up. Was he expecting me to talk about the timeslip? Bet he'd like that, then he could report back to Annabel, no matter what he'd said about everything being confidential, and say she was right. That I was mad. But I wasn't mad. If only I could bring back some proof. Next he'd be trying to section me. 'Look, Craig, I'm sure you're great at your job and all that but I don't need to be here.'

'Your boss thinks differently, and as she's paying me a hefty sum to listen to you, I think you should take up that offer. You have a sister, I understand?'

He'd done his homework. 'Yeah.'

'Is she older? Younger?'

'Younger.'

'Tell me about her?'

I relaxed back into the chair. Talking about Chloe would mean I didn't have to talk about myself. 'She's married. Expecting a baby just before Christmas.'

'Really. Sounds like she's going to be a young mum if she's younger than you.'

'Yep, nineteen. She should never have been allowed to get married, Mum and Dad...'

'Yes?'

'Nah, nothing.' I took another sip of water. 'Chloe's got this spectacular house on the seafront. Detached. Massive.'

'Chloe's your sister?'

'Yeah. I'd love to live in a house like hers. She has the most awesome view of the sea. And that lashing sound when the breakers crash against the rocks.' I smiled. 'Perfection. I love it.'

'I can tell. Why don't you live somewhere like that?'

'I could never afford it.'

The conversation went on like that and Craig took care not to pressure me into talking about anything I didn't want to. I was kind of enjoying his company. He was nothing like Scott, or Richard for that matter. Although Craig's dark curls fell across his forehead in the same way as Richard's. Butterflies danced in my stomach at the thought of Richard. Was I falling in love with him or was it a crush? Either way, he wasn't mine to have. He was to be Rebecca's husband not mine. I'd made up my mind that the wedding would go ahead. I trusted Richard. He was a kind gentleman. I'd seen his concern for those poor kids. Richard would protect Rebecca from that awful brother of hers. I was sure of it.

Craig's phone buzzed. He glanced over to the desk.

That was rather unprofessional having his phone go off during a session. I wondered who it was. Maybe his girlfriend or wife. By the looks of him he was itching to check.

He cleared his throat. 'Well, Zara, that's to let me know our hour is up. How did you find it?'

An alarm. I'd judged him wrongly. Gosh that time went quickly. 'Okay,' I said.

'So will you come back again?'

I shrugged.

He stood up and strode over to his desk, sank into the leather executive chair, and opened an appointment schedule on his PC. 'How about next week at the same time?'

'All right.' I smiled. 'Thanks.' I dug my hands into the velour upholstery to push myself to a standing position.

'Good.' He headed to the door and opened it for me to leave. 'I look forward to next week.'

'Thanks.' I made my way out. 'Bye then.'

It hadn't been as bad as I thought. Craig was nice and really easy to talk to. He had a lovely soothing voice too. Agreeing to another session would keep everyone happy and hopefully off my back. I glanced back at the lodge but Craig had gone in and the door was closed.

As I wandered across to the bus stop, I decided to go to the train station. Why wait until tomorrow when it was still daylight and I was already out and about? I smiled at the thought of seeing Richard again.

My head whirled. Light blinded me. Finally the dizziness subsided. Sunlight shone on my face and I was overcome by intense heat. My pale blue dress trailed the ground. How did women cope with clothes like this in these high temperatures? I thought of the skimpy shift I'd been wearing.

Footsteps came from behind me. A hand touched my arm. 'Sister, what are you doing out here? Mary's waiting to fit your gown before Sir Richard arrives. Hurry now.'

I turned to face Edward. 'Sorry, I needed a bit of air, but you're right, it's far too hot out here.' I headed to the house without stopping to gaze at the spectacular magenta dahlias.

The sooner I got the wedding dress fitted, the sooner I'd get to see Richard. I just prayed that I wouldn't teleport before having the chance to spend time with him.

The lustrous silk hugged my waist. I smoothed my fingertips down the fabric. It was soft to touch. I turned and stared into the full length mirror. Ivory suited me. The style clung to my body but widened below my knees and spread down to the floor into a short train. The top of the bodice and three-quarter sleeves were trimmed with lace. Richard wouldn't know what hit him when he watched me walk down the aisle, or should I say Rebecca? Richard would make a good husband, therefore, I'd let the wedding go ahead. I wondered who'd consummate the marriage, Rebecca or me, and I couldn't help hoping it would be me.

Mary gazed at me. 'You look beautiful, Rebecca. Sir Richard's a lucky man. I'll just add the finishing touch.' She stood behind me and fastened a choker around my neck. 'I remember your last wedding. Of course, you were nothing but a sweet young thing then, trembling at the thought of becoming a bride.'

I stroked the single strand of pearls.

'But Sir Samuel treated you kindly, as will Sir Richard, but I think you already know that, don't you?' She smiled into the mirror.

I smiled back.

'This time it'll be different. You're older and know what to expect.' She chuckled. 'If you and Sir Richard are blessed we could see a new little one arriving this time next year.' She looked at me for a reaction but without warning the flash came.

Although it didn't feel the same. Stars flashed in front of my eyes. My head whirled. I was being pulled.

'Rebecca.' Richard was at my side.

I was no longer in the wedding gown but a blue silk dress.

Richard touched my arm. 'My dear lady, are you sick? Are the arrangements proving too much? Ruby, bring some water,' he shouted, 'and hurry.' He steered me to the couch and took a seat beside me. What had happened? I was still here. I must've gone through the portal but boomeranged back again as all I'd done was move from the bedroom to the drawing room.

The maid rushed in with a glass of water. Her face paled. 'Mistress.'

'I'm fine,' I said. 'Please don't worry.'

Richard took the tumbler from Ruby and held it to my lips.

I wondered why I hadn't gone back. Was it because I'd resisted? Did that mean I was learning to control this thing, rather than it controlling me? At least now I'd get to spend time with Richard.

He placed the glass down on the small table and inched closer to me. 'I'm not happy about your condition, Rebecca. He turned to Ruby. 'Find Sir Edward and ask him to call the physician.'

Being this close to Richard made my heart race at twice its speed. 'No' – I rested my fingers on the back of his hand – 'there's no need. I'll be fine in a moment. It's my own foolish fault for missing luncheon. Ruby, ask Cook to prepare me a sandwich.'

'Yes, mistress.' She hurried out of the room.

'Very well, but if there's no improvement you must see the physician. Our wedding is only six weeks away. You must be in good health for that.'

Only six weeks and I still didn't know what his kisses felt like but I intended to find out. I gazed at him.

'Yes, yes, I know' – he grinned – 'you may still reject me. If Edward has been arrested before the ceremony, and you don't wish to go ahead with our wedding, then we'll part company and you'll never have to cross paths with me again. However, I can't help hoping that you'll agree to proceed with the marriage and become Lady Rebecca Cavendish.'

I inched closer to kiss him.

'Dear lady.' He held me at arm's length. 'You're obviously not feeling yourself.'

Richard and I strolled to the lakeside in the scorching heat. He lugged two folding wicker chairs and against his wishes I carried the picnic hamper. My blue-patterned linen gown had a contrasting sashed ribbon around the waist and fell loose to the ankle making it cool to wear.

'Are you feeling better now?' he asked.

'Yes, I was foolish to miss luncheon.' The sun was warm on my face but the wide-brimmed straw hat and parasol offered plenty of protection.

He stopped under a tree. 'Shall we picnic here? The cedar will offer shade and we'll have a perfect view of the wildfowl.'

Swans, including two black ones, several geese, and a trio of ducks were in our sight. I twiddled the large diamond ring on my left hand. 'This is an enchanting spot.'

'My fiancée deserves the best' – Richard unfolded the two wicker chairs revealing a deep cushion on each – 'even if it may only be for show.'

I smiled.

'Although, like I've mentioned before, I hope you do agree to become my wife.' He spread a rug onto the grass.

'Thank you.' I dropped the basket to the ground and sank into one of the seats although I'd rather have laid down next to him.

Richard flipped the lid of the hamper and pulled out two glasses. His eyes glinted. 'Champagne. Good girl, Ruby.' He popped the cork and sparkling wine rose to the top of the glasses. We laughed as they nearly overflowed.

As I sipped the sweet fizz, I gazed across to a small island towards the centre of the lake. 'Is that a heron?'

Richard looked up. 'It is indeed.' He rummaged among the red-checked lining. 'Now let's see what else Ruby's packed for us.'

I hoped there was something on the menu suitable for a vegetarian. If I didn't eat something then almost surely the bubbles would go to my head.

He unpacked the items one by one. 'Smoked salmon, asparagus,' – he licked his lips –'strawberries and small cakes.'

Thank goodness for the strawberries. 'I'm not that hungry as I had that sandwich earlier. Perhaps I'll just nibble a few strawberries.'

He frowned. 'I don't want you fainting on me again.'

'I promise, I won't. I'll eat a cake too.' I helped myself to a tea plate, a red linen napkin, a good helping of the fresh fruit and a jam tartlet.

Richard served salmon on to his plate accompanied by the asparagus. 'Edward's organised an engagement ball for us.'

'My brother has done that?'

'He certainly has. With my encouragement, of course.' Richard chortled. 'Once we're married' – he grinned – 'that's if you decide to go ahead with the ceremony, we'll fill the house with dancing. I imagine it was like that when Samuel was alive?'

I smiled in acknowledgement. I bit into the sweetest strawberry I'd ever tasted. Before I'd even had a chance to swallow it a light flashed in front of my eyes. My head screamed. I was going to pass out. I tried to resist the pull.

I heard voices around me, and opened my eyes. 'Where am I?' A young doctor hovered over me.

'It's all right, miss' – he shone a torch in my eyes – 'you're in hospital.'

Oh god, not again. This couldn't be happening. 'How did I get here?'

'The ambulance brought you in. Can you tell us your name, miss?' asked a woman who appeared a good twenty years older than me. Was she another doctor? She didn't look like a nurse but then she wasn't wearing a white coat either.

'Zara. Zara Wiseman.'

'Good. I'm Ms Emily Weybridge, the consultant on this ward. Are you able to tell me what the date is?'

Date. What was the date? '16th July 2023.'

'And have you been admitted to hospital before?'

Had I? Last time I'd discharged myself before being admitted. 'No,' I answered.

A doctor I recognised strode over. He glared at me. 'Ms Weybridge, this is the same patient brought in by the paramedics the other week. Remember I discussed her with you. She refused to stay in for observation.'

'Ah, yes. I remember. Similar circumstances to now. And once again all the tests have come back negative.' She turned to me. 'You're quite a puzzle, young lady. However, on this occasion I must insist that you stay in overnight so we can observe you.'

'No, I can't. I need to get home.' I went to sit up but my head spun, forcing me to flop back down on the pillow.

'You're in no fit state to go home.' She rested two fingers on the inside of my wrist. 'And you need to calm down as your pulse has shot up.'

I sighed. 'All right, but if I stay, can I go home first thing?' I looked around. 'My bag. Where's my bag? I need my phone.'

The consultant turned to the auburn-haired woman on her right. 'Nurse, can you get Zara's bag for her?'

'Yes, doctor.' The nurse bent down to the locker at the side of the bed. 'Here you are.' She passed me my rattan handbag.

'Thanks.'

'Now do as the doctor says and be a good girl.' The nurse patted my hand. 'Don't worry, we'll look after you.'

With only six weeks before the wedding I didn't have time to be ill. As soon as I was out of here I'd give it a couple of days and then go back to Bridge View Hall. I had to. I had to spend more time with Richard before Rebecca married him.

Chapter Fifteen

Mum and Dad hurried into the ward.

'Darling.' Mum wrapped her arms around me. 'What on earth happened?'

'I was a bit faint, that's all, and some busybody decided to call an ambulance.'

'Laura' – Dad tapped Mum's arm – 'the doctor's heading over now.'

Ms Weybridge stopped at my bay and took the chart from the bedframe. She glanced up at Mum and Dad. 'You must be Zara's parents.'

'Yes, we are,' Mum said. 'Is she all right?'

The consultant drew the curtains and smiled while examining the chart. 'Looking at her obs, she certainly seems to be. Although…'

Dad's eyes narrowed. 'What?'

'I'm afraid your daughter's a bit of a mystery to our medical team. This is the second time she's been brought in by the paramedics and both times with the same symptoms' – she glanced from Mum to Dad – 'and unfortunately we're still none the wiser.'

'The second time?' Dad squinted.

'Yes, she was in here recently. We did various tests which we repeated yesterday but all have come back normal.'

Dad glared at me. 'Why didn't you say something?'

'Because you already think I'm mad.'

'Zara' – Ms Weybridge faced me – 'is there something I'm missing here?'

I shook my head. The doctor turned from Mum to Dad.

'We lost our son in recent years and I'm afraid Zara's not coped well.' Dad fiddled with his tie. 'And since her sister got married last September and is now expecting' – he took a deep breath – 'I'm afraid Zara's become rather delusional.'

'No, I've not. And don't speak about me like I'm not here.'

'I beg to differ, darling.' He gazed up at the consultant. 'Our daughter believes she's some kind of Time Lord being sent back in time to save her ancestors.' He glared at me. 'I'm sorry, Zara, but it's no good you scowling at me like that. We're worried about you, and with just cause, even more so now it's landing you in hospital.'

How dare he? I wasn't a child. 'I didn't ask you to come. In fact, how did you know I was even in here?'

'Holly phoned.' Mum took my hand. 'She knew we'd want to know.'

Traitor. I'd be having words with her. I specifically told her not to tell anyone I was in here.

The consultant looked from me to my parents. 'Zara, I can make a referral for you to speak to someone?'

'That would be good.' Dad gave a half smile. 'Thank you, doctor.'

I coughed. 'I am here you know. Anyway, for your information, I'm already seeing someone, so that should shut you up.'

'You are?' Dad asked.

'Who?' Mum asked. 'You're not lying to us, are you?'

'No, I'm not bloody lying. If you must know his name's Craig Fields. Check him out if you don't believe me or ask Scott, he'll know, as Annabel arranged it all.'

The consultant nodded. 'Yes, I know Dr Fields.'

'Would you recommend him?' Dad asked.

'I would. He's very sought after.'

They were talking about me like I was invisible. I just wanted to get out of there. I turned to the consultant. 'Can I be discharged now?'

'Yes. I don't see why not as we can't find anything physically wrong with you. And in light of what your parents have said, I believe it to be your mental status. However, any more fainting problems, please contact your GP. I'll sort out the paperwork and then you can leave.'

'Great. Thank you.' I turned to Mum. 'Can you pass my clothes from the locker, please?'

The ceiling fans in Double Dee's coffee shop were a welcome addition in this heat. Dave brought over a steaming cup of coffee. 'One Americano.' He flopped down next to me. 'What's up?' He put his arm around my shoulder.

I broke down in tears and snuggled up to his chest.

'Hey, come on now.' He patted me on the back. 'Can't be that bad. Has that naughty Scott been upsetting you? Do I need to have words with him?'

I pulled a tissue out of my handbag and dabbed my nose. 'No.' I sniffed. 'Well yes, but not just him. Everyone's ganging up on me.'

'Ah, is that why Holly's not hanging with you today?'

'Yes.' I sniffled. 'They all think I'm mad.'

'Course they don't. Tell Uncle Dave all about it.'

'Not a lot to tell except I've been having fainting spells and now I have to see someone to talk about my feelings.'

'That's good, babe, isn't it?'

'Is it?' I sat up straight. 'How did you know Dan was right for you?'

Dave's pale blue eyes shone. 'I knew he was the man for me from the first moment I caught sight of him. He made my heart pound and when he brushed his fingers against my skin, my whole body tingled.' He gazed into space. 'I suppose it was missing him when he wasn't around, laughing at his corny jokes, I basically loved everything about him. That's why marriage, or living with someone is such a shock, because you have to learn to love the real them' – he chuckled – 'warts and all.'

That's how I felt about Richard. Not about warts, but I couldn't get him out of my head. I longed to be close to him all the time. Even in my sleep I dreamed about him.

Dave waved a hand across my face. 'Anyone in there?'

'Sorry.' I held his hand. 'You and Dan are made for each other.'

'Just like you and Scott.'

Were we? But if that were the case then why was Richard occupying my mind all the time and not Scott? These days all Scott seemed to do was irritate me. And since I felt like he'd betrayed me, I hadn't wanted him near me.

I lowered my head. 'No, I don't think we are, Dave. I don't feel all of that you just said.'

'If that's the case please put the man out of his misery because I'm telling you now, I know for a fact that's exactly how he feels about you.'

I lifted my head. 'He told you that?'

'Yes. And more than once. He's hanging in there hoping that one day you'll marry him. For God's sake, Zara, you have to tell him. He'll be cut up for a while but at least he'll have the chance to find someone else.' Dave patted my hand. 'Why don't I get you a nice blueberry muffin to have with that coffee?'

'Go on then,' I mumbled, feeling like a real cow to Scott.

The sky was on fire. It looked like it would be another scorcher tomorrow. I was half way home when I turned around. Should I go to the train station? But then I thought better of it. I really should let my body recover a little more. I'd go Monday after work. Holly was out with Adam this evening which meant I'd have the flat to myself. Scott wouldn't be turning up as we still weren't speaking. Mum said he'd wanted to come to the hospital but Dad had told him best to leave it.

I put my key in the lock, pushed the door open, and was surprised by the sound of the TV coming from the lounge. 'Is that you, Holl?' I called.

She peeped out of the doorway. 'Hi, Zara, how are you?'

'I thought you were out with Adam?'

'Should've been but I didn't want to leave you alone after your...'

'My what?'

'Your fainting spells.'

'Did my mum put you up to this?'

She grinned. 'She might've said it was a good idea.'

I clenched my fists. Why couldn't they leave me alone? 'How can it be a good idea, Holl, when I'm still bloody livid with you?' I headed for the kitchen but she followed.

'But you know I had no choice.'

I drew water from the tap and filled the kettle. 'You promised.' I flicked the switch, and took a mug from the cupboard.

'I know but... Would you mind making me a coffee?'

Yes, I bloody did mind, but there was no point being petty about it so I grabbed another mug and spooned instant coffee into both. 'You know one day you're all going to look pretty stupid not believing me.'

'How so?'

'Because I'll find a way to bring some proof back with me.' Would that be something I could control? The engagement ring, maybe?

Holly took a packet of Maryland Cookies from the biscuit barrel, ripped open the top, and filled a tea plate. 'You talk about promises, Zara, but what about your promises? You promised you wouldn't do the time travel thing anymore.'

Ignoring her I picked up the boiling kettle, poured water into the mugs and stirred the drinks.

'Well?' Holly raised her voice. 'What have you got to say about that?'

She was right. I was lecturing her on promises but I'd broken mine. I turned to face her. 'Yes you're right. I'm sorry. Here.' I passed her a mug. 'Truce?'

'Truce.' She put the mug down on the side and took me into a hug. 'You're my best friend and I love you. And that's why I let your mum and dad know you were in hospital. They've had enough worry over the years with losing your Michael. It's not fair to them, is it?'

I let her hold me. It wasn't fair but what could I do? It was my destiny. I pulled her to arm's length. 'Hey, why don't we go out tonight? Let's go for a curry, or a pizza? You choose.'

She smiled. 'I've a better idea. Let's order a takeaway, get into our PJs and crash in front of the TV. We can watch Mr Darcy if you say yes.'

'A brilliant idea.' I'd pretend Mr Darcy was Richard.

Chapter Sixteen

Sounds of girlie giggles travelled down the corridor. I stopped outside my office. What was going on? Feeling like an intruder I pushed open the door and stepped in. It didn't look like my office. Instead work stations had been installed. Two desks positioned face to face with only a small divider in-between for a minute amount of privacy.

Scott was leaning over a woman's shoulder as they both stared at the screen. She held onto his every word.

'What the heck's going on?' I asked. 'And who the hell is she?'

Scott spun around. 'Hi there, Zara. Welcome back. Meet Megan.'

I glanced at my desk. 'What's happened to my stuff?'

'We transferred everything from the drawers into these ones' – he pointed – 'and the paperwork in your filing cabinets into those.' He signalled with his hand. 'Cool, isn't it?'

'I don't bloody think so. I liked it the way it was. And why are you in here?' I glared at Megan.

'Don't be so rude, Zara.' Scott scowled.

Megan twisted to face me. She was striking. Platinum bleached hair worn short in a pompadour, perfectly shaped eyebrows, aquamarine eyes, and four tiny diamond studs in each ear. She smiled showing off her perfect teeth. 'Hello, Zara. I'm Megan Masters. I've heard all about you.'

'Well you have the advantage over me then.' I slammed my handbag down on the desk. 'This is the first I've heard about you.'

'Annabel said you knew all about it.' Scott put his arm around my shoulder.

'Get off me.' I pushed him away. 'Not this, I don't. She said she was employing a temp. Not someone to invade my space. How am I supposed to concentrate? This isn't on. Wait until I speak to Annabel.'

'Oh, I almost forgot' – Megan flashed her eyes at Scott – 'Annabel said to send Zara in to see her when she arrived.'

Annabel said to send Zara in to see her when she arrived. I was bloody here. She might've looked mature but acted more like a frivolous schoolkid. 'Why the hell are you telling him when I'm standing right here?'

Her face flushed. 'Sorry, I...'

'For fuck's sake, Zara. Leave the girl alone. It's not her fault that Annabel saw the necessity to get someone in. If you weren't off chasing fairies or whatever fantasy you're busy doing then there wouldn't have been the need.' He rested his hand on Megan's shoulder. 'Take no notice of her. She's not well.'

What did he mean I wasn't well? I wanted to shout at him but instead I picked up my handbag from the desk and stomped out of the office. *How dare Annabel do this to me?* Did my years of loyalty count for nothing? On reaching her room, I banged the door with my fist and stamped straight in.

'What's going on, Annabel? I come back and find my office space turned upside down and discover you've installed my replacement in there.'

Annabel rose from behind her desk. 'And good morning to you too, Zara. Now I suggest you calm down and take a seat.'

'And if I don't want to?'

She held out her hand signalling me to sit down. I plonked into the chair and she returned to hers. 'Coffee?' She poured two cups from the pot on her desk without waiting for my answer.

'I don't understand. I've done as you asked and I'm seeing Dr Fields. How could you do this and not even tell me?'

She pushed one of the coffees over to me. 'We did discuss this, Zara.' Her voice remained calm. 'I said my plan was to get someone in to assist with the editing.'

'You said a temp.'

'Yes, that's right but after serious consideration I came to the conclusion that we should get a young person in to train. This is a good thing. It'll allow you more time to write. Not just the serial but other articles. I thought you could have your own weekly column.'

'But I liked my private space.' I picked up the cup and took a sip of coffee.

'Megan needed a place to work. And as you and Scott are the only two members of staff who don't share an office, I concluded she should share with you.'

I slammed the cup back down on the saucer.

Annabel passed me an extra large tissue from the Kleenex box on her immaculate desk. 'Mop it up, Zara.'

'Sorry.' I soaked up the splattered beverage. 'Why me? Can't she share with Scott?'

'Zara' – Annabel twisted the gold pendant around her neck – 'I'm going to let your attitude pass because I know you're not well. Megan was the right decision for the magazine because once again you've been off sick. You must understand that at the end of the day Feminine Smile has to come first. You've always been a good worker and I know you will be again. Give yourself time to grieve. The weekly meetings with Craig will help.'

I frowned. 'What's he said to you?'

She shook her head. 'Paranoia doesn't suit you' – she took a deep breath – 'but then maybe that's all part of your illness. For your information and let me be clear. Craig hasn't mentioned your visit to me other than to let me know you attended. He's not allowed to, but also' – she reached for my hand – 'Craig would never break a client's trust.'

Annabel was right. I was being paranoid. What had got into me? This wasn't me. 'I'm sorry,' I said in almost a whisper.

'That's all right. I understand. Now, why not give Megan a chance? She's a nice girl but has a lot to learn and you'll make the perfect mentor.'

I nodded.

'Another reason I wanted her in your office.' She picked up the coffee pot. 'Would you like a refill as you splashed half across my desk?'

'Yes, please.' Maybe working with the girl wouldn't be too bad and it might be nice to have some company. Although, I didn't like the way she and Scott had been all over each other, not that it should matter to me, but it did. I drank the coffee just leaving the dregs. 'Thanks, Annabel.' I stood up from the chair. 'Once again, I'm sorry for my outburst and promise to try and get on with Megan.'

Scott picked up his pint of beer. 'Thanks for agreeing to come out with me.'

'You're right. We need to clear the air.' I sprinkled salt and vinegar onto a bowl of chips.

His hazel eyes glistened. 'I've missed us.'

'What did you expect? You betrayed me.'

'What are you talking about? I didn't betray you.'

'Yes you did. You went behind my back to Dad.' I blew on a chip before popping it into my mouth.

'Only because I care. So about you and me?' He squeezed my fingers.

I pulled my arm back.

'What? You can't even bear to hold my hand now? Is that it then for us? Because quite frankly I'm not sure how much more of this I can take.'

'Looking to replace me with Megan?'

'What?' He slammed his glass down.

'I saw how you held on to her every word.'

He shook his head. 'Well at least if I took her out she wouldn't be acting like this.'

'Take her bloody out then. See if I care.' I shot up and grabbed my bag. 'Ask her out. You may as well,' I raised my voice, 'because we're done, Scott Edwards. We're done.'

'Zara.'

I heard him call after me but refused to turn back. Instead I made my way towards the train station, not caring that it was dark. I had to see Richard.

Mary rolled my plaited hair, pinned it in place, and finished the style with a blue headband above my brow. I stared in the mirror. It didn't look like me.

She placed her hands on my shoulders. 'Sir Richard's a kind gentleman.'

'Yes, he is,' I said.

'I don't want to speak out of place, Rebecca but...'

'But what?'

'Just be careful of that brother of yours,' she whispered.

'Mary, what do you mean?'

She headed to the door, peeped outside, closed it fully and came back over to me. 'I don't believe Sir Samuel's death was an accident.'

Mary was reiterating what Richard had said. I turned to face her. 'Why are you saying this?'

She fiddled with her fingers. 'Rebecca, I've known you and Edward since you were babies and' – she blinked – 'that brother of yours...'

'What?'

'He's always been a bad un. From a young age he got himself into trouble. The amount of times your father bailed him out.' She sighed. 'And then when your father refused to help anymore, suddenly your parents are in an unexplained accident.'

'What are you saying?'

'Nothing. I've probably said too much.'

'Are you suggesting Edward had something to do with that?'

She stayed silent.

'Mary. Tell me, please.'

'Nothing could be proven. And then once he'd drawn all funds from the house, he sought a husband for you. Sir Samuel was a good man. Stepped in when Edward had creditors knocking at the door, until one day he refused to do it anymore.'

'How do you know all this?'

'Sir Samuel, as did your dear mother, took me into his confidence. Also it's the reason your father changed his will and made you sole beneficiary.'

Things were becoming a little clearer. So Rebecca and Edward were brought up in this house, and Richard's suspicions about Edward were right.

Mary pulled up a seat next to me. 'Before Sir Samuel died, he asked me to protect you should something happen to him, and then the next day he had that awful supposed accident.' She rubbed her eyes. 'And now' – she sniffled – 'I'm concerned Sir Richard will be next, and maybe you too. That way Edward can take ownership of Bridge View Hall.'

'That's a strong accusation, Mary.'

Footsteps echoed outside in the hallway. Mary held a finger against her lips. There was a knock on the door.

Mary got up and opened it. 'Sir Edward, can I help you?'

'The guests are starting to arrive. Is Lady Rebecca ready?'

'Almost. She'll be there in due course.'

'Don't be too long. Sir Richard won't want to be kept waiting.'

'She'll be there soon.' Mary closed the door, and put a hand to her chest.

'Are you all right, Mary?'

She nodded. 'I will be.'

'If what you suspect is true, then why wasn't he arrested?'

'There was no proof. He's too clever for that.'

I wondered whether I should tell her about Richard's suspicions but decided against it.

Mary held out the gown for me to step into. Blue and gold lace overlapped turquoise chiffon which floated to my ankles with a short train. I stared at my reflection. The bodice was flattering and the colour suited me.

We joined the dance floor and glided around like the other couples. It was odd because I wasn't a very good dancer yet my feet knew exactly where to go.

'You look beautiful, Rebecca,' Richard whispered.

My stomach bubbled. His breath was sweet and inviting. I wished he'd kiss me. 'Thank you,' I finally managed to say.

After numerous rounds on the dance floor, Richard led me out of the French doors onto the veranda and down the stone steps to a quiet spot in the garden. He brushed his fingertips across my cheek. My skin tingled. 'I'm besotted with you, Rebecca.' He caressed my neck. 'I think I'm falling in love with you.'

I stroked his rough chin. 'I feel the same.'

His lips touched mine. My heart quickened. His kisses tasted fruity from the wine. My whole body yearned for him but he pulled back. 'Forgive me, dear lady. I shouldn't have done that.'

'It's all right. Kiss me again.'

'I can't risk soiling your reputation. We'll be married soon. That is...'

I grinned. 'Yes, Richard, I'll marry you. Come to my room later.'

'My dear lady. That would be most improper.'

'But I need to speak with you.'

He gazed at me. 'I can't do that.'

'Yes, you can. We shan't be alone. Mary will be there. She has some information about Edward and my room's the safest place to talk.'

'Very well but not until our guests have all left.' He led me back into the ballroom and onto the dance floor.

⋆

Mary helped me out of my gown.

'I'd like you to tell Sir Richard what you told me earlier.'

'I'm not sure, Rebecca. He's a good friend of your brother. If this gets back to him then' – her posture tightened – 'my life could be in danger too.' She slipped an ivory cotton robe over my blue nightdress.

I turned to look at her. 'It's all right, Mary. You can trust him. I promise.'

There was a tap on the door.

'That'll be him now.' I headed over to the door and inched it open. 'Come in. Mary's waiting.'

'I'm not comfortable being in here and especially when you're in night attire.' He glanced over at Mary. 'Is the kitchen empty?'

'Yes. The staff have all retired. We can speak there, but...'

'There's a problem?'

'How do I know I can trust you?'

'You can. I promise.'

'Very well. I'll go downstairs and check the coast is clear. I don't think you should be in here though. It's improper.'

'I agree. I shall come with you.'

I held him back. 'He'll be there in a moment, Mary. I need to speak to him.'

She frowned. 'Very well, but be careful.'

Once she'd gone I put my arms around Richard and placed my lips on his. For a moment he returned my kiss before holding me at arm's length. 'Forgive me. This is most inappropriate. I must go.'

'Tuck me in first.'

'Don't do this to me, Rebecca.' He held his hand on the door knob.

'Please. And then you can go.' I climbed the step to the four-poster, pulled back the covers, slid into the satin sheets and laid my head on the squishy pillow.

He came over to the side, stroked my arm, and kissed me on the cheek. 'Sleep well, dearest.'

I closed my eyes. His footsteps echoed as he clicked the door shut on the other side.

Shivering, I opened my eyes. Dazed, I gazed down at my clothes. I'd been transported back. I wore my skimpy shift and was curled up on the cold floor near the ticket machine. No wonder I was cold.

A man came through one of the turnstiles and dropped a few coins by my feet. 'Buy yourself some breakfast, love.'

'No.' I tried to pick up the money to give back but he'd gone. I finally managed to scramble to my feet. My legs felt like jelly. The station was deserted. I checked the time. Five o'clock. I wondered how long I'd been there? Had I arrived back unconscious like other times but escaped the hospital because no one was around to call an ambulance? I had to get out of there before someone saw me. With my handbag across my shoulder, I headed for the exit and watched the sky turn orange as the sun came up.

A taxi driver pulled on to the forecourt. I headed over to the empty cab.

Chapter Seventeen

The alarm buzzed on my mobile. I rolled over to turn it off and check the time. At least I'd managed a couple of hours sleep after staggering into the flat just after five am. I forced myself out of bed and on stumbling to the bathroom I caught my reflection in the hallway mirror. Blimey, I looked like death warmed up. Felt like it too. I didn't dare miss another day from work though or Annabel would definitely be booting me out of the door.

I threw off my nightie, switched on the shower, and stepped under the steamy flow. After lathering my hair, I rinsed and added conditioner, inhaling the vanilla fragrance to try and liven myself up. My stomach rumbled. I was starving. No wonder I was feeling rough. I turned off the shower and grabbed my towel.

The office door swung open. I peered up from the computer screen. 'Oh it's you.'

'Good morning to you too.' Scott stared at me. 'Crikey, babe, you look dreadful.'

'Thanks.'

'Are you ill?'

'What do you care?'

He sighed. 'It doesn't have to be like this.'

Megan breezed in. 'Morning, Zara. Morning, Scott.' She grinned at him before heading to her desk.

I leaned back in the chair. 'You two an item now then?'

She tossed her head back in laughter, 'No way. I mean, he's proper old.'

Scott glared at her. 'Cheers, Megan. Love you too.'

'Oops, sorry,' she said, 'I didn't mean it to come out like that. It's just...'

'I know. I'm only teasing.' He turned to me. 'Not sure what you're smirking at, Zara. If I'm proper old then you must be too.'

I chuckled. 'You're right. I suppose I must be.'

His eyes sparkled and for a moment my heart gave a little leap. Maybe there was still something there, but what did it matter when we'd already ended things? I twisted the alexandrite birthstone ring on my index finger. It was such an unusual ring, appearing emerald throughout the day and ruby at night. Scott had given it to me on my birthday with the words, 'The next one will be a diamond when you say yes'. What was wrong with me? When he was mine, I didn't want him, and now I was reminiscing about what we'd had. I gazed up at him. 'What can I do for you?'

'I brought you this.' He passed me a buff file. 'It's about the mansion. I thought it might be of interest.'

'Awesome.' I beamed. 'Thanks, Scott.'

'No worries. I'll leave you girls to it.'

'Actually' – Megan rose from her seat – 'I'll come with you as I've got an appointment with Annabel.' They both left the room giving me the opportunity to browse through the house details. I opened the folder.

The five-hundred acre property had been purchased in 1829 by an Albert Harrison who built a simple Regency house on the land. Over the years it had gone through several transformations and in the mid-nineteenth century Karl and Marta Hoffman came over from Germany, taking up residence at Bridge View Hall. Karl, an architect, extended the building to include a conservatory, billiard room and tower. Twelve years later the property was sold to an English couple, George and Elizabeth Pendleton.

Pendelton? They were Rebecca and Edward's parents.

Scott must've spent a fair time researching as I hadn't managed to uncover any of this during my initial searches. He obviously still cared. Could there be hope for us? After all, Richard would never be mine. Richard was Rebecca's love. I popped the paperwork back into the file, leaned back in my chair and thought about Scott when Richard popped into my head.

Someone shook my arm. I opened my eyes and stared up at Megan.

'Zara, are you all right?'

'Oh' – I pulled myself upright – 'what's going on?'

'You were asleep. I was getting worried. I've been shaking you for five minutes. I thought you were dead.'

'That's a bit of an overreaction.'

'No, it wasn't.' Her hands trembled. 'You looked so pale and you weren't moving and then when I couldn't wake you ...'

'Hey. It's all right. I'm sorry, I didn't mean to give you a fright.' I poured a glass of water and took a huge swig. 'Look, Megan, you won't mention this to anyone, will you?'

She squinted. 'I don't know.'

'Please.'

'But...'

'Please,' I said again.

'If you're sure you're okay.'

'I am. I didn't sleep well last night, that's all.' I got up from my chair and pushed it around to her desk. 'Tell you what, show me what you're working on and I'll see if I can offer some guidance.' Annabel wanted me to mentor so that's what I'd try to do.

'Thanks, Zara.' Smiling, Megan hurried over next to me, took her seat, unlocked the PC, typed on the keyboard and brought up a Word document on the screen. 'This is Ben's film review of *Indiana Jones and the Dial of Destiny*. Annabel's asked me to proof it.'

'Ben?'

'You know, the guy who started just before me.'

'Ah, yes.' I was surprised Annabel hadn't introduced me. 'Did Annabel explain what you have to do?'

'Sort of, but she went quickly so I wouldn't mind if you could go through it again.' Megan scratched her ear.

'Sure, don't worry. I'll explain. When you're proofing you need to look for several things. Firstly, make sure there are no typos or spelling errors. And check for formatting issues and inconsistencies. You know what I mean?'

'Think so.'

'Great. Also, make sure it reads well as some of our reporters can be a bit slapdash. Not Scott though. He's meticulous.'

She nodded.

'Tell you what, I'll sit with you while you complete this.'

'Thanks.'

We had our heads together when high heels clicked into the room.

'Now this is what I like to see.'

I looked up at Annabel. 'Hi there.' She looked stunning in her white blouse and burgundy floral skirt. 'Love your outfit,' I said. 'Is it new?'

'Yes, it is. Thank you.' The skirt swirled as she stepped to my side.

I touched the sleeve of her gypsy top. 'Where did you get this from?'

'Seasalt.'

'It's gorgeous. So soft. Feels almost like silk.'

She smiled. 'Yes, I like it. Viscose, apparently.' She looked from me to Megan and back at me. 'Zara, are you free for a catch up in my office' – she glanced at her watch – 'say, ten minutes?'

'Sure.' I nodded. 'That works.'

In good spirits and less fatigued, I meandered along the corridor towards Annabel's office. That quick doze had really helped. It was weird how I suddenly felt at ease with everything. I'd enjoyed mentoring Megan and wondered why I'd been so reluctant? Had I been threatened? She seemed a nice enough girl. I breezed past Scott's door, held open with a wedge, and gave a little wave. He waved back. I continued walking until reaching Annabel's room and tapped on the glass door.

She pulled it open. 'Thanks for coming, Zara. Coffee?'

'Cheers' – I chuckled – 'and I promise not to spill it over your desk this time.'

'I'm pleased to hear that. Do take a seat.' Her skirt swayed as she sashayed to her desk. She poured coffee into a mug and placed it in front of me before sitting opposite. 'Dare I say that we seem to have our old Zara back?'

'If you like.' I smiled.

'Watching you with Megan reassures me that I made the right decision bringing her in. You'll make an excellent mentor. Your sessions with Craig must be helping.'

'Yes, I think they are.' I took a sip of the drink and replaced it on the coaster. It was wonderful to have Annabel off my back. Hopefully the rest of them would leave me alone soon too.

'How's the project going?'

'You mean the time travel story?'

'Yes.' She picked up a pen and flicked open her notepad.

'Really well. Actually, Scott did some research for me.'

'That's what I like to see. Working as a team. That's what Feminine Smile's all about.' She scribbled something on the paper. 'And how about you and Scott? What's happening there?'

I shrugged. 'Not sure.' I took a sip from the cup.

'I heard you were going through some rough waters.'

I clenched my fist. 'From Scott?'

'Yes, but before you start blaming him, I prised it out of him.'

I relaxed my fist and took a deep breath. 'That's okay. I wasn't going to. He was awesome providing me with lots of history about the house. By the way, is it all right if I leave a little earlier tomorrow as I've got a session booked with Craig?'

'Of course. Your appointments with Craig must always take priority. The main thing is your recovery.'

Megan and I were heading out of the building when Scott called from behind us. 'Wait up, Zara. You got a minute?'

I turned to Megan. 'I'm just going to have a chat with Scott so I'll see you tomorrow. Well done for today.'

'Okay. Bye then.' She gawked at Scott. 'Night, old man.' She hurried down the steps giggling.

Scott chuckled. 'Cheeky minx.'

'She's all right. Now what can I do for you?'

'I wondered if you had time for coffee?'

'Coffee. Hmm...' It would be nice to spend some time together. I'd been angry for far too long. 'Okay. Double Dee's?'

'Cool.' He linked his arm in mine.

I smiled and let him lead me around the corner to the cafe.

'You're looking better than you were first thing.'

I wasn't going to tell him I'd fallen asleep so I just said, 'Thanks. I'm feeling better too. Work was more like it used to be today.'

'It's good to see you getting on with the new girl.'

'She's okay. I think I misjudged her.' I glanced ahead at the coffee shop forecourt. 'Isn't that Dan?' I waved. He waved back and stubbed out a cigarette into an ashtray as we reached the premises. I nudged his arm. 'Isn't it time you quit?'

'Yeah, you're right. Told Dave come my birthday, I'm going to stop. Anyway, it's cool to see you two together.' He pushed the door open. 'One black Americano and a cappuccino?'

'Thanks,' we answered in unison and made for the comfy furniture.

I sank into the leather sofa and Scott flopped down next to me. 'I've missed you,' he said.

'I've missed you too.'

He brushed the back of my hand. 'Do you think...?' He shook his head. 'Nah, don't worry.'

'What?'

'You and me' – he squeezed my fingers – 'do you think there's any hope?'

I shuffled closer but then Richard was in my head so I slid back. 'I don't know. I mean, I don't want to lead you on.'

'Then how about we take things slowly as friends?'

'Sounds like a plan.'

He grinned. 'Friends with benefits?'

'A black Americano for the lady, and a cappuccino for sir,' interrupted Dan. 'Can I get you anything else?'

Scott squinted. 'Blueberry muffin?'

'Go on then.'

'Two blueberry muffins coming up.' Dan made his way to the counter swaying his slim hips.

Scott took a gulp of his drink.

I grinned.

'What?'

I pointed to the froth on his upper lip.

'Oh.' He ran his tongue across the foam. 'Now. About my suggestion or was it a question? Anyway, what do you reckon? Friends with benefits?'

Friends with benefits didn't sound like a bad idea. I took a sip of coffee. 'Maybe,' I answered from behind the cup pretending to be coy.

'Cool.' His hazel eyes twinkled.

'Actually, Scott, I'm going to Chloe's this Sunday. Fancy coming with me? As a friend of course. Mum and Dad will be there too. I'm sure they'd all love to see you.'

'I'd like that. Let me know what time.'

Chapter Eighteen

It had been a good week at work and I was feeling more like my old self but I'd been itching to get back to Bridge View Hall. However, because I didn't dare take any more time off work I'd waited until Friday evening to head to the station. Peak time was over and although quiet, there were still a few commuters coming in from the trains. I headed for the platform and almost immediately the flash hit me.

Where was I? A voice I didn't recognise. The smell of wood, the kind typical of old properties, travelled to my nose. I shivered. Disorientated, I opened my eyes and took in my surroundings. Edward was on one side of me, Richard the other, and we were sitting in a church pew. I touched my head revealing a wide-brimmed straw hat trimmed with lace.

'And now,' the minister announced, 'we shall stand and sing Hymn Number 283.'

After a rustle of gowns and shuffling of feet the congregation led by the soprano boys' choir sang 'Abide with me'.

Afterwards the minister cleared his throat. 'I will now publish the banns.' He read out some names which I didn't take in until he got to '...between Richard John Cavendish of the Parish of Lambridge and Rebecca Anne Pendleton of this Parish.' The minister peered around the room. 'If any of you know cause or just impediment why these persons should not be joined together in Holy Matrimony, ye are to declare it.'

The church went silent. I glimpsed at Richard. He smiled, taking my hand. His eyes gleamed. Butterflies flipped inside my stomach. Edward let out a deep breath when no one objected.

At the end of the service the minister, curate and choir boys filed out of the church. The organist played an exit piece as the congregation filtered out pew by pew with each person stopping in the vestibule to say a few words to the minister and shaking his hand.

We reached the front of the queue. The minister smiled, peered over his round metal glasses and said, 'Lady Rebecca, I'm looking forward to conducting your wedding ceremony in three weeks. Your parents would be so proud if they were still here and could see the woman you've grown into.'

'Thank you.' I returned his smile.

After shaking hands, and thanking him for a lovely service, Richard linked his arm in mine, and we moved on to make way for the parishioners behind us. We were sauntering alongside the graveyard, when he came to a halt at one of the graves. 'The minister's right. Your mother and father would be proud of you.'

I read the words on the headstone.
Treasured memories of beloved parents.
Sara Mary Pendleton (nee Blackwood) 1869-1905
A tender mother: a faithful friend.
Peter Simon Pendelton 1864-1905
A beloved father: a protector.
Although they sleep their memories live on.

An involuntary tear fell to my cheek. Richard passed me a handkerchief. I dabbed my moist face.

'I apologise, dear lady, I did not mean to upset you. Come.' I let him guide me down the path. Once away from the church, he stopped again and took my hand. 'How would you like a boating trip on the lake? A friend of mine has given me permission to use his rowing boat.'

'Yes, please. That sounds wonderful.'

Edward hurried from behind us. 'Did I hear you mention a rowing excursion, Richard?'

'You did, sir, but I'm afraid it's an outing for two. My fiancée and I would prefer to have some time alone.'

Edward frowned.

Richard's eyes widened. 'You don't mind do you, Edward?'

'No' – he huffed – 'that is, providing my sister feels comfortable without a chaperone.'

'I feel quite comfortable, brother. Please don't worry. Richard will take care of me.'

Richard squeezed my fingers. 'I will indeed.' He guided me along the path but when it came to turn into the road to the mansion, he turned to Edward. 'We're going this way so we'll see you this evening.' He twisted back to me. 'I have a surprise for you.'

I wondered what the surprise was and where he was taking me as I thought the lake was in the opposite direction. He stopped outside the Langham Hotel.

'What are we doing here?' I asked.

'This is my home when I'm not in London.'

Was he going to take me to his room?

He grinned. 'Don't look so worried.' He strode up to an indigo car and opened the passenger door. 'This is my surprise.' He held out a hand to assist me.

I sank into the bucket seat of the Daimler convertible. 'It's lovely. Is it new?'

'Yes' – he cranked the engine and jumped in behind the steering wheel – 'it was dropped off yesterday. I thought you'd like it.'

As we drove through Horam and Amblehurst, I marvelled at the gorgeous green countryside. Richard pulled the car to the side of the road. 'We need to venture the rest of the way on foot. Have you been to Worthwood Lake before?'

'No,' I answered admiring the wildflowers, recognising the thistles and harebells but not the yellow blooms.

'Not a lot of people know about it. You'll adore it.'

'Is it far?' I asked, fanning my face.

'No' – he pointed – 'just up there. Once we're over the top, I promise to find us shade.'

I peered down at my light blue gown. Lovely, but hardly practical for hill climbing. I held the skirt above my ankles.

'Don't worry, there are steps and a rail.' He lugged the hamper from the back seat and linked his arm in mine. 'Just a little walk. The view will be worth it. You'll see.'

I ambled up the wide rustic steps with Richard at my side. Once we reached the top, I gasped at the secret valley below. Shades of reds and green surrounded glinting water. It reminded me of a blue lagoon, like a piece of Heaven, secluded and only available to the meagre few who knew of its whereabouts. Richard and I were alone. Had he brought me here to seduce me? My insides bubbled.

He put his arm around me. 'Do you approve?'

'It's spectacular.'

'And the best is yet to come. Are you ready?'

'Yes.' I hitched my skirt up a couple of inches away from the ground.

'Let me help you down' – he held onto my arm – 'as it's a lot trickier.'

We took the steep steps at a snail's pace and once we reached the flat the stunning vision was worth it. A pair of black swans veered towards us. I peered out across the amber tinted ripples.

Richard relinked his arm in mine and we strolled across a timber bridge to the jetty. He pulled a small rowing boat into position, placed the hamper inside, stepped in and held out a hand to assist me.

I grabbed hold of his waist to balance and boarded the vessel. 'Thank you.' I giggled, lowering myself onto the bow seat opposite him.

He removed his blazer, laid it in front of him, and rolled up his sleeves. 'You don't mind, do you?' His brownish gold eyes twinkled.

'No, of course not.' I wanted to stretch across to pull off his necktie and undo the top buttons on the crisp white shirt but instead I just smiled.

My heart doubled its beat as he took hold of the oars, leaning forwards and backwards repeatedly, turning the oars with ease. 'You've done this before,' I said.

He laughed. 'Yes. It was a regular pastime my father and I shared.'

'Shared?'

'Alas, yes. He died last year.'

'And your mother?'

He shook his head. 'No, she's gone too. Like you, I am an orphan.'

'I'm sorry.' I leaned across to touch his hand making the boat rock. 'Sorry.' I sat back sensing my face turning the colour of beetroot.

Once the boat had settled, he said, 'Maybe not a good idea to do that again.' He chuckled.

I laughed to cover up my embarrassment. After moments of silence I said, 'I can't believe Edward played a part in Mother and Father's accident. How could any son do that?'

'Rest assured he'll not go unpunished. Your parents' deaths and my good friend Samuel's will be avenged.' Richard signalled with his head. 'I'll make for that island over there to have our picnic.'

'That sounds lovely.' He was handsome, kind and considerate. A recipe for the perfect husband.

When we reached the bank, he tied the boat to a post, got out, pulled the boat closer for me to disembark, and then leaned in to pick up the picnic basket. 'Splendid,' he said, 'we have this beautiful willow to protect us from the sun's strong rays.'

'A wonderful beauty spot.'

He took a rug from the top of the hamper and spread it on the ground. 'Dearest, are you fine with this? I'm sorry, I should've thought of bringing chairs.'

'This is perfect.' I lowered myself onto the mat.

He kneeled down, took a bottle of fizz from the basket along with two glasses, popped the cork making us both laugh, and poured a sparkling wine for each of us. 'For you.' He handed me a champagne flute, with bubbles rising from the bottom, and clinked it against mine. 'To us.'

'To us.' I took a sip of the chilled alcohol, enjoying the smooth creamy taste on my tongue and on swallowing experiencing a buzz.

Richard moved into a sitting position with his legs stretched out in front. He took my glass and placed it, along with his own, on a tree stump. 'Would it be too forward of me to remove your bonnet?' he asked.

'Not at all. We have lots of shade so I don't really need it.'

'I feel so at ease with you.' He unpinned my hat and unclipped my chignon, allowing my hair to fall freely across my shoulders. 'This marriage idea may have started out as a farce, something neither of us thought would actually happen, but' – he ran his fingers through my hair – 'my dearest, Rebecca, I've fallen deeply in love with you and it would break my heart if you decided not to go ahead with the wedding.'

'I feel the same.' I laid my head back against his chest and gazed up at him. 'The day I become Lady Rebecca Cavendish will be the best day of my life.'

'You're so beautiful.' He brushed my hair behind an ear and caressed my neck. I lifted my head, moved my face to his, and kissed him on the lips. For a moment he kissed me back before pulling away.

I frowned. 'Don't stop.'

'I apologise, I should never have done that.'

'It's all right, we're alone. Kiss me, please.'

He leaned closer, loosened my bodice, and moved downwards from my neck, smothering me with kisses. My skin tingled with excitement. Before reaching my breasts he moved back up towards my face and gently pressed his lips on mine. Passion screamed inside me. My body urged him to kiss me harder, and take me, but he took care not to touch me in any way that would be seen as improper.

He slid my bodice back onto my shoulders. 'I can wait.'

'But we don't have to.'

'Yes, we do. I respect you far too much to take advantage. In three weeks we will say our marriage vows and you'll become my wife, then my dearest, I'll come to your bed and make you mine. Come, sit up.' He re-opened the hamper. 'Let's explore the cuisine delights the hotel has packed for us.'

Mary brushed my hair. 'How was your day on the lake?'

'Perfect. Richard brought a picnic and we had champagne.' My heart skipped a beat when I mentioned his name.

'Well I hope you ate some food too.'

'We did. It was divine. Salads, breads, strawberries. Oh and Richard had lobster.'

'You didn't? Lobster's normally your favourite which is why I made a point of letting Sir Richard know to ensure it was packed.'

'I didn't feel like it today. The excitement was a little too much.'

'Understandable. Sir Richard will make you a good husband. You're going to be happy with him.' She placed the hairbrush down on the dressing table, rested her hands on my shoulders and stared at me through the mirror. 'But once you're wed, you and Sir Richard need to take care.' She blinked. 'I overheard your brother talking earlier in the drawing room with a gentleman I didn't recognise and they appeared to be plotting about money Edward was due to inherit. I fear once you've become Lady Cavendish that both yours and Sir Richard's lives will be in danger.'

Suppose Edward was too clever for Richard. Edward was responsible for Rebecca's mother and father's accident and had managed to get away with it. I turned my head to face Mary. 'Sir Richard says he has a plan to prevent Edward harming either of us.'

'Even so, things can go wrong. So, please, Rebecca, you must warn Richard.'

'I will.' I made for the bed, stepped up into the four-poster, and laid my head on the comfy pillow.

'Sleep well, my child.' She pulled the satin sheet over me before leaving the room.

Mary was right, we needed to be careful. Why hadn't Edward been arrested yet? Supposing he managed to worm his way out of the charges. I'd speak to Richard again. My stomach curdled. Richard needed to be ahead of Edward.

Unable to sleep I lay staring at the ceiling. All I could think of was Edward and the harm he could cause us. In my mind's eye I pictured the Daimler turned upside down, my dress soaked crimson, and Richard's lifeless body caught in the shattered windscreen.

No, Richard wouldn't let that happen. To distract myself from the scenes in my head, I closed my eyes, and imagined Richard kissing me all over.

The sound of coins clinking on concrete aroused me. I opened my eyes. The station foyer was almost deserted. I shivered. Goose pimples covered my bare arms. I attempted to stand but stumbled. My stomach rumbled. Yet again the time travelling had left me not only dizzy but weak from hunger. Finally, I managed to stagger up and headed over to the vending machine. I popped twenty pence pieces into the slot and pushed the button. Steaming vegetable soup dripped into the paper cup. I lifted it out, blew on the broth, and took a sip. It might've been thin and tasteless but my stomach gurgled in appreciation. Dazed, I managed to zigzag out of the train station and climb into a cab.

Chapter Nineteen

Holly glared at me. 'My god, you look ghastly.'

'Cheers for that.' She was right though. I spooned Weetabix into my mouth, fighting to keep it down.

'Do I need to have a word with that Scott for keeping you out all night on Friday? I mean you never left your bed yesterday and you still look like you've not slept a wink.'

'Oi. Mind your own business, otherwise I'll start interfering with your love life.' The last thing I wanted was her to discover I hadn't spent the night with Scott. I blew over the coffee and took a sip.

'Looks like you need a double espresso, never mind an Americano.' She pressed the button on our newest toy, brought a cup of cappuccino to the table, and sat down to drink it.

'Espresso's too strong for me.'

'Yeah. Know what you mean. By the way, what time are you leaving?'

'Scott's picking me up in a couple of hours.'

'It's brilliant how you two have managed to sort things out.'

'We're trying.' I gathered my dirty dishes and took them to the sink. 'What are your plans today?'

'Adam's coming round to make me lunch.'

'You're lucky he's such a great cook.' I rinsed out the glass, cup, and bowl, and placed them in the drainer. 'I wonder what delights my sister's cooking for us, or should I say Mum as she's bound to be in charge. She'll be fussing over Chloe. "Sit down, darling. You need to rest." Still at least if her focus is on my sister it hopefully won't be on me.'

'That's true. You know though, you should be glad. I wish my mum lived close enough to fuss over me.' Holly's mum had remarried and emigrated to Australia with her new husband last year.

'Sorry.'

'It's not your fault. Anyway, Adam reckons he's got enough cash saved to take me out there soon.'

'Awesome.' I caught sight of the time on the microwave clock. 'Right, I'd better hurry if I'm going to get into that shower before Scott gets here.'

My face looked like I needed a blood transfusion. I had to do something otherwise I'd have Mum saying how I resembled a vampire again and then fussing around me. I'd just dabbed another layer of blusher on my cheeks, and traced a rose tone pencil over my lips, when Holly knocked on the bedroom door, opened it slightly, and peeped from behind. 'How you doing in there?'

'Almost ready. Come in.'

She strode in. 'Well you're looking a little more human. What you wearing?'

'Not sure.' I got up from the dressing table and rooted through the wardrobe and pulled out a sundress. 'What do you reckon?'

'Yeah. I like that. Let's see it on.'

I threw off the bathrobe and stepped into the dress.

'You look a million dollars but' – she shook her head – 'have you lost weight?'

'A bit. That's why I went shopping.'

'What size is that?'

'Eight.'

'Bloody hell, Zara. You're making me look huge and I'm only a twelve.'

I stared into the mirror, swaying from side to side.

She sighed. 'Look, take no notice of me. I'm just jealous. You look stunning. The bright red is perfect against your dark brown hair and electric-blue eyes.'

I sat back down at the dressing table, pulled up the top half of my hair, twisted it into a loose bun, clipping it in place, and let the rest of the hair flow down my back.

'Cool. You look so sophisticated. Just one more thing.' Holly rushed out of the room and was back in a second. 'This.' She fastened a gold rope chain around my neck. 'Scott won't be able to keep his hands off you.'

'Thanks, Holl. You're a brilliant bestie.'

'That's what friends are for.' She took me into a hug. 'I hate it when we fall out.'

'Me too.'

'Anyway, looking like that should stop your mum going on about your weight. She'll just see a gorgeous woman.'

'Yeah?' I stood up and stared at my full length reflection in the mirror. Holly was right. I looked amazing.

A horn beeped from outside. I peeped out the window. 'That's Scott,' I called, 'so I'm off. Have a nice day with Adam.'

'Cheers,' Holly shouted from her bedroom.

I slammed the front door behind me, hurried down the path, and opened the passenger door to the Porsche. 'Hi, Scott.' I pecked him on the cheek.

He gasped. 'Wow. You look…?'

'Yes?' I grinned.

'Stunning.'

'Thanks. The dress is new.'

'You look healthy too.' He started up the car and pulled away. 'I reckon your mum will be pleased.'

'Hope so.'

'Now, listen, see if you can get through the day without a row, and that includes with Matt' – Scott steered into the second lane as he overtook a line of slow vehicles – 'okay?'

'Sure.'

After driving in silence for most of the way, Scott said, 'It's another scorcher.' He rested his right arm on the open window. 'So did you have a think about my proposition?'

'I'm still thinking.' He looked so sexy in a white T-shirt and denim shorts showing off a gorgeous tan. Butterflies in my stomach fluttered on overdrive. If he hadn't been driving I'd have kissed him there and then. 'I thought we were supposed to be taking things slowly.'

'Friends with benefits don't need to go slow. Happy for you to use my body anytime.' He beamed.

Maybe if Richard stayed out of my head then I'd seduce Scott this evening. 'Let's see how things go.'

He pulled up outside my sister's. I gazed out at the ocean imitating the Mediterranean Sea with its vibrant blue shade. Amber rays reflected on the sand. 'I wish I lived here.'

'Marry me, my darling, and I'll buy you a place just like this.'

'Scott, what did we just say?' I got out of the car and slammed the door.

Dad was standing by the window staring out at the view when I headed into the lounge.

'Hi, Dad.' I put my arms around his waist. 'Gorgeous, isn't it?'

He patted my hand. 'It is indeed, darling. My favourite place. I wish I could get your mother to move somewhere like this.'

'What?' I frowned. 'You mean you've asked her?'

He nodded. 'Oh yes, several times but she doesn't want to move from the family home.'

I peered out at the tranquil waves as the golden sphere sank into the sea. The whole sky burned, reflecting orange into the water, and my anger at Scott fizzled away. 'I must get the love of the ocean from you.' I kissed Dad on the cheek. 'I've brought Scott' – I gave a little laugh – 'or should I say Scott brought me.'

Dad and I continued to stare at the sunset in silence.

'There you are.' Mum clip-clopped into the room breaking the serenity. 'Didn't I teach you that it's manners to come and greet your host, never mind your mother?'

I twisted around. 'Sorry, Mum. Dad and I were just sharing a moment.'

She glared at me. 'The only reason I knew you were here was because Scott came and found us.'

I pointed to the window. 'We were just watching the sun go down. Look at it. Glorious.'

Mum shook her head. 'Well never mind that now.' Footsteps on the laminated flooring made her turn. 'Ah, Chloe. As you can see I've found your sister. She and your dad are both getting soppy-eyed about the sunset.' What was the matter with Mum? Why couldn't she notice beauty around her? All she cared about was having a spotless house and making sure Dad kept the garden in an equally immaculate state.

'It is rather stunning, Mum.' Chloe wrapped her arms around my waist. 'Wow, look at you. You're so skinny, making me feel even fatter.'

I touched her stomach. 'You're not fat. You look incredible. Do you know what you're having yet?'

Her eyes twinkled. 'You'll have to wait and see.' She brushed her fingertips down my dress. 'This is stunning. Did you have it made?'

I giggled. 'No way. I bought it at Blue Flamingo in the sale. Cost me twenty-two quid.'

'Awesome. It fits you like a glove. You look sensational.' She folded her arms. 'Anyway, dinner's ready. Mum's been working really hard so we don't want to spoil it.'

⋆

After taking the final bite of the vegetarian wellington, I put my cutlery in the finished position. 'That was gorgeous, Mum, you'll have to give me the recipe.'

'I agree,' Scott said. 'Your mum's a brilliant cook.' He rubbed his stomach. 'Your pastry is so light, Mrs Wiseman.'

Her face shone. 'Why, thank you, Scott. I love cooking and it's always nice to have people appreciate it.'

Matt rose from the table and gathered everyone's empty plates.

'What about you, Matt?' I asked as he took mine. 'What did you think?'

'It was yummy. The flavouring was to die for. I loved it all but particularly the beetroot and butternut squash. Keep making meals like that, Mum,' he said, 'and you'll convert me to vegetarianism in no time at all.'

I smiled. 'That's really good to hear.' Maybe he wasn't that bad after all.

'In fact,' he continued, 'I think I'd like the recipe since I've taken over the role as chief chef in this house.'

'He's a fabulous cook' – Chloe stood up and took the dishes from Matt – 'much better than me. Beans on toast is my speciality. Apple crumble everyone? Matt's creation, not mine.'

'I think we could all do with a few minutes before dessert,' Matt said. 'Let's do our little announcement first.'

'Oh, all right.' She placed the dishes back down on the table. 'Mum.' Chloe's eyes twinkled.

Wide-eyed, Mum waited.

'You'd best get knitting in pink.' Chloe put her hands on her small bump. 'It's a girl.'

Matt stood behind her, wrapping his arms around her shoulders. 'Amelia Jane.'

They looked the perfect couple. Had I misjudged him? Maybe he was right that day when he said I was jealous, not jealous of Chloe having him, but what they shared.

Scott parked the Porsche outside the flat. 'Thanks for a lovely day.' He kissed me on the cheek. 'And well done for not starting any arguments.'

'Yes, I surprised myself. And did you notice, Matt never ventured outside for a smoke once?'

'He's given up, that's why.'

'He has?'

'Yes. He told me when I was in the kitchen. Can't have been easy.'

'No, it can't have been. You know I think I may have got him wrong. He does really seem to care about Chloe.'

'Dare I say you're growing up?'

'Maybe I am. See you tomorrow then' – I fluttered my eyelashes – 'unless you fancy a cuppa?'

'You don't need to ask me twice.' He was out of the car, around the passenger side and opened the door. 'My lady.'

'Cheers,' I said, stepping out. Was I doing the right thing inviting him in? Richard popped into my head again. *But you're not mine. Scott is.*

We sloped up the path hand in hand. I stuck the key in the lock, turned it, and pushed the front door open to a hushed silence. 'Holly and Adam must've gone to bed.'

Scott looked at me and I knew what he was thinking although he kept his thoughts to himself. Instead he said, 'I'll put the kettle on,' and headed for the kitchen.

I followed him. 'If that's what you want or...'

'Are you saying what I think you are, Zara?'

'Mm-hmm.' I put my arms around his neck.

He bent his head and brought his lips to mine. 'You sure?'

'I'm sure.'

He scooped me in his arms and carried me to my room, gently dropped me on the bed, and kissed me hard. 'God, I've missed you,' he said.

I returned his passionate kisses, slowly moving my hands down his body, caressing every inch, thinking only of him. 'Missed you too.'

Chapter Twenty

Holly barged into the kitchen. 'Morning.' She glanced around the room. 'Where's Scott? I thought I heard his voice earlier.'

'You did. I've made you a tea.'

'Cheers.' She squinted. 'Where is he now?'

'He had to go.'

She picked up the mug and blew on the drink. 'That's a bit daft. He could've given you a lift or...'

'Or what?'

'You've not fallen out again, have you?'

'No. Nothing like that.' I took a sip of coffee. 'He's on a conference for a couple of days so had to go home to pack. Anyway, where's Adam? I thought he stayed over last night.'

Her eyes filled.

'He didn't stay?'

She shook her head. 'We had a row.'

I put my mug down on the worktop and hugged her. 'Oh, Holl.'

'Careful,' she said, 'I've got a hot tea in my hand.'

'Oops.' I dropped my arms. 'You two are always arguing so what made this one different?'

'Grr...'

'What's that all about?'

'Adam. He never stopped going on about this woman at his work place. Brittany this and Brittany that. If you could see her, Zara. Long blonde hair and legs a mile long.'

'You've met her then?'

'Yeah. At one of his work's socials. She's single and kept flashing her eyes at him all night.'

'But, Holl. Adam loves you. You know that.'

'I know, it's just…'

'Let's sit down.' Taking my coffee, I headed over to the table and put my drink down. 'It's just what?'

'I was already feeling fat and ugly yesterday after you looking like a model in your new dress' – she perched on a chair next to me, took a sip of the tea, and placed the cup on a coaster – 'and then him going on about Brittany half the night really got to me.'

'You mad cow. You're gorgeous. And Adam knows that too.'

'Well in the end I told him to clear off and go and be with her.' She took a tissue from the Kleenex box on the table and blew her nose. 'He stormed out and told me that my jealousy would be the death of our relationship. And he's right. Maybe it is already. I thought he'd text but nothing.'

'He's probably giving you time to cool off.'

'Anyway' – she swigged the rest of her drink – 'I'd better get ready for work. How about you?'

'I'm in a little later today because I've got a session with Craig.'

'Right now, I could do with going in your place.' She sniffled. 'Why hasn't he messaged me?'

'Text him.'

'Do you think?'

'Yeah, I do. Someone has to make the first move.'

'Okay.' She picked up her mobile and typed a message. 'There. I've sent it.'

Almost immediately her phone bleeped. She checked the text and smiled. 'He said he's sorry too.' She rose from her seat and hugged me. 'Thanks for giving me the push. Good luck with your Craig appointment. I'd better get cracking.'

'Glad to help.' Shame Scott had to rush off. I thought back to last night. It had been wonderful. And I'd even managed to keep Richard out of my head.

※

Craig passed me a second glass of water before sitting on a chair opposite me. 'You seem to be doing well.'

'Yes, I am.'

'But I have to ask, Zara' – he took a deep breath – 'are you still under the impression that you're some kind of time traveller.'

'Definitely not.' Edward popped into my thoughts. I should be at Bridge View Hall now warning Richard. I peered down to hide the truth. 'Like everyone said, I was delusional. Not thinking straight and I mixed up fiction with what was actually happening. Maybe I needed that escape?'

'Look at me, Zara.'

I lifted my head and hoped my face didn't reveal my lies.

Craig held eye contact. Almost like he knew.

I swigged a gulp of water. 'I'm back to my old self. Just ask Annabel if you don't believe me.'

'Zara, I never said I didn't believe you and I wouldn't dream of asking Annabel anything. Like I told you from the beginning, our sessions are completely confidential. I suppose my next question is where do we go next?'

'I don't understand.'

'Do I discharge you? Or if I do, will you slip back into your fictional world?'

'Discharging me sounds like a good idea. I'll be fine, honestly.'

His gaze remained fixed. 'You know, I think I'll book you in for one more session next month.'

I shrugged. 'If that's what you think is best but honestly, I'm fine,' I repeated.

He headed over to his computer and opened up the online diary. 'Let's say October 5th. I'll email you the appointment.'

I rose from the chair. 'Thanks. I should get off to work.'

It was dark by the time I got home. 'You in, Holl?' I headed for the lounge and flopped onto the sofa.

She wandered into the room dressed in her night clothes. 'You're late.'

I yawned. 'Work was manic. We had to get everything ready for this month's edition to go to print. Where's Adam?'

'He's busy tonight.'

'But you're okay?'

'Yeah. We met up for coffee after work. It was always planned that he wouldn't be around tonight.' She hovered in the doorway. 'Fancy a glass of vino?'

'I'd love that.'

'Have you eaten?'

I kicked off my sandals, put my legs up on the couch, and rubbed my feet. 'No. Too damn tired to be honest.'

'I'll make you some toast. You can't drink on an empty stomach.'

'Thanks.' Once she'd left the room I picked up the remote control and flicked on the television. All I could think of was getting back to Bridge View Hall. It was torture. I had to warn

Richard. Having to work until gone nine was too much. How did Annabel manage it? She was thirty years older than me and it hadn't phased her at all. Even Megan was flagging before we'd finished. My eyes refused to stay open so I didn't fight them. With my eyes closed I daydreamed about Richard and Scott. Torn between the two. Both handsome, both kind, and both made my heart skip. How could I feel like this about both of them? Was it because when I was at Bridge View Hall, I wasn't me but Rebecca? Talk about a love triangle.

'Zara?'

I shook myself back to the here and now. 'Oh, I must have dozed off for a moment.' I laughed. 'I was having a weird dream. Scott was about to have a duel with an Edwardian gentleman. They were fighting over me.' I grinned.

She glared at me. 'It's not happening again, is it?'

'What?'

'You? You don't think you're a time traveller again, do you?'

'Crikey. Can't I even have a dream like a normal person?'

Her muscles relaxed. 'Of course you can.' She passed me a plate. 'Here's your toast. I'll just get the wine.'

'Thanks. It smells divine.'

She gave a little laugh. 'It's just toast.'

'I know.' I nibbled on the hot buttered toast. Hopefully I'd managed to fob Holly off. I had to get back to Bridge View Hall. There was no way I could wait until the weekend. I'd go tomorrow after work and hope that I wasn't too tired the next morning.

Chapter Twenty-One

As I entered the station the last of the commuters bustled past me.

'Zara, is that you?'

I peered up at the porter who'd looked after me when I'd fainted. 'Hi, there,' I said. 'How are you?'

'I'm well. Just knocking off. How are you doing these days?'

'All right, thanks.'

'Where are you off to at this hour?'

'To my sister's. She's expecting a baby in a couple of months. Her husband's away so I'm staying with her overnight as I don't like the idea of her being on her own,' I lied.

He patted me on the arm. 'Well you take good care of yourself. I'd better get off otherwise my missus will wonder where I've got to. Don't want my dinner ending up in the bin.'

'See you then.'

The porter waved. He hurried out of the exit as I headed to the platform and waited.

Where was I? I was being led into a ballroom by a gentleman with blond hair whom I didn't recognise. My gown rustled as I moved. The taffeta fabric was cool against my skin.

'Thank you for allowing me the first dance.' The stranger guided me onto the chequered dance floor. It reminded me of a giant chess board. Once again, although I didn't know the steps, my feet knew where to go. Who was this gentleman? And where was Richard?

The room was magnificent. Huge brass chandeliers hung from the tall panelled ceiling. Was this Bridge View Hall? And if so, how come I hadn't seen this room before?

'It's a pleasure to finally meet you, Lady Rebecca?' he said spinning me around and managing to avoid the other couples.

'And you.' I answered, wishing I knew who he was.

'Richard has talked incessantly about you since your engagement.'

Not knowing what to say, I smiled.

'He wasn't exaggerating your beauty.'

I sensed my cheeks heating up.

The music stopped. He stayed close. 'So what secrets can you tell me about Sir Richard?' he asked.

I was wondering how to answer when Richard came along and took my hand. 'I see you've met Charles. My best man.'

Again I just smiled.

The band started the music. 'This dance is mine, I believe.' Richard led me away from Charles and into a quickstep.

Couples spun around the room. Gorgeous gowns provided lustre and colour in luxurious fabrics of emerald, rich burgundy, cobalt blue, pink, sage, and peach. Mine was azure blue but I wished for the rich burgundy worn by the blonde girl who stood out amongst everyone. Not only was she stunning but she appeared regal. I had to know who she was. 'Richard, who's the lady dancing with Charles?'

'Dearest, that's your best friend, Melinda. Although I can understand why you didn't recognise her as she looks particularly beautiful this evening, although not as beautiful as you, my love.'

'Of course it is. How foolish of me not to recognise my own friend.'

'I believe it's the burgundy, darling. Normally her attire is paler, not quite as striking.'

Melinda. And she was not only gorgeous but my best friend. I wondered how long she'd been my friend for. 'Charles appears besotted.'

'He does indeed.' Richard guided me into a turn. 'Once we're married we shall have lots of events like this. This room has been closed for far too long. Mary mentioned there hasn't been a ball at Bridge View Hall since Samuel died.'

'That's right.' If Mary had said that then it must be right. I was loving the dancing because my feet knew where to go, but struggling to recognise Rebecca's friends and acquaintances. Was I only partly experiencing Rebecca's memory?

I searched the area for Edward. 'Who's that gentleman my brother's in deep conversation with?'

'I'm not sure but I've an inkling he's the villain Edward's been plotting with.'

My stomach churned. 'We need to be careful. I wonder if he's the same gentleman Mary overheard chatting about Edward's upcoming inheritance.'

'No doubt, but do not fear, dearest, I'm watching him carefully. He'll not get a penny from my estate, and neither you nor I will come to any harm. Once the police have gathered enough evidence they'll arrest him and we'll be safe.'

Mary's words kept going around in my head. *Things can go wrong.* 'But...'

'Shh. Enjoy the moment. I've missed you. Unfortunately I must leave again for London tomorrow.' He moved me into a natural turn towards the corner.

'You're leaving?'

'I know I've only just come back, darling, but there's a lot to be done in preparation for my move down here on a permanent basis. Do not fear, I'll be back in a couple of days.'

⁂

Melinda took my arm and led me to the corner with a group of ladies. A girl around fifteen tittered. 'Sir Richard is so handsome, Rebecca. You're so lucky.'

'You're right, Caroline. She is.' Melinda beamed.

'Have you noticed the way Sir Charles has been looking at you?' I asked.

'No.' Melinda blushed. 'Really?'

'He's besotted with you. Did you know he's Richard's best man?'

She shook her head.

'Which means you'll be in close contact with him at the wedding. I'll make sure I throw you my bouquet.'

Caroline nibbled on a wafer. 'My guardian's looking for a husband for me.' She dropped her smile.

'Really?' I asked. 'But you're so young.'

'Not too young at all,' a girl in a silk sage dress answered. 'She's sixteen. I think it's exciting. I wish my father would start looking for a husband for me.'

'It would be if it were someone nice' – Caroline blinked – 'but only last week he invited a widower over for dinner.'

I touched her arm. 'A widower?'

She nodded. 'Yes, and not just a widower who's looking for a wife but one who wants a mother for his children too.'

'How many children?' I asked.

'Four.'

I rested my palm on her shoulder. 'And is that what you want?'

'No.' She sniffled. 'He's fat, bald, and ugly. I always hoped I'd get the chance to be married to someone handsome like Sir Richard or Sir Charles but my guardian will marry me off to anyone who needs a wife.'

'Then you must stand up to him and say *no*.'

The girls in the group all stared at me.

⋆

I spent the last hour or so getting to know Melinda and Caroline. They were so easy to get on with. No wonder Melinda was Rebecca's best friend, and Caroline was such a sweet girl. I had to find a way to help her.

Richard made his way over. 'Rebecca, our guests are starting to leave. We should wish them all goodnight and thank them for coming.' He led me to the opened door at the main entrance where we stood ready to shake hands with the ladies and gentlemen as they left the hall. After thanking us for a wonderful evening, they climbed into their carriages or cars, until there was no one left. I'd no idea where Edward was, in fact he'd barely mingled with the guests at all.

I glanced up at the full moon and stars. 'It's bright tonight.'

Richard put his arm around me. 'Ideal for a moonlight stroll in the garden.'

'I'd like that.'

'Perfect.' He stepped into the hall for a moment and returned with a shawl. 'You'll need this.' He draped a lace wrap around my shoulders and led me around the back of the house to the lit gardens where Victorian lampposts lined either side of the footpath like sentries.

As we meandered a *twit woo* came from up high. 'An owl,' I said.

'A barn owl, I believe.' He pointed. 'If you look at the top of that elm you can just about make him out in the hollow.'

I squinted. 'Oh yes.' I wrapped my arms around Richard's neck and brushed my lips against his.

For a moment he kissed me with passion but then, as he'd done previously, drew back. 'Not long now, my darling. Soon you'll be mine.'

'Don't stop, please. We're not doing anything wrong.'

'And as I've told you before, sweetheart, I respect you far too much.' He kissed me gently before drawing back again. 'Come, it's time you retired to your room.'

'Before we go in, Richard, there's something I wanted to speak to you about.' I pulled him towards the nearby bench and sat down.

'Anything, my dear.'

'Did you know that Miss Caroline's guardian is trying to marry her to a fat, bald, ugly widower?'

'I did hear something, yes. Poor child.'

'Exactly, she's not much more than a child.'

He squeezed my fingers. 'Neither were you when you married Samuel.'

'That was different, he wasn't a monster old enough to be my father.'

'In this instance, I'm afraid you're right about him being a monster. Rumours have it that he made his late wife's life brutal.'

'Then we have to do something.'

'What is it you want from me, Rebecca?'

'You must have a friend who'd like to marry her? She's attractive. Kind. Young. She'd make any gentleman a good wife.'

'Hmm. Actually I may know someone.'

'You do?'

'A cousin of mine. He was left a widower a couple of years ago.'

'Another widower. How old is he?'

'Around my age and handsome, but...'

'But what?'

'He's also looking for a mother for his young son.'

'How old is the boy?'

'Just two. His mother died in childbirth.'

I squinted. 'Poor little mite.' I took a deep breath. 'But don't you know someone who isn't a widower?'

'I'm afraid not, sweetheart. Miss Caroline is an orphan and from a lower class and if it hadn't been for the kindness of Miss Melinda's uncle taking on her guardianship, who knows where she might be right now?' He stroked my fingers. 'Harsh as it may sound, Miss Caroline's not the type of young lady a gentleman of worth is looking for. However, I think William would be drawn to your young lady because she's parentless. He's a kind man, and nothing like the ogre her guardian has lined up. Let me speak to William while I'm away.'

William certainly sounded a better catch than the monster proposed. 'Yes, please. If he's anything like you then I know he'll make her happy.'

Mary helped me out of my gown. 'Next time when the house is full, like this evening, it will be your wedding day.' She wandered over to the wardrobe and took out my wedding dress. 'You're going to look beautiful. Your mother and father would be so proud of you.'

'Thank you.' I brushed my fingers down the lustrous ivory silk. It was gorgeous. 'I think that gentlemen you mentioned plotting with Edward was here tonight. Edward was certainly in deep conversation with someone.'

'You're right. He was here. Did you speak to Sir Richard?' Mary hung the gown back up.

'I did. He said we're not to worry.' I slipped a nightdress over my head and fastened the buttons. 'And he's going to help me find a husband for Miss Caroline so she doesn't have to marry that horrid widower her guardian has in mind.'

'You always were a bit of a matchmaker, Rebecca. Come now, you should get into bed and I must get to mine.'

I climbed into the four poster. She kissed my cheek. 'Sweet dreams, Rebecca.'

'Good night, Mary.' Caroline and William would be perfect together, I was sure. It seemed like the perfect answer. As soon as possible I'd contact Melinda and put my plan to her to see what she thought.

Chapter Twenty-Two

After staggering into the house in the early hours I managed a few hours sleep before heading off to work. I was first to arrive so I unlocked the premises and made my way to the office. Megan wouldn't be in for another half hour at least which would allow me some quiet time to get down my story.

I switched on the PC, loaded the Word document, sank into the chair and took myself back to Bridge View Hall. I thought about Caroline with Richard's cousin, imagining another Mr Darcy, and gave him a soft voice with a gorgeous smile. Yes, he'd make an ideal husband for Caroline. I'd send word to Melinda that Caroline was to be a bridesmaid which would allow her some time at the wedding to become acquainted with William.

Tapping the keyboard with speed, I typed *Miss Caroline* as the chapter heading, and immersed myself into the story.

'Crikey, Annabel, I didn't hear you come in.'

'Sorry to make you jump. You're sounding very industrious. What is it you're working on?'

'The serial for the next edition. It'll be ready for you by lunchtime.'

'Wonderful. Well done, Zara. Are you okay though? You're looking a little peaky.'

'I'm fine. Just didn't sleep that well last night.'

'Tell you what, once you've finished, take the afternoon off. Go home and get some rest.'

'Are you sure?'

'Absolutely. In fact, take tomorrow off too. There's not much to do and you're way ahead of schedule.' She patted my arm. 'Keep up the good work.'

I took a leisurely stroll home. When I pushed open the flat door, I almost fainted from the heat. It was stifling. I flicked off my heels and inserted my feet into the pink fluffy slippers Mum had bought me when I came out of hospital. Almost unable to breathe I padded into the lounge and flipped open the double aspect windows. It didn't take long for a breeze to run through. Food. TV. Sleep. That should be my order of things. I made for the kitchen, where it was a lot cooler, ran the cold water tap and filled a glass. My stomach rumbled. I took a couple of wholemeal slices from the storage bin, a container of grated cheese from the fridge, and sprinkled a handful onto the bread, topping it with a heaped spoonful of pickle. A tube of Pringles winked from the corner of the worktop teasing me. I pulled out a few and placed them on the side of my plate to nibble with my sandwich. The lounge would be fresher by now. I gathered my lunch onto a tray and headed in there, flopping on the sofa.

It had been generous of Annabel to give me time off to catch up on rest. My first thoughts had been to go to Bridge View Hall but what would be the point? The likelihood of Richard being there was remote. Strange how Scott and Richard were both away at the moment. Scott would be back from his conference tomorrow and I was looking forward to seeing him again. He'd always been dishy, a guy who had girls chasing after him, but since he'd grown his hair a little, loose strands curled against his brow, making him look even cuter. I took a bite of the sandwich. My stomach made rumbling noises in appreciation.

I picked up the remote control and flicked on the TV.

I awoke shivering. The sun had gone from the front of the house turning the room chilly with the windows wide open. I got up and closed them, returned to the sofa, and turned the channel over to Netflix but I couldn't get into watching anything. It was no good, I had to get out. Holly wouldn't be home for ages. I padded to the bathroom, gave my face a quick splash, combed my hair and scooped it up into a ponytail.

The park was busy. Mums with pushchairs chatted on benches while their toddlers amused themselves on the grass. Older children were playing footie when a ball came flying at me and just missed my face. 'Hey, be careful.' I scowled.

One of the mums rushed towards me. 'I'm so sorry.' She caught hold of a red-headed boy. 'Tommy, say sorry to the lady.'

He lowered his head.

'Now, Tommy, or I'm taking you home and you can go straight to bed.'

His cheeks turned almost the same colour as his hair. 'Sorry, lady.'

'That's okay,' I said, my anger fizzling away. 'It's all right,' I said to the woman, 'no harm done.'

I headed to the pond where a young mother was on a bench watching her identical twins feed the ducks. The blonde-haired little girls dug into a plastic pot and threw out seeds to the ducks, giggling each time one of them came closer.

'How old are your twins?' I asked.

'Three.' The mother beamed.

'They're so cute. Are they yours?'

'Yes. I had them young.'

I pointed to the bench. 'Do you mind?'

'Not at all. It's nice to have someone to talk to. I love my girls but it's always nice to have a bit of grown-up conversation.'

I took a seat. 'I'm Zara.'

'Katie. Nice to meet you.'

'My younger sister's expecting a baby.'

'How lovely. Her first?'

'Yes, due end of November, early December.'

Katie was petite and pretty with mouse-coloured hair. 'She's only nineteen,' I said.

'Age doesn't matter. I'm only twenty.'

'How did your parents react when you told them you were pregnant?'

'Alarmed at first but they soon saw how happy me and my Billy were so came around. And they love these two.'

'I thought my sister was too young but she seems so content with her husband that I think maybe I was too quick to judge.'

'Sounds like you may have been. How about you? You married?'

I chuckled. 'Not me. I'm not ready to settle down. My mum keeps telling me I'll run out of time to have kids, but quite frankly I'm not interested in starting a family. Probably too selfish as I love my life how it is. Is that bad?'

'Course not. Everyone can't be the same. You're very easy to talk to. What do you do?'

'Thank you. You are too. I'm an editor for Feminine Smile, although recently I've taken on writing a serial for the magazine.'

'Ooh, I get that mag. I can't believe I'm sitting here talking to Zara Wiseman.'

'You've read it?'

Katie's face lit up like a lamp. 'You're joking, aren't you? I love it. The hardest part is waiting for the next month's issue. So tell me, which man will she choose?'

'Secret, I'm afraid. If I let the cat out of the bag then my boss wouldn't be happy with me. Besides,' – I grinned – 'I'm not sure which way it will go yet.'

'Exciting.' She glanced at her watch. 'Oh, I'd better go. Need to get dinner on as Billy will be home soon. Girls,' she called.

'Do we have to?' they asked in turn.

'Yes, Daddy will be home.' She turned to me. 'I've loved chatting. Thank you for perking up my day. I look forward to the next episode.'

'And thank you,' I said.

She took the girls' hands. 'Say goodbye to Zara.'

'Bye, Zara,' they said in unison as Katie led them away.

⋆

Splinters of light beamed in front of my eyes. I held my head as I deciphered my whereabouts. I was on the couch in the drawing room of Bridge View Hall.

There was a tap on the door and Ruby entered. 'Miss Rebecca' – she paused – 'you look pale. Are you all right?'

I pulled myself upright. 'A little headache. Nothing to worry about.'

'I'll ask Mary to make you up a tonic.'

'There's no need. I'll be fine. What is it you wanted?'

'Miss Melinda's here but perhaps you'd prefer me to send her away?'

'No, don't do that. I'd love to see her.'

'Oh' – she handed me a small envelope – 'and this came for you by messenger.'

'Thank you. Give me a couple of minutes before showing Miss Melinda in, and please bring some tea.'

'Yes, Miss Rebecca.'

I ripped open the envelope and read the note.

Dearest, Rebecca,

William has agreed. Please speak to Miss Melinda and Miss Caroline. I'll be back at Bridge View soon.

Forever yours,

Richard.

So this was the reason the pull was so strong. The house knew I needed to be here to fix things for Caroline.

Melinda sashayed in. 'Rebecca.' She kissed me on the cheek. She looked delightful dressed in a pink damask gown. It had a high collar, loose bodice, and frilled layers. 'I know we hadn't arranged to see each other,' she said, 'but it's such a lovely day I thought you might like a wander in the park.'

'That would be lovely but should we have tea first?' I needed some nourishment before I could go anywhere.

'You know I can never resist a slice of your cook's Victoria sponge.' Melinda took a seat next to me.

'I'm glad you're here as there's something I'd like to put to you.'

'Sounds intriguing.'

Ruby came in with a tray. 'Tea, Miss Rebecca.'

'Thank you.' I thought about offering to pour but then I'd have had the dilemma of not knowing how Melinda drank her tea.

After pouring the teas and cutting the cake into slices, Ruby asked, 'Is there anything else, Miss Rebecca?'

'No, that will be all. Thank you, Ruby.' Once she'd left the room, I passed a slice of cake to Melinda and took one for me.

'Thank you.' She took a bite. 'Mmm. Wish our cook baked as good as yours.'

'Since the ball I've not been able to get Caroline and that widower out of my mind.' I nibbled on the sponge too.

'I know. Me too but it can't be helped. My uncle won't back down.' She dabbed the napkin on her lip. 'In strict confidence, Rebecca, my uncle's struggling financially. His stocks and shares took a huge loss a few months back, and Caroline has become just another mouth to feed.'

'Can't your father take her in?'

'Goodness, no. Anyway, this is a good match for Caroline. The groom in question is affluent. She'll want for nothing.' Melinda sipped from the china cup.

Want for nothing except love. No, I wouldn't let that happen. 'Supposing someone younger and handsome could be found?'

She shook her head. 'That's not going to happen, Rebecca. Caroline has nothing. No gentleman would be prepared to wed her.'

'But supposing...' I smiled.

'You have to accept it. You were only sixteen when you married Sir Samuel.'

'But that was different. He wasn't old and ugly, or' – I sighed – 'he wasn't a widower who had a bad reputation of treating his previous wife badly.'

She frowned. 'How do you know that?'

I wasn't going to mention Richard. 'It's common knowledge.'

'Well there's not much we can do.'

'But there is. I think I've found an alternative solution.'

'You're always trying to be a matchmaker, Rebecca.'

'But this can work. I spoke to Sir Richard and he has a cousin, also a widower but much younger than the one your uncle has lined up. This gentleman has only one child, and he's happy to meet Caroline. If they get on then he'll marry her. Do you think your uncle will agree to this plan?'

She shrugged. 'I don't see why not. Tell me more.'

'I don't know much except that his name's William and he's handsome and kind.'

'If he's anything like Sir Richard then I'm sure Caroline will definitely agree, and my uncle won't care so long as she's not his problem anymore.'

'Perfect.' I took a bite of the sponge to quash the nausea. 'I'd like Caroline to be my bridesmaid too. That way she has a reason to be at the reception and she and William will have the chance to get acquainted. What better place than a wedding to kindle love?'

She took my hand. 'You really are the perfect matchmaker. Please can you put a spell on Sir Charles. It's time I had a husband. You're the same age as me and about to marry for the second time.'

'I think you're halfway there. At the ball he was besotted with you.'

Chapter Twenty-Three

Scott wandered up the path wearing a huge grin. 'What's going on?' I asked. 'You look like the cat who's got the cream.'

'I've a surprise, but let me get in first.' He pushed the front door closed behind him and straight away took me into his arms. 'I've missed you.'

'I've missed you too.' I pulled him away slightly. 'But friends, remember?'

'I remember.' He glared at me. 'Are you okay? Only you're looking tired?'

I'd hoped my foundation would've covered up my exhaustion, following the last timeslip, even though that had been two days ago. 'Just a bad night,' I said. 'Anyway, out with it, what's going on?'

'You remember Dark Chaos, the old guys I reviewed earlier this year?'

'What about them?'

'Well...' He smirked.

'Tell me.'

'Remember I spoke about the journalist who put them on the map?'

'Rachel Webster. Course. I was inspired by her.'

'Well she's agreed to do an interview with me.'

'I thought she lived up north somewhere.'

'She does. She's just outside Chester in a little place called Woodhaerst in North Wales.'

'I don't understand then. Are you doing it via Zoom?'

'Nope. Here's the best bit.' He put his arms around my waist. 'You and me, babe, are going on a little trip up there.'

'What do you mean, you and me?'

'Exactly that. You and me are off for a nice long weekend. And Rachel mentioned we might like to visit Chester Zoo as it's so close.'

'The zoo?'

'Yes. They have a lovely giraffe house there.'

'Giraffes?'

'Yep. I knew you'd like that.' He nodded. 'So you'd get to see the giraffes, and I'd get the interview with Rachel. Two birds with one stone.'

'Really? And when am I supposed to have said that I have this thing for giraffes?'

He frowned. 'I'm sure you did' – he took my hand – 'but aside from that, you'll love it up there. And don't worry' – he grinned – 'I've cleared it with Annabel.'

'What do you mean you've cleared it with Annabel?'

'Just what I said. She's given you leave so you don't have to be back in work until Wednesday.'

I held my hand up in front. 'Let me stop you right there. Are you telling me that you've gone behind my back and asked my boss to give me time off from my work place without even discussing it with me?'

He stared at me.

'Well?'

'I don't see your problem.' He blinked. 'It'll give us a chance to have some special time together and get close again.'

'You don't see the problem.' I glared at him. 'You're unbelievable, Scott Edwards. How dare you decide to book time off from work on my behalf?' I gritted my teeth. 'How bloody dare you?'

'But, babe?' He rested his fingers on my arms.

'Don't babe me.' I pushed him at a distance. 'What part don't you understand about friends? I told you I wanted to take things slow. Well, I'm not even sure I want to do that now.'

'I'm sorry. I just wanted to surprise you.' He stared at me with those puppy dog eyes but I was too angry to let them melt me.

'Just go. And oh, before you do, as you seem to like sorting out my life, you can bloody well let Annabel know that I'll be in work as normal on Monday morning.'

He took my hand. 'Babe.'

I pushed his hand away. 'Just go.'

His eyes filled. 'I'm sorry. Please.'

'Go now, otherwise I'll be slamming the door in your face.'

He rubbed his brow before turning away. 'I'm sorry,' he said again as he got in the car.

Without waiting for him to drive off, I slammed the front door closed. *Who the hell did he think he was?*

Holly was washing up when I barged into the kitchen. She turned towards me. 'What's up? You had a row with Scott?'

'Bloody cheek of the man.'

She sighed. 'What's he done now?'

'He only had the nerve to go behind my back to Annabel and clear it with her that I'd go to bloody North Wales with him.'

'North Wales, eh? Why there?'

'To meet that retired journalist. Rachel Webster.'

'Rachel Webster. Isn't she the writer you were raving about the other week? The one that put Dark Chaos on the map?'

'Yes. That's her.'

Holly squinted. 'But I thought you'd want to meet her?'

'I would under other circumstances. But I don't intend letting any bloke sort out my life for me.'

'I see.'

'I don't think you do.' I clenched my fists. 'Taking things slowly doesn't mean going behind my back and booking a weekend away together. That's the last thing I want.'

'Although…'

'What?'

'You might've had a good time.'

'No, I wouldn't. I'd already decided that I wanted to chill this weekend. I need some space.' I relaxed my fists. 'Anyway, what are your plans?'

'Off out.' She peered up at the clock. 'In fact, Adam's picking me up any time now. Oh, and I'll be staying at his tonight unless…'

'I don't need you to babysit me if that's what you're asking.'

The doorbell rang. 'That'll be him now.' She wiped her hands on a towel. 'Well so long as you're sure.'

'I am. Off you go and have fun.'

'Cheers. Will do.' She picked up her shoulder bag from the chair and headed out of the kitchen. 'Bye then.'

The slamming of the front door echoed in the otherwise quiet space. My stomach rumbled. I checked the fridge. Nothing much in there except half a slab of cheddar along with a few slices of wholemeal in the bread bin, that would do for cheese on toast. I flicked on the kettle, turned on the grill and set to work with slicing the cheese, placing it on the bread, and sprinkling paprika and tarragon before putting it under the heated grill. While the cheese sizzled, I threw a teabag into a cup and made myself a tea. Once everything was ready I carried it through to the lounge and flopped down on the sofa.

As I nibbled the toast, I came up with a plan. Holly wouldn't be home before late afternoon tomorrow, so if I was out for the night, no one would know. And I'd have Sunday to sleep all day if necessary, and be recovered sufficiently to make it to work on Monday. Yes, that was what I'd do.

Chapter Twenty-Four

I was back in Bridge View Hall but it can't have been my wedding day as I was wasn't wearing a bridal gown. Instead I was dressed in a gorgeous azure silk fabric which overlapped a light blue chiffon, and the fitted bodice was trimmed in gold lace. My waist appeared tiny and the puffed sleeves showed off my slim arms. The corset was uncomfortable and restricted my breathing. I let out a breath. The price Edwardian women paid to look good.

A tap came on the door. I turned around and spotted Ruby in the doorway. 'Your guests have arrived Miss Rebecca.'

'She'll be there shortly.' Mary twisted me back towards her, and combed the front of my hair.

'Very well.' The maid closed the door behind her.

I gazed into the mirror at the transformation. Mary had rolled my hair into a bun leaving small ringlets falling at the side. I put a hand to my head. 'It's lovely,' I said before rising from the dressing table stool. Once again I stared back at my reflection. This time standing and swaying from side to side. 'Thank you.' I hugged Mary, unsure whether that was something Rebecca would do or not.

'You look beautiful, my dear. Every man's eyes will be on you this evening as you enter the room.' She headed across to the wardrobe. 'Although maybe not as many as tomorrow when' – she held up the shimmering ivory gown – 'you'll be wearing this.'

So it was the eve of Rebecca and Richard's wedding. I wondered which guests had arrived. Melinda and Caroline? Charles and Richard's cousin?'

'Come along, dear.' Mary opened the door. 'Don't keep your guests waiting in the drawing room any longer.'

I headed out of the door and strolled along the landing, stopping when reaching the winding staircase. Here I held my dress up, taking extra care not to trip on the dress falling below my ankles, or its short train at the back. On reaching the bottom of the stairs, I peered both ways wondering which way. Luckily, Ruby came out of a double doorway on my right. That must be the place.

'Mistress,' she said, 'you look beautiful.'

'Thank you, Ruby.' I took a deep breath, held my head high, sauntered into the drawing room and searched for Richard. In no time at all he was at my side.

'Darling, you look divine.'

I smiled, glancing around at my guests and recognised Rebecca's best friend, Melinda, deeply engrossed in conversation with Charles. She was in burgundy again. It suited her. I wondered what that colour would look like on Rebecca who always seemed to wear blue.

Over to my left I caught Caroline. Who was that she was speaking with? He turned towards me. William. It had to be William because he was a clone of Richard. Spellbound, William turned back to Caroline. Did that mean he'd marry her?

Richard took my arm. 'Come and meet my cousin.' He led me across to William and Caroline. 'Will, my dear cousin, meet my betrothed, Rebecca.'

William tore himself away from Caroline, took my hand and brought it to his lips. 'Good evening, Lady Rebecca. Richard did not exaggerate your beauty. I'm delighted to be part of your celebration.' He released my hand.

'We're pleased that you could make it. And I see you've met my young friend, Miss Caroline.'

'Indeed, I have, and fear I'm bewitched by this fair maiden. We don't want to take precedence over your evening, but from what Richard has told me, I'm sure you'll be delighted to hear that I've spoken to Miss Caroline's guardian who's agreed that we may wed.'

'This news make me joyous.' I hugged Caroline. 'I told you things would work out.'

She blushed like a ripe strawberry. 'Thank you, Miss Rebecca. I'm forever in your debt.'

I squeezed her fingers. 'No need. You're my friend and I'm just glad that Sir Richard and I managed to find a solution. I wouldn't have been able to sleep at night knowing that you were going to marry that monster.'

A couple of girls dressed in the same uniform as Ruby circled the guests handing out goblets of champagne. Richard took two full glasses from the small tray and passed one to me as Ruby approached with hors d'oeuvres.

'Sir.' She offered up the selection.

'Thank you.' Richard helped himself to a salmon mousse.

'Mistress Rebecca?' She lifted the platter towards me.

I stared at the fish appetisers and breathed a sigh of relief on spotting mushroom tartlets on the other side of the platter. 'Thank you.' I bit into the snack. 'Mmm. Tasty.' I swallowed it down with a sip of sparkling wine.

The guests filtered out couple by couple as Richard and I stood at the door. It had been such a wonderful evening. The soles of my feet stung from gliding the dance floor all night. There'd been no sign of Edward though. *Where was he?*

Escorted by Charles, Melinda was the last to leave. She pulled me to the side. 'Thank you for a wonderful evening. I can't believe you made it happen for Caroline. I don't know how you managed it, but thank you. She can now have her wish to marry a kind, handsome gentleman.' She hugged me.

'And it looks like you could have your happy ever after too,' I said, signalling to Charles.

'I do hope so. Imagine, the three of us sitting in your drawing room enjoying tea, no longer spinsters but married ladies.' She giggled. 'And maybe we'll all become mothers the same time too.'

I shivered at the thought of babies. 'Yes, imagine.' I kissed her on the cheek.

'Are you worried about tomorrow? You seem nervous.'

I thought about Edward, and yes, I was nervous he was up to something, but nervous about marrying Richard. No. This was the right thing for Rebecca. She'd be safe from her wicked brother. I imagined lying in Richard's arms, making love. 'No,' I answered truthfully, 'I'm not nervous but looking forward to it.'

'Miss Melinda,' Charles said, 'our carriage awaits.' He took my hand. 'Good night, Lady Rebecca. Richard is a lucky man.'

I smiled. 'Good night, sir.'

Richard put his arm around me as Charles led Melinda to the Landau. Before climbing in she looked back and smiled.

'They make a delightful couple, don't they?' Richard said as the horses trotted down the driveway.

'They do. Wouldn't it be wonderful if they were to get married too?'

He gave a small laugh. 'It would indeed.' Not dropping his hold, he walked me back inside the house and closed the front door behind us. My legs trembled. My body yearned for him. 'Escort me to my chamber,' I said.

'I'm not sure that's appropriate, Rebecca.'

'Please.' I lifted my lips to his. 'I'm concerned Edward may know something.'

He dropped his arm and faced me. 'How can this be so? Has he said something?'

'No. Nothing like that, but didn't you notice his absence tonight?'

'You're right, but there is nothing to fear, darling. It's more likely that he's out with his cronies planning how he can spend my money.'

'I'd still like you to walk me to my room. We won't be alone. Mary will be there.'

'Very well.' His eyes twinkled. 'How can I refuse you?'

My heart pounded as he led me down the corridor, up the winding stairs, and along the landing, stopping at Rebecca's bedroom. He kissed my cheek. 'Goodnight, dear lady. Tomorrow I will make you mine.'

I turned the knob. 'Come in, please.'

'No, that would not be appropriate. Sleep well, my heart. Tomorrow will be here soon when Edward will get his just deserts and we will say our vows.'

'Miss Rebecca. Miss Rebecca.'

I rolled over and opened my eyes. Where was I?

'Miss Rebecca.'

I looked up. 'Mary.'

'Ruby has brought you breakfast.'

This was Rebecca's bed. I should've been back in my own time, curled up on the station cold floor shivering, but I was still here. This had never happened before. What did it mean?

'Come along, Miss Rebecca.'

Breakfast in my room? I struggled to sit up. 'It's all right, Mary, I'll come downstairs to eat.'

'Much better to have it here. This way you can eat in your night attire instead of requiring another change into your bridal wear.'

That made sense I supposed. I glanced across to the small table stacked with food. 'Very well.' I pulled myself up further and perched on the edge of the bed before stepping off and making my way to the breakfast. I glared at the feast. Porridge, and sardines. My stomach churned. I hated porridge and there was no way I'd eat the sardines. An omelette and fried potatoes but bacon was added. I had no intention of eating them either with me being a vegetarian.

'Come, dear,' Mary coaxed, 'you need to eat a nourishing breakfast to give you strength for your big day.'

I covered my tummy. 'I feel too sick to eat anything.'

'You'll feel better once you start eating.'

I spotted crumpets with melted butter. I picked one up. 'I'll try this.' I took a bite and held a hand across my mouth to stop me throwing up. 'Sorry, Mary. I simply can't eat a thing.'

'Very well, dear. I'll get your bath ready.'

Mary brushed my hair with a silver-engraved hairbrush before rolling it into a pompadour and left loose strands at the side, which she later teased with tongs – nothing like mine at home – into small ringlets.

Why hadn't Edward been arrested? Richard said the police had enough evidence?

As if Mary could read my mind she squeezed my hand. 'I'm sure they'll come for him.'

'But supposing something has gone wrong?'

'No one knows of Richard's plan except you and me. And I haven't uttered a word to a single soul.'

'Me neither.'

'They'll come for him. You'll see.'

I stepped into the ivory wedding gown and stared at my reflection in the mirror not recognising this stunning lady. The style was more comfortable than I'd remembered. Softer too, and the cream lace trimmings gave it an even more luxurious look. I ran my hands down the front of the fabric. 'It's beautiful.'

'As are you, my child.' She slid my fingers into a pair of silk gloves before positioning a velvet headband, adorned with tiny white satin ribbons, on the top of my hair.

I went to pick up the purple aster bouquet from my dressing table.

'Not quite.' She fastened a single string pearl choker around my neck. 'Now, are you ready to become Lady Rebecca Cavendish?' She handed me the flowers.

'Yes, I am.' I may not have been ready for marriage, but Rebecca certainly was.

※

The carriage pulled up outside St Mark's church. Edward got out, headed around to the other side, and opened my cab door. He took my hand. 'After today,' he said, 'our financial troubles will be over. You've done well, my sister.'

He led me through the decorated lychgate. My nose prickled at its white rose and green foliage decorations, but thankfully I didn't sneeze. The thought of standing next to Richard saying our vows made my heart race, while at the same time it pounded in case our plan had gone wrong.

'You're very quiet, sister.' Edward glared at me.

'I'm just taking everything in.'

'If you know what's good for you, you won't mess this up.'

What was he talking about? Did he know? Had he somehow discovered our plan and managed to wheedle himself out of the charges?

'Do you understand, Rebecca?'

I peered up at him. 'I won't mess it up, brother. Rest easy.'

The sun almost blinded my eyes as we headed up the pathway to the porch entrance where Melinda and Caroline waited.

Melinda gasped. 'You look beautiful, Rebecca.'

'Thank you. As do you and Caroline.' Like me, they wore ivory gowns but theirs were in an empire line style and boasted a wide deep pink sash under the bodice.

'Less tittle-tattle, ladies.' Edward grunted. 'You've an important job to do.'

'Sorry, Sir Edward.' Caroline gave a little curtsy as William came out of the church door and spoke to Edward.

Edward nodded, turned to us and said, 'It's time.'

We walked down the aisle in procession to 'Here Comes the Bride.' William first, next Melinda and Caroline dropping petals from their flower baskets, followed by Edward and me.

Scott popped into my head. I wondered what my wedding would be like if I said *yes* to him. Was I being disloyal? But if that's what I wanted, why couldn't I commit?

Richard was standing at the front row. His eyes lit up when he turned towards me although it was hard not to miss the frown as Edward led me towards my groom. Richard had obviously expected Edward to have been arrested by now too.

On reaching the bottom step, he and William moved alternately to the left, and right, then Melinda and Caroline did the same, thus making a space in the middle. Richard took me by the hand and guided me to the altar where we kneeled down on a deep cushion.

⋘

Richard parted the slit in my glove. He touched the gold band from Rebecca's first marriage, before sliding an almost identical one next to it on my finger, and said, 'With this ring I thee wed, with my body I thee worship, and with all my worldly goods I thee endow...'

The authorities hadn't arrested Edward. Did that mean that Rebecca and Richard's lives were in danger? Would I be here to help save them? Or would I be here and Edward killed me? What of my family back in my own time? It would crush Mum and Dad.

The minister continued with a prayer before joining our right hands and said, 'Those whom God hath joined together let no man put asunder.' He continued speaking to the people.

I waited for the flash but nothing happened, I was still standing by Richard's side when the organist played the chords to the intro of 'All Things Bright and Beautiful'. The congregation joined in with the hymn as Richard and I, along with Charles, Will, Caroline and Melinda, were led into the vestry where we were asked to sign the register before heading back down the aisle to Mendelsohn's 'Wedding March'.

I hadn't been sent back so what did this mean? Was I to become Rebecca forever? What about my old life. My career? And more importantly Chloe? Who'd look out for her? I'd been wrong about Matt, he loved her, so he'd take care of her, and soon she'd have her new baby. No, she didn't need me. But what would this do to my parents? They couldn't lose another child. Mum, in particular, had struggled since Michael's death. Would this push her over the edge?

No, I must be here because my mission wasn't finished. Rebecca and Richard still needed saving.

Crowds of villagers cheered as we reached the opened iron gates. The people joined our procession as the horses trotted up the driveway. We pulled up outside Bridge View Hall. Richard got out first and came to my side to assist my exit from the carriage. Villagers cheered congratulations throwing rice. The front of the house was adorned with white rose garlands.

I gripped Richard's hand. Yes, this was what I wanted. I had my new friends, Melinda and Caroline, both soon to be married too.

We stopped at the ballroom entrance. Our guests were already seated inside at a large rectangle table. Richard kissed me on the cheek. 'Ready, Lady Rebecca Cavendish?'

'What happpened?' I whispered. 'Why hasn't he been arrested?'

'I'm not sure, but keep smiling so he doesn't get suspicious.'

'But supposing he knows?'

'Shh, there's no way he could.'

As we entered, our friends rose from their seats, clapped and cheered. We headed for the throne-like chairs at the head of the table. Richard pulled one out for me before lowering himself to the other. Once we were both seated our friends sat back down.

A three-tier white iced wedding cake took pride of place in the centre of the table with cold meats, breads, and salad distributed around it. I imagined Rebecca's first marriage. The room would've likely been crammed with guests, but that then made me think of Samuel's murder. Now Richard was in danger, and maybe even Rebecca.

Distracting myself from my thoughts I glanced around the room at my friends who'd become more like family. I spotted Mary next to a man with a white beard. Was he a servant? Either way, it made me smile that she'd been invited.

The ballroom was packed. Servants from the house and villagers had seemingly been invited. A small orchestra played from a manmade platform. The large table we'd all sat around earlier had been cleared and moved to the side.

Richard took my hand. 'May I have this first dance, my dearest wife?' Without waiting for an answer, he led me on to the dance floor and spun me around in a waltz. As we circled the room, guests rumbled a large applause, clapping hands before joining us.

During the evening I participated in lots of dances, including the cake walk, turkey trot, and the castle walk, my feet knowing exactly where to go. Afterwards the musicians took a break, and refreshments were served to our guests.

A maid I didn't recognise offered up a tray. Richard took two flutes of champagne and passed one to me. 'Would you like to spend a little time with your friends,' he asked, 'before the dancing recommences?'

'That would be nice. What will you do?'

'I have a little business to chat over with Will and Charles.'

'Business?'

'Don't worry, dearest. It won't take long.'

'If you're sure.' Was this business to do with Edward? Looking back at Richard, I headed across the ballroom towards Melinda and Caroline who were now also absent their partners.

'Hello, ladies,' I said.

'I wonder what that's about?' Melinda glared across to the men.

'I think perhaps they're plotting a surprise,' I lied.

'How thrilling.' Melinda's eyes sparkled.

'Caroline,' I said, 'how are you getting on with Will?'

'He's adorable, Rebecca. I can't thank you enough for making this happen. We will be married within a month and I hope you'll be my matron of honour.'

'I'd love that, but' – I looked across at Melinda – 'wouldn't you rather...?'

Melinda giggled. 'She's already asked me to be her bridesmaid and when it's my turn you can both be my attendants too. This is so exciting. A few weeks ago I thought I'd end up as a spinster for the rest of my life. And now look.'

I felt so at ease with these two ladies. It was like I'd known them all my life but then maybe Rebecca had.

The music started up again. This time it was a mazurka. I wasn't sure how I knew that but maybe it was coming from Rebecca's memories. After many spins around the floor, and another waltz, Richard glided me outside to the terrace. Under the warm moonlight, he took my face in his hands, and kissed my lips. 'All is in hand,' he said.

'How can you be sure?'

'Trust me,' he said as Edward strode towards us.

My legs trembled.

Edward smirked. 'Now, dear brother-in-law, perhaps you and I may conduct some business.'

'Sir, there is plenty of time for business. This is my wedding celebration.'

'Please accept my apologies. My pleasure of you becoming part of our family got the better of me. I can wait,' he mumbled as he marched off.

'He knows,' I said.

'No' – Richard squinted – 'he can't. It isn't possible.'

The villagers, guests, and servants had left with Will, Caroline, Melinda and Charles being the last to leave. Edward was hovering around Richard when the front door slammed with an almost deafening sound followed by a hustle and bustle as uniformed officers marched into the drawing room. What had taken them so long?

An inspector resembling Hercule Poirot slapped his hand on Edward's shoulder. 'Sir Edward Pendleton?'

Edward peered around him. 'What's going on?'

'Answer the question, sir. Do you go by the name of Sir Edward Pendleton?' He signalled to the uniformed officers who stepped closer.

'That is my name. Now, I insist you inform me of the purpose of this outrage.'

'Sir Edward Pendleton' – the inspector cuffed him – 'I'm arresting you on suspicion of murder, fraud and illegal activities.' He turned to the policemen. 'Take him away.'

Edward wriggled but their grip was too strong. 'Sir Richard,' he shouted, 'do something.'

Richard held his head high. 'I'll do nothing, dear sir. You'll pay for what you did to my good friend, Samuel.'

Edward glared at me. 'Rebecca, help me. I'm your brother.'

I looked directly into his dark eyes and answered how I thought Rebecca would. 'No, brother, I'll not save you. You'll pay for not only murdering my first husband, but for Mother and Father's so called accident too.'

Once the uniformed officers had led Edward out of the drawing room, the look-alike Poirot shook Richard's hand. 'Sorry it's so late but we didn't want to interrupt your wedding celebrations.'

'Thank you, I appreciate that. Forgive my curiosity, but why has it taken so long for you to take him in? You had enough evidence.'

'We needed more witnesses, but don't worry, sir, he won't be able to escape these charges. He'll hang for what he did.'

'Finally,' Richard said, 'time to make you mine.' He scooped me into his arms and carried me up the winding stairs and along a corridor in the opposite direction to the one I was expecting. Where was he taking me? This wasn't the way to Rebecca's room.

Edward had been arrested, Zara's mission was complete, yet I hadn't been transported home. Was this my life now? Had I become Rebecca? Had Zara Wiseman gone forever?

Richard halted outside a double door, pushed it open, and carried me over the threshold into this elaborate bedroom. He stroked my cheek and neck before replacing his fingertips with lips and gradually slipped my gown away from my shoulders, smothering me with kisses. I stepped out of the gown and allowed my husband to remove all my garments until I stood naked. He scooped me up again, and laid me on the huge four-poster bed before removing his own clothes.

This was my life now. I had become Rebecca, and ready to experience my husband's lovemaking for the first time.

The flash came. *No, no, please don't send me back.* I tried to resist the pull.

Chapter Twenty-Five

Voices. Footsteps. *Where am I?*

'She's waking up,' a woman said. 'It's okay, Zara. I'm here. Open your eyes, darling. Someone, get the doctor.'

'It could just be like before, Laura,' a man said. 'She may slip back again.'

'No, this is it this time,' she answered. 'I can sense it. Where's the doctor?'

The man spoke again, 'She's here now. Stand back, love.'

A bright light shone in my eye. I pushed a hand away.

'It's all right, Zara. I'm Ms Weybridge, your consultant.'

'She is waking up? Isn't she?' The woman asked.

'It looks like she is, Mrs Wiseman. I believe your daughter's back with us.'

Daughter?

'Zara, can you open your eyes? You're waking up from a coma.'

Zara? No, I'm Rebecca. Lady Rebecca Cavendish.

'Your mum and dad are here,' the doctor continued.

Someone stroked my face. 'Zara, it's Dad. You gave us a hell of a fright.'

Someone else wailed. 'My baby. I thought we'd lost you. We've been here every day for the last two months waiting for you to wake up. Thank God you're back. Everything's going to be all right.'

Back? Not all right. Two months. No, I had to get back to Richard. He was about to make love to me. I squeezed my eyes to force the flash but the only flash that came was a light being shone in my eyes. *I'm Rebecca. Not Zara. I want to be Rebecca.* With blurred vision, I looked up at the lady doctor. 'I have to get back. Please, help me go back.'

'It's all right, Zara.' The doctor moved the torch away from my eyes. 'You are back and your parents are here. They've been so worried.'

'I'm not Zara. I'm Lady Rebecca Cavendish.'

'What's she saying?' the woman asked.

'Don't worry, 'the doctor said. 'She's a little confused. This will right itself in time.'

'She'll be okay then?' came from the woman.

'I believe so. This is a perfectly normal reaction for patients waking up from a coma but we'll do some tests to make sure there's nothing untoward going on.'

This can't be happening. 'I must get back.'

'Shh. You are back,' the doctor said. 'Look, here's your mother.'

Someone stroked my arm. 'It's over now, darling. You're back here with us, thank God. We thought we'd lost you.'

I peered up at the woman. 'Mum?'

'Yes love, it's me.' She squeezed my hand.

'Mum, I need to go back.'

'It's all right, my love,' she answered. 'The nightmare is over for us all.'

It was futile. I wasn't going anywhere. I closed my eyes.

Chapter Twenty-Six

Mum, Dad and Scott circled my bed. 'Here's the doctor now.' Dad moved out of the way to allow the consultant to get close to me.

'Good afternoon, Zara, how are you feeling?'

I shrugged. 'How do you think I feel when I'm still here?'

Without commenting on my statement she said, 'We've had the results from the latest brain scan and I'm pleased to say it's clear.'

Mum squeezed my fingers. 'Then why is she still confused?'

The doctor addressed me, 'Zara, do you remember earlier in the year when you thought things were happening to you?'

I didn't answer.

'And you attended sessions with a psychiatrist?'

Again I didn't answer.

'What are you saying?' Dad asked. 'That this is all related to her being delusional?'

'It's the only acceptable conclusion we can come to. We believe that Zara could no longer cope with the situation so regressed within herself. There was no physical reason for her comatose state.'

'So, what does this mean?' Mum asked.

Ms Weybridge looked directly at me. 'Zara, I recommend that you recommence your sessions with Dr Fields.'

'When can she return to work?' Scott spoke for the first time.

'It's going to take you a few weeks to regain your strength' – the doctor smiled at me – 'but I'm confident with the right aftercare you'll make a full recovery.'

'That's good news, Laura. Isn't it?' Dad put his arm around Mum. 'How long before she's discharged?' he asked the doctor.

'I'm happy to discharge you today, Zara.'

'Thank you.' The first thing I'd do was get down to the train station.

'However,' she continued, 'I think I'd prefer it if you weren't alone.'

'I'm not alone. I have a flatmate.'

'I'd rather you had someone with you full time.' She turned to Mum. 'Zara needs healthy meals, light exercise, fresh air, and professional mental health care.'

'Yes, she can stay with us. I'll make sure she get's all that as I'm home in the day and can take care of her.' Mum rested her fingers on Dad's wrist. 'And Tim, if I have the car, I can drive her to see the psychiatrist.'

'That sounds ideal. I'll sort out the discharge papers now.' Ms Weybridge faced me. 'Let your mum take care of you, Zara, as I'd rather not see you back on my ward anytime soon.'

'Thanks, Doctor.' Dad shook her hand.

Once the consultant had moved away, I said, 'I'm not coming back with you.'

'Now, Zara,' Dad said. 'It won't be for long. Just until you're strong again.'

If I had one more cup of tea thrust at me I was sure I'd scream. It was stifling in this house with Mum fussing round me like a mother hen. And Scott was almost as bad. He'd turned up every day. And today I was in a more foul mood than normal.

I glared up at him. 'Why are you even here? You're always hanging around me like a lapdog.'

He pulled away his hand. 'Sorry, Zara, but I thought we'd lost you for good. I didn't mean to hang around you like that. I'll go.'

You wicked cow. I grabbed his arm. 'No, Scott, I'm sorry. I should never have spoken to you like that. Don't go.'

Dad rose from the armchair. 'Come along, Laura, let's give these young people a few moments on their own.'

'Oh. Er. Oh. All right.' Mum stood up from the other chair. 'I'll just get these washed up and put the kettle on again.' She gathered the mugs on to a tray before leaving Scott and me alone.

'God, Scott. She's suffocating me. I've been here for two weeks now and barely had a second to myself. She even drives me there and back to see Craig. Told her I can get the bus home but–'

'She's just worried about you, babe. We all are.'

'But this isn't helping me. Being back in my childhood bedroom, and Michael's ghost. Do you know his room is like a shrine? She's not moved a thing. No wonder she can't get past his death.'

Scott gripped my fingers. 'Wait until Chloe's had her baby. Your mum's focus will change then. You'll see.'

'I can't wait that long. Talk to my dad. Tell him I'm well enough to go back to the flat. And I want to get back to work. I can't cope with all this smothering.'

'All right. I'll have a word. Maybe you're right and all this isn't helping you.'

Scott had managed to convince Dad that it was doing me more harm than good having Mum fuss over me like a mother hen so I got back here two days ago.

Holly finally went off to work this morning, slamming the door behind her. I peered out of the window and watched her lift drive off. At least it wasn't raining. I slipped on my black parka and headed out into the biting wind. I needed to get back to Richard. It had been far too long. No one could understand because they all thought I was crazy.

The road was fairly quiet as it was gone nine and the kids would be settled in classrooms at school and commuters would be sitting at their desks. I stopped at the mansion remembering my last night there almost three months ago. My wedding night. My friends, Melinda and Caroline. The music. The dancing. Richard's tender kisses. I'd been cheated.

I hurried across the road at the pedestrian lights and into the station foyer. The porter who'd looked after me on more than one occasion headed my way.

'Zara, I heard you've been poorly?'

Had he? Who'd told him?

'Sorry, I wasn't stalking you, there was a note in the magazine you write for.' He patted me on the shoulder. 'Good to have you back, young lady. Where are you off to today?'

'My sister's,' I lied.

'Well have a nice day. I'd better' – he pointed towards a platform – 'the nine-thirty is due in for London.'

'Sure.' I gave a little wave. 'See you again soon.'

Once he was out of sight I headed for Platform 2 and waited but nothing happened so I headed back to the foyer. Again nothing. Back to another platform. Nothing happened. What was wrong? Why wasn't it sending me back? I sloped out of the exit and strode back home.

My mobile vibrated. I glanced at the number. *Mum.* She was probably checking up on me. I answered the call. 'Hi, Mum, you okay?'

'Chloe's had a baby girl,' Mum answered. 'When can you get here?'

'Which hospital?'

'No, not at hospital. She had the baby at home. Your sister's asking for you. Can you get Scott to bring you down this evening?'

'Sure. See you later.' I ended the call. Chloe a mother, Mum a granny, and me an aunty. Glad I hadn't missed the chance of meeting my new baby niece, I hurried into town and headed for the mall.

Monday morning meant it was quiet. Where was the best place to go for baby clothes? I'd no idea. I peered up at the frontage of the shop in front of me. Next. Yes, I think they sold them. Making my way inside I spotted an assistant.

'Do you sell baby clothes?' I asked the female assistant organising ladies T-shirts on the rail.

She looked up and smiled. 'Indeed we do. Straight ahead.'

'Thanks.' I strode to the end of the shop and peered up at the signs. 3-6 months. 12-18 months. Ah, newborn. Yes, that's what I wanted. Um. I should've asked Mum what the baby weighed. In fact, I hadn't even asked if Chloe was okay. Probably because I was so shocked that she'd had the baby at home. I'd no idea she was even considering a homebirth. Mum never said, and neither did Chloe or anybody else for that matter. Each to their own I supposed. No way would I have wanted that.

Little outfits hung on the hangers begging to be bought. What should I buy? Maybe a variety of things. I selected a pack of five spotted bodysuits, a Jo Jo crisp white bodysuit with a silver-thread embroidered elephant, a pack of three patterned sleepsuits, one of them in rose, a white hooded knitted cardigan with crimson buttons, a pale pink stripey dress with decorative strawberries across the smocked bodice, and finally a pack of neutral lace socks. That should do for now. I headed to the checkout where the cashier cashed them up and loaded them into a huge carrier bag.

'That's eighty-five, ninety-nine.' The salesperson smiled.

'Thank you.' I tapped my credit card on the machine. Under a hundred quid for that lot. I thought I'd done well.

The baby garments lay spread on the sofa. I picked up the little dress and wondered what my baby would've been like if I'd had one with Richard. My eyes filled. I had to try the station again. I'd keep going until I found the portal and it took me back to my husband. Sniffling, I wrapped up the baby items a packet at a time.

Scott pulled up outside just as I'd finished writing out a congratulations card to Chloe and Matt. I gathered the gifts into a shopping bag and hurried out to get into the Porsche.

The raging rollers foamed. I put my scarf across my mouth. 'She's angry,' I said.

'Certainly looks that way.' Scott took my hand. 'Don't think we'll be going for a swim today. 'Come on, let's get inside.'

We hurried up to the house, knocked and waited.

Dad answered. 'Hello, Zara.' He kissed me on the cheek. 'You're looking a lot better. Come in quickly and let's get this door closed.' Once it was shut he turned to Scott. 'Good to see you again, son. Matt's in the kitchen, and Chloe, your mum and the baby are in the bedroom.'

'I'll go and find Matt' – Scott passed me my bag of gifts – 'and let you get acquainted with your new niece.'

'Thanks, Scott.' I headed to the bedroom. 'Knock knock,' I said. 'Okay if I come in?'

'Zara, glad you got here okay. It's wild out there.' Chloe was propped up in bed cuddling a bundle of pink with a head of dark hair peeping out.

'Look at you,' I said. 'Can't believe you're a mummy.'

Her blue eyes twinkled. She patted the bed. 'Come and meet Amelia Jane.'

I wandered over, dropped the bag to the floor, and perched myself on the covers next to my sister. 'She's gorgeous. How much did she weigh?'

'Six pounds seven ounces.'

'And what time did you have her?'

'Four-fifteen this morning.'

'I'll leave you girls to it for a while and make us some tea.' Mum left the room.

I stroked Chloe's arm. 'You must be tired.'

'Just a bit.'

'I hadn't realised you were having her at home?'

'I didn't fancy going to hospital and the midwife was more than happy for me to have a homebirth. It meant no worries about packing a bag and getting to the hospital before she was born. Just as well too. She was really quick for a first baby.'

'Yeah?' I peered over to glance at Amelia's little face. 'She looks like a little angel.'

'She's lovely, Zara. I can't believe she's mine. Want a hold?'

'Can I?'

'Yeah.' She passed me the tiny bundle and Amelia gave a tiny cry.

'How are you?' I asked.

'Bit sore. Matt's been great. He's been in charge of feeding and changing her so far. Wanted me to rest.'

'That's nice. You're not feeding her yourself then?'

'Thought about it. Even gave it a little try but' – she shook her head – 'it really wasn't me. Amelia doesn't object to the bottle. And look at her. She's so contented.'

Mum came back with tea and biscuits. She placed the tray on the chest of drawers. 'Why don't we put Amelia in the crib, Chloe? That way we can have a cuppa in peace.'

'I'm okay holding her.' I rocked the swaddled baby.

'It would be a good idea,' Mum continued. 'After all, we don't want Zara dropping her.'

I frowned at Mum. 'Why would I?'

She tapped my shoulder. 'Because you've been very poorly and still building up your strength.'

I looked at Chloe.

'Maybe it's for the best. You can have another hold later. Anyway, I want to see what you've got in that huge sack.' Chloe grinned.

'Oh all right then.'

Mum took Amelia and laid her in the mesh fabric crib next to the bed. 'Zara, pass your sister a cup of tea.'

'I've had that many cups of tea, Mum,' Chloe protested. 'In fact, I've rested long enough. I'm going to get up and come into the lounge and open our pressies with Matt.'

'But...'

'Mum, it's not like in your day. They like us new mums to move about. I had a normal birth, not even any stitches. I'm fine.'

Mum shrugged. 'If you say so. I'll get your father to carry in the crib.'

'No need.' Chloe pulled the covers back and climbed out of bed. 'We have a baby monitor. We'll stick the TV on and we can watch her from in there.'

Mum pulled a funny face, went to say something but obviously changed her mind. I laughed. 'Cool. Can you record it?'

'I don't know. We'll have to ask Matt. Come on, and bring those pressies.'

After I'd finished hugging Mum, Dad, and Chloe, I followed Scott outside to the car and inhaled the salt air. 'Shall we have a little stroll along the front first.'

'You sure? It's pretty bitter.'

'Just for a few minutes.'

'Okay.' He took my hand, I wanted to pull it back but let it stay.

'I noticed you got upset when cuddling Amelia. I didn't take you for the broody type.'

'I'm not. You don't know what you're talking about. I didn't get upset.'

'Zara, you had tears. I saw them with my own eyes.'

'Just shut up.' Anger rose within me. I imagined myself foaming from the mouth like the sea.

He put his arm around me. 'Hey, I didn't mean to agitate you. I'm just worried.'

'Well there's no need. I'm happy for my sister so if you saw tears then they were happy tears.'

He grunted. 'If you say so.'

'I just did, didn't I?' I picked up a pebble and tossed it into the water. 'There's something about being close to the sea that makes me feel free. Do you feel it?'

Scott put his arms around me. 'I do. Although, darling, I have to say you're not showing the actions of a person feeling free. You seem stressed. How are you really doing?'

I hadn't realised he'd been watching me so closely while I was holding the baby. My stomach fizzed as anger raged inside me. I pushed him away. 'How the hell do you think I'm doing? Everyone thinks I'm crazy, and I know I'm not.' I didn't want to be here. I wanted to be back in bed with Richard so I could experience his lovemaking on our wedding night. It wasn't fair. 'And no one gives me any space. Even you?' I glared at him. 'Why are you watching my every move? Did my mum put you up to it?'

'Babe.' Scott frowned before taking a deep breath. 'This is what I mean. You're not yourself. I know it's hard for you but maybe if you talk to me about how you're feeling then I could try and help.'

'Well you can't. And you and everyone else continually smothering me isn't helping. I need to breathe.' I was behaving like a real cow but I couldn't help it. It was all too much. I longed to be with Richard. Not back here as Zara Wiseman.

'Just take me home, will you.' I strode towards the car. Tomorrow I'd go back to the station and I'd keep going until the portal opened. I was meant to be with Richard. I was meant to be Rebecca.

Chapter Twenty-Seven

A cyclist pushed into me as he bustled out of the station, but otherwise it was quiet. I headed for the usual platform. Nothing. I hurried back into the foyer. Nothing. I charged upstairs, across the bridge, and down the other side. Nothing. I dropped onto the bench and sobbed into my hands. Why wasn't it happening?

'Hey, Zara.' Arms went around me.

I looked up and it was the porter who'd rescued me many a time.

'What is it, dear? Are you ill?'

I pulled a tissue from my pocket and dried my eyes. 'No, I'm okay. Just having a funny moment.'

'Where are you off to? Not normal to see you on this platform.'

I shrugged. 'It's not working.'

He sat down next to me. 'What isn't, love? Is there someone you'd like me to call?'

'It isn't working.'

'It's all right, Zara. Everything's going to be all right. Do you have a number so I can call someone?'

I rose from the seat. 'No, I don't need anyone. I'm fine.'

He glared at me.

'Really, I am. I was just getting into character for my story.'

'Oh, I see. Sorry to have disturbed you then, love. If you need me' – he pointed to the other side of the platform – 'I'll be over there.'

It wasn't going to happen. Maybe everyone was right and I was crazy.

※

Scott pulled up outside the station. I climbed into the Porsche.

'Thanks,' I whispered.

'I was pleased to get your call. Where would m'lady like to go? Home? The beach?'

'Double Dee's? Holly's at home and I want to talk to you alone.'

'Sure.' He pulled the car away and headed into town.

I stayed silent. How did I admit that I'd been wrong? That I'd imagined the whole thing when I didn't want it to be true but if it had been real then I'd have gone back.

'Here we go. How lucky is this?' He parked in a bay across from the café.

'Yes. Great.'

We crossed the road and entered Double Dee's where Dan greeted us. 'Zara. Good to see you, girl.' He gave me a hug. 'Me and Dave have been so worried.'

Dan looked from me to Scott. 'Tell you what, I'll give you guys a few mins to get settled.'

'He didn't know what to say.' I slumped into the leather sofa. 'He's like the rest of you and thinks I'm mad.'

Scott flopped down next to me and took my hand in his. 'None of us think that, Zara. We're all just worried. Now, what was it you wanted to talk about?'

'You were right. You all were. I must've imagined the whole thing. Not sure why but I must've done.' Even while I said those words doubt still crept within me as I remembered the sensation of Richard naked lying next to me. I didn't know what to believe.

Dan was at our table. 'Cappuccino for madam and sir.'

He put a tall ceramic mug in front of each of us. 'And extra chocolate and marshmallows for the lady.' He beamed a wide grin.

'Thanks.' I couldn't help but smile.

'Now that's the Zara we all know and love.' Dan winked. 'You know, darling, you're so pretty when you smile.'

The next thing, tears streamed down my face. 'Sorry.'

'Oh no, I'm sorry. Bless you darling.' He sat down next to me. 'Whatever it is, this guy here' – he nodded towards Scott – 'he'll look after you.'

'I know. Thanks.'

Dan rose from the sofa. 'Now, I'll leave you two to it. Give me a yell if there's anything I can get you.' Swaying, he headed over to greet some customers coming through the door.

Scott put his arm around my shoulder. 'Why don't I take you away for a few days?'

'Where? How? What about work?'

'Wherever you want to go. Annabel will be more than happy to give me a few days off.'

'It's a bit cold though.'

'We could head down to the New Forest. Get a cabin, light a roaring fire, spend some time with nature.'

That did sound welcoming.

'And get to know each other all over again?'

'All right. But first, I'd better ask Craig what he thinks. Will you drive me over there once we've had these?' I pointed to our drinks.

'Anything for you. You know that.'

※

The windscreen wipers swished backwards and forwards making me sleepy. Scott pulled up on the road outside Craig's. 'Want to borrow my brolly?'

'Please.'

He passed me the umbrella from the door pocket. 'Should I come in with you?'

'No, you're all right. If you don't mind waiting for me here.'

'No probs.' He switched on his music.

I got out of the car and erected the umbrella. 'Shan't be long.' As I headed up the wooden steps I took care not to slip on the loose twigs. I finally reached the top and found Craig locking up.

He peered across. 'Zara?' He furrowed his brows. 'Did we have an appointment?'

'No, but I wanted to see you. Is that okay?'

'Of course, of course.' He unlocked the door and pushed it open. 'Come on in, take a seat.'

'Ta.' I collapsed the umbrella.

'You want a drink of something?' He placed his keys down on the desk.

'No, thanks.'

'Right' – he took the armchair opposite – 'tell me. What is it?'

'I...' I fidgeted with my necklace. 'I...'

'Take your time.'

'I realised something today.'

'Yes.'

'I realised that everything I thought had happened to me, you know, about going back in time, well um, I realise now that it can't have done. It must've been my imagination. I've no idea why but it must've been.' I peered down at the floor.

'Zara, do you realise what a big jump forward this is for you?'

'Is it?' I was standing next to Richard in church saying my wedding vows.

'Zara, look at me.'

I lifted my head and faced him.

'Recognising this was in your imagination is the first step to recovery. I'm proud of you.'

'Thanks.'

'Would you like to talk more about this?'

I glanced out of the window at the pouring rain. 'Not really. Scott's waiting outside for me.'

'Ah, I understand. So, let's have a look. I believe I'm due to see you on Wednesday. Is that correct?'

'Yes, but that's really why I needed to speak to you.'

'Oh?'

'Scott wants to take me away for a few days.'

'Anywhere nice?'

'He thought somewhere like the New Forest but we've not decided yet. But I wanted to check with you first as it means I won't be able to attend my session.'

'That's all right, Zara. It'll do you good to get away for a while.' He rose from his seat, went over to the desk and opened his online diary on the PC. 'How about I see you the week after next?'

'Yes, that should work.'

'Okay. Four-thirty a week Wednesday.' He headed back over to me. 'Now if you have any problems before then, my mobile number is on here.' He passed his business card. 'Call me day or night if you need me.'

'Thanks, Craig.' I got up from the chair. 'Well, I'll let you get off home. Like I said, Scott's in the car.'

Chapter Twenty-Eight

We drove down a narrow lane into Rosdorn, a hamlet not too far from Brockenhurst, consisting of a few picture-box dwellings, a pub, a couple of small shops to buy essentials, and a café. 'That's ours, straight ahead.' Scott pulled the Porsche into the driveway of a small cottage with *Angel's Haven* swinging on a slate sign from a wooden post.

'It looks lovely,' I said, admiring the white picket fencing surrounding the eighteenth century property. This was a brilliant idea of Scott's. It would be good to get away for a while and allow me space to sort out my head.

'We were lucky to get it at such short notice.' Scott got out of the car and opened the boot. 'It was only because they'd had a last minute cancellation. If you look across there,' he said as I joined him, 'you can see the forest.'

'I love walking among the trees.'

'I know you do, and this is less than a five minute stroll.' He lifted the bags out of the boot. 'Come on, let's go and explore.'

We wheeled our small cases up to the white front door. Scott tapped the pin number into the keypad, took out the key and unlocked the door. As we stepped into the warmth, I gasped at its beauty. Unlike the old redbrick frontage with Georgian windows, inside was completely modernised. The lounge was huge, light and spotless. A log fire blazed in its black-brick housing under an oval mirror.

I sank into the large cream sofa, finished with rose-patterned scatter cushions, and a white throw hung over each arm.

'That looks comfy. May I join you?'

'It is.' Richard popped into my head and I wanted to shout *no* to Scott but instead answered, 'Do.'

He flopped down at my side. 'You like?'

'I do.'

He moved closer, put his arms around my neck and kissed me on the lips.

No. This wasn't right. I was Richard's wife. I backed away.

'Too soon?' He squeezed my fingers. 'I understand. Let's look around the rest of the place.' He led me into the kitchen. 'Wow, check this out.'

It was modern yet had kept some antique touches with its old pine table. I pulled out the single drawer. 'Table mats.'

'And come and look at this.' He opened up a cupboard. 'It's even got a dishwasher and a washing machine/dryer.'

'That's good.' I smiled. Why had I agreed to this?

He opened the fridge. 'Look, they've even left us some goodies. Cheese, milk, croissants, butter, strawberries, and this.' He waved a bottle of Chardonnay. 'Brilliant.'

We continued the tour to the bathroom. 'Wow,' he said. 'Check this out. A bathroom to die for.'

It was rather lovely with a *his and hers* sink unit, walk-in shower, toilet, and freestanding bath with gold taps.

Scott took my hand. 'And now the bedroom.'

The word bedroom took me back to my wedding night. I was lying in the four-poster with Richard. My skin tingled remembering his naked body touching mine.

Like the rest of the property, the bedroom was amazing, and under normal circumstances I'd have been wowed. But it wasn't right. How could I share the super-king size bed with another man when I was married. I didn't care what they said. It can't have been my imagination. It was too real.

Scott perched on the edge of the bed. 'Come here.' He patted the blue throw.

I stayed where I was.

'You know,' he said, 'if it's too soon, I'll take the couch.'

'You sure you don't mind?'

'No problem.' He turned away but not before I caught the sad expression on his face. He was such a kind, gentle and considerate man, but he wasn't Richard.

I made for the rose flowery drapes and peered out of the wide window. 'We can see the forest from here.'

He moved next to me. 'It's perfect. Fancy a walk?'

'Now?'

'Yes. Why not?'

I shrugged. Maybe it would be easier being together if we were out and about. 'Okay. Let's go before it refreezes.'

A couple of cars on the road were brought to a halt by two tan and three off-white ponies.

'The ponies take precedence on the road here,' Scott explained.

'Aren't they lovely?' I wanted to go over and stroke them but I'd heard they weren't used to being handled so better to leave them alone. 'I wonder if we'll see some more once we get inside the forest.'

'Quite possibly.'

We crossed the road while still admiring the small horses and within no time at all we were among the trees, crunching on the iced ground, still frozen from the morning frost. I blew into my woollen gloves to try and warm my face. 'It's bitter.'

'Just a bit. Come on, let's go for a ramble. Take care not to slip with this ice.'

We wandered along the frosty track moving deeper into the forest. I inhaled the earthy scent from the nearby oaks. After a while of walking in silence, Scott asked, 'How you doing, Zara? You're awfully quiet.'

'Okay.' I felt far from okay though. I wanted to be back at Bridge View Hall. I wondered what Richard was doing. Was Rebecca there in my place?

Scott gripped my fingers. 'I think we should be turning back soon before it gets dark.'

'You're probably right. But let's take it at a slow pace because looking at this sunshine I reckon we could be in for a gorgeous sunset.'

'All right' – Scott huddled up closer – 'but you'll have to keep me warm.'

I backed away.

'Sorry,' he said.

'Look.' I pointed at the ponies ahead. 'And check out that sky over them.' The sky had turned orange with pink and purple hues. 'Now isn't that a picture worth staying out a little longer for?'

'It is.' He took his mobile from a pocket and snapped the image. Afterwards he said, 'Let's go and have some hot chocolate by the fire.'

⁎

The hot shower had been refreshing and warmed me up. I wrapped a large fluffy towel around me and stepped out of the cubicle. I imagined Richard patting me dry and caressing me gently. I turned towards him to kiss his lips but he wasn't there. My head was messed up. Were they right and everything was in my mind? If only I knew. Part of it made sense that it hadn't happened, because it seemed so far-fetched, but everything was too vivid for it not to have been real. I wasn't wrong. I was sure. I needed to get back home and keep going to the train station until it sent me back to Bridge View Hall. Richard wasn't a dream. He couldn't be. He was my love. My soulmate. He was my husband and I was his wife. I was Lady Rebecca Cavendish. I had to get back.

Over the next few days Scott and I'd filled our time with walks in the forest. We wrapped up warm as the freeze wasn't letting up. We visited a nearby spa. Here we enjoyed a massage, swam in the heated pool, and lounged on sunbeds listening to music through headphones, but I couldn't relax. I kept wishing it was Richard here with me and not Scott. It was then it hit me. I'd been right. What happened to me at Bridge View Hall had been real. And that's why I was still unable to commit to Scott. It didn't matter how handsome he was, or how considerate, it was Richard I loved, and now I'd found him I wasn't going to lose him. No matter what they all said. He wasn't in my imagination.

Scott loved me there was no doubt. He'd put up with a lot from me over the last year, sat by my bedside when I'd laid in a coma for two months, stuck with me when I'd been a real cow to him. But it wasn't Scott I wanted. And it was wrong of me to keep him dangling. We could be close friends but that was all I could offer.

Thank goodness we were returning home tomorrow. Once there, I'd try and put some distance between us.

Chapter Twenty-Nine

A car hooted outside. I peered out of the window. It was my parents so I picked up the black sack full of presents, headed out of the door and down the footpath to where Dad was standing with the Puma boot open. I threw the sack in.

He kissed me on the cheek. 'Merry Christmas, love. Hop in the back.'

'Thanks, Dad.' I climbed into the back. 'Hi, Mum. Merry Christmas.'

She held her gaze for a moment. 'You're still looking peaky.'

'I'm fine.' I fastened the seatbelt.

'Ready in the back?' Dad asked.

'Ready.'

'Great. Let's get on then and fingers crossed we get to your sister's before it snows again.' Dad started the car up and pulled away. 'You know, Laura, I'm still wondering if we should cancel and just go back to ours.' He turned left out of the road. 'The last thing we want is to get stranded down there.'

'What, and miss our granddaughter's first Christmas Day. It'll be fine. If you have a problem driving then I'll take over.'

'That's not what I said, love.'

Mum seemed to pick an argument with Dad all the time these days. Had she always done that and I hadn't noticed? She twisted her head to speak to me. 'It's a shame Scott won't be here this year.'

'I told you, Mum, we're not seeing each other anymore.'

'That's a mistake if there ever was one.'

'Laura. Leave the girl alone, please. I'm trying to concentrate in this weather.' He flicked on the windscreen wipers.

The sky turned black and the next thing huge hailstones smashed down on the windscreen. Today was the first day I'd not managed to get to the train station since returning from the New Forest last month. Supposing today was the day I was meant to find the portal.

It was three months since I'd said my vows to Richard. I held my stomach. If I hadn't been sent back I could've been pregnant by now. Would I ever get the chance to look into those gorgeous mahogany eyes ever again? Or feel his fingertips caressing my skin? I closed my eyes and imagined him kissing my lips. Our tongues mingled. I groaned.

Dad brought me back with a jolt. 'You all right in the back?'

'Just a little travel sick,' I lied.

Mum turned her head. 'I thought you'd grown out of that years ago?'

'Me too. It's just today I'm feeling a bit queasy. Probably the windscreen wipers knocking me for six.'

Mum passed me a plastic container. 'Here. If you think you're going to be sick, use that.'

'Thanks.' I took the rectangular receptacle knowing that there was no way I'd need it as I didn't feel nauseous at all. Just lovesick.

'Almost there, folks.' Dad pulled onto the slip road, turned right off the roundabout and continued on the same road until we reached the seafront where we parked behind a Porsche that looked a lot like Scott's.

The waves were wild. I climbed out of the car and headed towards the shoreline. Hail hurled at my cheeks but I didn't care. I wished I could just stay out there.

'Zara,' Mum called. 'What are you playing at? Get yourself inside before you catch your death.'

※

Chloe greeted us at the open door. 'Hurry up and come in. You're letting out the warmth.' She gave me a huge hug. 'How are you doing now?'

I shrugged. 'So so. You know.'

'Go through to the lounge. Scott's here already.'

I touched her arm. 'What do you mean Scott's here?'

'What? You didn't invite him? I assumed you had. Someone did, anyway.'

I scowled at Mum and Dad. 'Do you know something about this?'

'It was for your own good,' Mum said. 'You two belong together. And once you're fully recovered you'll see that. Just stick with it, darling. He's great husband material. Loyal. Considerate. You could do far worse than him, my girl. Tim, tell her?'

Dad held his hands up in front. 'I'm staying out of it. This is your mother's doing, love. Nothing to do with me. She just can't help herself.'

I was seething and about to shout at Mum when Chloe pleaded with me. 'It's done now, Zara. Let's not spoil today. Please. This is Amelia's first Christmas.'

'Okay. But only because of Amelia.' I turned to Mum. 'This isn't over.'

Matt and Scott came into the hallway. 'We thought we heard voices,' Matt said before kissing Mum, and shaking Dad's hand. 'Zara.' He nodded at me.

'Scott,' I said. 'I hadn't realised you'd be here.'

He squinted. 'But you invited me.'

I shook my head. 'Actually, I didn't.'

'Oh, sorry. Your mum said you'd asked for me to be here.'

'Never mind, you're here now and we won't spoil Christmas. Nothing's changed between us though. As long as you know that?'

'Yes. Sure.'

Matt rubbed his hands. 'Follow me into the dining room and be prepared to be surprised with the feast I have in store for you all.'

'Vegetarian, I hope?' I glared at him.

'Naturally. And' – he grinned at Mum – 'I'm looking forward to your verdict.'

The table was beautifully set. Matt placed some kind of pastry dish on an oval platter in the centre and cut it into slices. 'Help yourselves,' he said smiling before taking a seat.

'This looks good,' Dad said. 'What do you call this, son?'

'It's a chestnut, spinach & blue cheese en croûte. I got the recipe from the Good Food site.'

'It certainly looks tasty. Shall I sort yours for you?' Dad asked Mum.

'If you don't mind, love. It'll save me getting up as my knees are giving me a lot of jip today.'

'Anything for my lovely wife.' Dad picked up two plates in turn and served a decent sized wedge on each, along with crispy, golden roast potatoes, sprouts, carrots, parsnips and peas. He set a plate down in front of Mum.

'Thank you, Tim. This looks very appetising, Matt.'

'I did the roasters.' Chloe beamed. 'I was Matt's sous chef. Wasn't I?'

'Yes, darling.' Matt waited until we'd all helped ourselves before serving his and Chloe's. 'Now to wait for everyone's verdict.'

I had to admit it was gorgeous. This confirmed to me that I'd got Matt wrong. He was a good husband and dad.

Once the dinner was over the Monopoly came out as usual on Christmas day in the Wiseman household. I really wasn't in the mood. 'Do you mind if I skip this?'

'Come on, sweetheart,' Dad said. 'You know how much I look forward to this.'

I sighed.

'Actually, Mr Wiseman, I wouldn't mind a bit of time with Zara.' Scott turned to me. 'Perhaps you and I can clear up the dishes?'

'That's an excellent idea,' Mum answered for me. 'That's settled then. Off you go, Zara, if you don't want to join in the game the least you can do is give Scott a hand clearing up.'

Seemed like I didn't have a choice. I followed him out to Chloe's kitchen which was like the ones you'd find in a Home and Garden magazine. Black and white chequered flooring. Black ceramic worktops over white cupboards. It was gorgeous. I dropped the dishwasher door. 'Do you want me to load?'

Scott pressed his fingertips on my arm. 'Leave that for now and sit down for a minute. Surely you owe me that.'

Maybe I did. 'Okay.' I climbed onto the high-backed vinyl stool at the breakfast bar. 'What is it you want?'

'An explanation I suppose.' He took the seat next to me. 'I don't really understand where I went wrong. We had a lovely break together and then out of the blue when you're getting out of the car you announce that we're done. What did I do wrong?'

'Nothing. It wasn't you. It's me. You and me, well, we weren't working, and it would've been wrong to keep stringing you along. I don't love you, Scott. Not like that, anyway. I love you as a friend, and maybe in time we can be close friends again.'

His eyes filled. 'You sure about this? I can give you space?'

'I'm sure.'

'But maybe once you're well again? I'll wait for you.'

'I don't want you to. I want you to get on with your life and find a nice girl who is worthy of you, and that's not me.' It was harsh but there was nothing else to do. I had to be honest with him. Even if I never found my way back to Richard, I'd not settle for second best as I knew that I'd never feel that way about Scott.

After cuddles from us all, Amelia was back sleeping in her cot. She was such a contented baby. I wondered what mine and Richard's baby would've been like. Tears trickled down my cheek. Chloe spotted me dabbing my face. She came and sat down next to me. 'You okay?'

Nodding, I managed to say, 'Yep.'

'Want to go for a walk? Just you and me?'

I nodded again.

'Mum,' she said, 'would you mind keeping a listen out for Amelia? Zara and I are going for a quick walk along the front.'

'I'm not sure that's a good idea.' Mum frowned. 'It's wild out there, you'll catch your deaths.'

Dad got up and peered out of the window. 'Well it looks like it's dried up now, at least. Wrap up girls.' He turned to Mum. 'They'll be fine.'

Arm in arm we strolled along the shingle shore. 'How are you really doing, sis?' Chloe asked me.

I shrugged. 'Okay.'

'I spotted you crying. You know you can talk to me about anything?'

'I know.'

'Mum and Dad said you broke up with Scott? What was that about?'

'I realised he wasn't right for me.'

'So today isn't a reconciliation then?'

'No. That's Mum just interfering as usual.'

'She just worries. How's it going with your psychiatrist?'

'Okay.'

'Do you still think the timeslips were real?'

I shrugged again. 'Honestly, I don't know. Sometimes I think everyone's right and it was in my head but other times it's still so vivid, Chloe. I mean if it didn't really happen how come I can smell Richard? Feel his kisses? Sense his fingertips brushing over me?'

She stopped walking and took my hand. 'How could it be real? It's too far-fetched.'

'I know but...'

'Come on, Zara. I reckon you realised that Scott wasn't right for you so therefore your subconscious dreamed up this perfect guy.'

'You're probably right.' Was she? I wished I knew.

Chapter Thirty

It was my first week back at work. I'd insisted I was ready to return after the new year bank holiday. Megan was still on leave so I had the office to myself.

I was editing an article from a new trainee reporter. His writing was flat. How this young man had managed to get the job was beyond me. He'd done a review on a local theatre production. Where was the colour of the costumes? What did they look like? How did their voices sound? I marked the Word document with my comments. I sighed.

'Everything all right?' Annabel was behind me.

I sighed again. 'Not really. It's this.' I signalled to the computer screen. 'Where did this guy train? I mean did he even have any journalist training?'

'He's a trainee, Zara. He's looking to you to mentor him. Of course...'

'What?'

'You could always look at getting back to finishing your serial for the magazine.'

I blinked. 'I'm not sure.'

'Think about it.' She pulled up Megan's chair next to me and sat down. 'So how's it going with Craig?'

'Good thanks.'

'And you're now understanding what you thought had happened didn't?'

'If you're asking me am I still delusional, no. And yes, I understand.' Reluctantly I'd tried to accept it had all been in my imagination after going to the train station every day for the last four weeks and nothing happening.

'Good girl. Have a think about what I said. I'm prepared to offer you a full time position as a writer which means you won't have to work on any more of this stuff.'

'Now that sounds appealing.'

'If you're struggling, Zara, why not finish early as it's Friday. It's been hard for you, I'm sure, being back this week. Use the time to get a walk in and some fresh air. It's a lovely day.'

I glanced out of the window. 'You know what, Annabel? I think I will. Thanks for that.'

⋆

The park was quiet except for a few dog walkers. Pulling my coat closer to my chest, I headed for the duck pond. The wind was bitter despite the blue sky. I spotted a figure with two children by the bench. As I got closer I recognised Katie.

She smiled. 'Zara. Is that you?'

'Katie.' I hugged her. We'd only met that one time but we'd built up a wonderful rapport. 'Do you think we'd be too cold sitting down?'

'It's not too bad here as it's sheltered. I only got up for these little madams.'

'Great.' I took a seat on the slatted bench. 'How are the twins?'

'They're good thanks. Wouldn't leave me alone though until I brought them to feed the quack quacks.'

The two little girls giggled as they threw bird feed to the wild fowl. Some children would've been nervous at the gaggle of geese but not these two.

'Play nicely now.' Katie sat down next to me. 'How about you, Zara? Are you better?'

I frowned. 'Sorry?'

'I heard you were poorly.'

'Oh. Where did you hear that from?'

'The magazine. They put a message in when the serial was delayed. Oh hang on.' She jumped up from the bench. 'Ella. Stop that.' She hurried over to the twins. 'Now what have I told you about snatching? Say sorry to your sister.'

'Sorry, Emma.' Ella kissed her sister on the cheek.

'That's all right.' Emma tipped some of her feed into Ella's container. 'You can share mine as yours has all gone.' Emma grinned.

'She's a sweetheart,' I said. 'How do you tell them apart?'

'You mean apart from one is sweetness and light while the other's a little rascal?' Katie chortled.

'Yes.' I smiled at the girls.

'If you look closely, Emma has a little mole on her chin.'

'But how did you know it was Ella snatching?'

'Because she's always doing it.' Katie laughed again. 'Like I said, she's a little rascal.' She sat back down next to me. 'Anyway, you didn't say how you're doing?'

'Not bad, thanks. Today's my first week back at work. I won't lie, it's been hard.'

'Do you think you'll finish the story?'

I shrugged. 'Not sure. Strangely enough my boss was asking me a similar question earlier, she even offered me a permanent position as a writer.'

'Really.' Katie blew into her hands.

'Yep. And I have to say after reading some of the rubbish I had to edit today' – I sighed – 'I'm sorely tempted.'

'You should do it. You're an excellent writer.'

One of the twins screamed.

'Not again. Hang on.' Katie rushed over to the girls. 'Ella, why do you always have to be so mean to your sister?'

'She hurt me first.'

'No, I didn't.' Emma sobbed.

Katie took a hand of each of the twins. 'Look, I'm really sorry, Zara, but I'm going to have to go.'

'That's okay. I can see you have your hands full.'

'I think maybe they're getting a bit cold. See you again though, I hope.'

'That would be nice.'

'Hang on' – she took out her mobile – 'tap your number in and I'll text you so you have mine too. That way we can meet again. Maybe even without these two little rebels.'

'That would be nice.' I keyed in my number. 'See you again soon.'

***

The station was empty. Too early for the commuters. I headed for the platform. Would today be the day? No flash appeared. I tried another platform. Nothing. Over the bridge. Again, nothing. Once again I acknowledged that I had to accept what they were all saying. It couldn't have been real.

With the biting wind slapping my cheeks, I was hurrying home when a hand on my shoulder made me jump. 'What the hell?'

'Hello, stranger.' It was Dave from Double Dee's.

'Gawd, you almost gave me a heart attack.'

'Sorry, darling. What's up?'

'Nothing.'

'Tell your face that. Look, come across to our place and I'll buy you a coffee and I'm pretty sure there's a blueberry muffin with your name on it.'

'Go on then. You've sold it to me.' I hooked my arm in his.

He tightened the striped scarf around his neck. 'It's been raw today. I'm looking forward to a nice hot drink to warm me up.'

'You're not working then?'

'Nope. My afternoon off. Come on.' He pushed the door open and made his way to a table near the front. 'Kelly,' he said to a waitress, 'get us two coffees and a couple of blueberry muffins will you, love?'

'Sure thing, boss.' Swaying her hips in tight black jeans, like a model, she made for the counter.

'So,' Dave said, 'what's happening with you and Scott?'

'There is no me and Scott.'

'Since when?'

'Since we got back from the New Forest last November.'

'But I thought…'

'Here you go.' Kelly placed a tray with the coffees and cakes onto the table. 'Can I get you anything else?'

'No, you're all right. We're good,' Dave said, 'but did Dan say what time he'd be back from his meeting?'

She looked at her watch. 'About five, so I reckon in about an hour.'

'Great stuff.'

Kelly moved to the only other occupied table.

'It's quiet in here.' I took a bite of the muffin.

Dave frowned. 'Unfortunately that seems to be the trend of late.'

'With homemade muffins like these, I'm surprised.'

'You'd think so, wouldn't you? But since that Coffisio chain moved across the road last month our trade has dropped.'

'But that's so unfair. I mean you don't get delicious homecooked treats over there or all these lovely comfy extras like sofas and scatter cushions. I just don't understand.'

'It all comes down to money, love. That's why Dan's gone to see a new supplier. If we decide to use them, it could mean some new goodies at a lower cost.' Dave took a gulp of his coffee. 'Anyway enough of that. About you and our Scottie. What gives?'

'I did like you and Dan suggested and told him straight that he should find someone else.'

'Poor guy. No wonder he's been looking so miserable.'

'To be honest, my mum didn't help matters. She invited him over to my sister's on Christmas Day, saying it was my idea which of course gave him hope. But there is no hope as I don't love him like that, but I hope one day we'll be able to be good friends again.'

Dave put his hand on top of mine. 'You did the right thing telling him, and fingers crossed, one day soon he'll find someone new. Someone who'll love him like that.'

The flat was empty when I got in. Holly wouldn't be back for at least another hour. It was clear now that I was never going to make it back to Bridge View Hall. I had to get on with my life, and maybe becoming a full time writer was just what I needed. At the very least I should finish the serial. I owed my readers that.

Memories of Richard's touch and kisses were becoming blurry. It was clear that I had to accept he was Rebecca's husband, and I wasn't Rebecca, I was Zara Wiseman.

I grabbed my laptop from the table, switched it on, opened up the Word document and typed the ending of *The Girl in the Ticket Office Window*.

Chapter Thirty-One

Chloe carried Amelia into my flat. 'Now you're sure you'll be okay?'

'Yes, of course.' I touched the pink furry coat and hat. 'Doesn't she look gorgeous in this?'

'It's what you bought her. You have good taste.'

'I know.' I grinned. 'Isn't she getting big?'

'She sure is. And she gets heavier each week. She'll be four months next week. Won't you little one?' Chloe kissed Amelia. 'I mean, where's the time gone?'

Matt pushed the stroller into the hallway and placed a grey patterned backpack onto the floor. 'Everything's in here, Zara. Bottles, nappies, wipes, etc. You do remember how to change her?'

'Of course I do.'

'Come on then, Chloe. Pass Amelia to your sister.'

'I'm just a little nervous leaving her.'

'Don't worry, sis. I'll take special care of her. If I have any problems, I'll ring you. I promise.'

Chloe handed me the baby. 'Promise you'll ring.'

'Promise. I see what you mean about weight. What's your mummy been feeding you on?' I tickled Amelia's chin making her laugh. 'Oh wow, when did she start doing that?'

'Just last week. It's lovely, isn't it?' Chloe's face lit up. 'Matt, show Zara how to fold up the buggy just in case.'

'There's no need, honestly.' I bobbed Amelia in my arms making her giggle.

'It won't take long,' Matt said. 'Watch. It's ever so easy. Firstly' – Matt flicked on the brake with his foot – 'make sure this is on. Then pull down the hood, push it forward, like this' – he demonstrated – 'then lift this handle and it all folds up. You can do it with one hand.'

'Ta, but can you open it up again as I plan to take this little one straight out to the park to see the quack quacks.'

'Ducks please, Zara,' he said. 'We're teaching our daughter to speak properly.' In seconds the pram was up again.

'Whatever.' I laid Amelia on the padded seat. She looked snug and comfy.

'Don't let her get cold out there though, will you?' Chloe stroked the baby's cheek.

'I won't, don't worry. It's warm right now, and I'll be back before it turns cold. Go and have a fun afternoon shopping with Matt's credit card.' I opened the door to let them out.

'Bye bye, baby girl.' Chloe peeped her head under the hood. 'Be good for Aunty Zara.'

'She will. Go, will you? I've arranged to meet my friend at two.'

Matt took Chloe's hand. 'Zara, don't forget to take the changing bag.'

'I won't. Go.' I closed the door behind them. 'Now then, little one. Are you ready to see those quack quacks?'

Amelia beamed a huge smile.

It was like a summer's day for March. I slipped off my coat and peeped in the pram to check on Amelia. I hoped she wasn't too hot. I'd ask Katie what she thought. I spotted her and the girls at the bench as I pushed the stroller towards the pond.

Emma and Ella ran towards me. 'Aunty Zara, can we see your baby?' They peered under the hood in turn. 'Mummy,' one of them said, 'please can we have a new baby brother or sister?'

'Maybe one day.' Katie grinned.

'Are you?' I winked.

She held a finger to her lips. 'Shh. I don't want them getting wind of it. Early days if you know what I mean. Now let me look at this little cutie.' She peered into the pram. 'You're gorgeous, aren't you?'

Amelia giggled.

'Oh wow. I love that. How old is she?'

'Coming up to four months. Chloe said she only started doing that the other day.' I held my stomach. 'Shall we eat first then feed the ducks only I'm starving as I normally have lunch before twelve.'

'Sure, we can picnic now. I'm pretty hungry too. The girls had a bite before we came out but they just graze so they'll have room for a bit more now. How about under that tree?' She pointed.

We headed across the mound and Katie threw a blanket under the large oak. 'We usually park ourselves here. It's a nice spot as it means you and I can sit on the bench and the kids can still see the ducks.' She passed the girls each a personalised lunch box. Both pink but Ella's had rainbow unicorns on it and Emma's coloured mermaids.

'At least while they have them I'll know which twin is which.' I laughed. I took Amelia from the pram and laid her down on the soft blanket so she could have a kick about. 'I can't believe it's only March. Do you think I should take Amelia's coat and hat off?'

'I wouldn't. Not while she's out of the pram, anyway.'

The girls plopped themselves down on the blanket next to Amelia and each of them munched a crustless cheese sandwich. I'd just dipped a carrot stick into a tub of red pepper humous when Amelia started screaming.

'Oh dear. She probably wants her milk.' I dug into the changing bag and pulled out the bottle and a muslin cloth. 'Come on then, baby.' I leaned down and swooped Amelia into my arms and held her close to me as I fed her from the bottle. She immediately stopped crying and made a smacking sound sucking on the teat.

'You've done that before. I can tell.' Katie popped a cherry tomato into her mouth.

'Yeah, a few times, otherwise believe you me my sister wouldn't have let me look after her. She was so nervous leaving her today.'

'She has no need. You're a natural.'

'Thanks.'

'By the way, I read the end of your story. Not quite the ending I'd expected but I loved it, nonetheless.'

'What did you think would happen?'

'That she'd have chosen the other man.'

'I thought about it.' My eyes filled.

'Then why?'

'I suppose... I don't know.' A tear dropped on Amelia's face. I wiped her cheek with the muslin. 'Sorry, sweetheart.'

'You know something though?'

'What?'

She shook her head. 'Not sure I should say. You'll think I'm daft.'

'Go on.'

'Okay, but promise not to think I'm barmy? Oh hang on.' She jumped off the bench. 'Emma, don't give your sandwich to the duck.'

'But he's hungry,' Emma answered. 'See, he's eating it.'

'No more. Bread's bad for ducks, remember. That's why Mummy always gives you special feed to give them.' Katie took another sandwich from Emma's lunch box. 'Now finish your lunch and then you can feed the ducks.'

Ella wagged a finger at her sister. 'But not with your sandwich. Isn't that right, Mummy?'

'Yes, it is, Ella.' Katie returned to her seat. 'Now, where were we?'

'You were about to tell me something.'

'Oh yes. Promise you won't think I'm daft.'

'I promise.'

'Well, I thought you were telling the story from experience. That you really did go back in time.'

'You don't think that might be a little far-fetched?'

'Some might think so, but maybe I'm a bit weird, only I reckon it's possible.'

'You do?'

'Yeah, I do.'

Katie believed it. Maybe it was true then. I took a deep breath before saying, 'To be honest I thought it was real too.'

'Thought or know?'

I shrugged. 'They told me I was delusional when I woke up from being in a coma for two months. Since they let me out of the hospital I've spent almost every day down the train station trying to go back but nothing has happened so I'd resigned myself to the fact that they must be right. I was delusional.'

She touched my hand. 'I don't think so. Have you tried searching for Bridge View Hall and the Cavendish family on the internet to see what comes up?'

'Not since it all happened as I didn't think it would be worth it.'

'It could be. That's what I'd do if it were me.'

'Really? You don't think I'm mad?'

'Not at all. I think you've been given a gift. Listen, the girls are having a birthday party next month. Why don't you come? Billy, his brother, and our parents will be there to help out so I should have a few minutes to speak to you without interruptions.'

'I'm not sure.'

'Go on. The girls love you and you can fill me in with your findings at the same time.'

'Okay. Text me your address and time etc.'

Chapter Thirty-Two

Megan tapped away on the keyboard at her work station across the low partition between us.

'How are you getting on there?' I asked.

'Good, thanks. I'm loving my job. How about you? Are you enjoying being a full time writer?'

I screwed up my nose. 'Not what I'm doing right now. No. I think I'm more of a fiction writer than this review work. This really isn't me. I've a meeting with Annabel shortly and I just know that she's going to ask if I'm ready to start a new serial.'

'And are you?'

'Not sure.'

'You should. The last one was a sell-out.'

'That's the problem.' I got up from my desk and headed over to the coffee machine. 'Want one?'

'Ta.'

I pressed the button to dispense each of us a coffee. Black for me and white for Megan. She'd become quite good company these last few months, and was a quick learner. 'Here you go.'

'Thanks. Why a problem?' She curled her hands around the mug.

'Supposing I can't do it again.'

My phone pinged. It was a WhatsApp message from Annabel. I opened it up. 'Goodness, I'd better go.' I popped the mobile into my pocket. 'I hadn't realised the time and Annabel's wondering where I've got to.'

'Good luck.' Megan put her head down and returned to her typing as I left the office.

Scott's door was propped open. I stopped for a second and gave him a wave. He smiled back. It was good how we'd both been able to move forward, slowly becoming friends again.

I knocked on Annabel's door before entering. 'Sorry, I lost track of time.'

'Not to worry. Take a seat.'

'Thanks.' Lowering myself into the chair the other side of her desk, I couldn't help but marvel at how immaculate her desk was. How did she manage it? She looked perfect as usual too. Her blonde waves were tied back into a French twist, and a purple swing skirt and lilac V-necked T-shirt accentuated her brilliant figure.

'How are you doing, Zara?'

'Good, thanks.'

'And your sessions with Craig?'

'Good too. He reckons I shouldn't need many more.'

'Really?'

'Yep.'

'And you and Scott seem to be working together better.'

'We are.' I smiled.

She stood up from her desk. 'Coffee?'

'No, thanks. I've just had one.'

She poured herself a cup. 'How are you getting on with the reviews?'

'To be honest, I don't think they're really me.'

'I'm glad you said that.' She sat back at her desk. 'I've noticed that your heart isn't in them. Have you thought any more about writing another serial?'

'Yes, but I'm not sure?'

'What's stopping you?'

I remembered I'd promised Katie that I'd research Bridge View Hall on the internet. That was over two weeks ago. Why hadn't I done it? What was stopping me? 'Inspiration for one.'

'You know we have a hoard of old newspapers up in the attic, don't you?'

'No.'

'Well we do. They go right back. Pre eighteen hundreds. I bet you could find something up there that would get your muse going.'

'Can I think about it?'

'Yes, but not too long as I'm getting a pile of letters and emails from readers each day asking when they're going to get more stories from Zara Wiseman.'

I laughed. 'I bet.'

'Seriously.' Annabel's face was straight. 'Check them out.' She passed me a wad of letters. 'I'll forward some of the emails on to you too.' She took a sip of coffee. 'If you don't feel ready to do another serial, why not start with a short story? Think about it at least.'

'I will. Is there anything else?'

'No, that's about it. Have a good weekend.'

'And you.'

I headed back to my PC and tapped history of Bridge View Hall into the search engine. Lots of detail popped up. This hadn't been there before. Not right at the beginning when I'd first gone back in time.

What was this? A wedding photo. Underneath was an article.

On the 24th September 1910 Sir Richard John Cavendish and Lady Rebecca Anne Pendleton became husband and wife. Later that evening after the wedding celebrations, uniformed police officers barged into Bridge View Hall and arrested the bride's brother, Sir Edward Pendleton, on the charges of murder, fraud, and illegal activities. Handcuffed, he was dragged away screaming, begging his sister, and new brother-in-law, to help him. Neither did, although according to a witness, the bride's complexion turned the same colour as her luxurious ivory silk wedding gown.

I studied the picture. That was definitely me on my wedding day standing with my husband, Richard. Therefore, I wasn't going mad. I really was there and this was proof. I continued to read the article.

In December 1910 Pendleton was found guilty of murder at the Old Bailey and hanged at Pentonville Prison on January 19th 1911.

He was hanged. My tummy curdled. I covered my mouth to stop me throwing up. Along with Richard, I'd been responsible for another person's death. How had Rebecca reacted to that? Would she have done the same as I did? Surely that must've been my purpose of being there. Perhaps I wasn't supposed to fall in love with Richard.

My hands shook as I lifted a glass to take a sip of water. Hanged. It was only what he deserved, but hanged? That was so final. I thought he'd rot in a cell for life. That was what he deserved for the crimes he'd committed. Putting him to death meant he didn't have to suffer.

'Thank you, Katie,' I whispered. If it hadn't been for her believing in me I'd have let the matter go and admit to being delusional. I wasn't mad. It had really happened. Wait until I showed Craig. After saving the images and articles, I pressed print. I tapped his number into my mobile. An answerphone. I left a message. 'Hi, Craig, I know I'm not booked in to see you but any chance you can fit me in? I've something urgent to discuss with you.'

Craig opened the door as I hurried up the steps. 'Come in, Zara.' His eyebrows furrowed. 'What is it that couldn't wait until next week?'

'I was right, Craig.' I grinned. 'Look, this is proof.' I passed him the printouts.

He flicked through the pages. 'You found this information on the internet?'

'Yes. So don't you see. It's everything I said. How would I have known all that if I hadn't been there?'

'Zara. I thought you agreed that it hadn't been real? We were making so much progress too.'

'But that was before I found this. This proves it wasn't all in my imagination.'

'It proves nothing, Zara. Take yourself back to right at the beginning when you researched your story. You used the internet, didn't you?'

'Well, yes, but none of this came up.'

'Not that you remember. This is likely what happened. You read it, forgot about it, but your subconscious stored it.'

'No, I don't agree. I remember being there.'

'You remember reading about it. The rest was your mind playing tricks.'

'No, I can prove it. Look at the wedding photograph. That's me.'

He shook his head. 'There's a likeness but that's all it is. Look again, Zara.' He passed me the photo printout.

I studied the picture again. 'But...'

'I'm sorry, Zara. But it wasn't real.'

Chapter Thirty-Three

The taxi pulled up outside a large detached house. 'Are you sure this is the correct address?' I asked the driver.

'Yes, this is Carpenter Way and that house there' – he pointed to the left – 'is number seventy-one.'

Katie must've been holding the party at her parents' home.

'That will be fifteen-pounds-fifty,' The driver said.

'Blimey.' I hadn't expected it to cost me that much. 'Can I pay by card?' I got out my purse.

'Yes.' He turned around and held out the keypad for me to tap my card.

'Thanks.' I climbed out of the car. At that cost there was no way I could afford a tip too. I headed down the long driveway as the vehicle drove off. Two bunches of pink balloons with Ella and Emma's names printed on them hung either side of the porch. This was the right house then. I rang the doorbell.

Katie answered. 'Zara. So glad you could make it. Come on in. The girls will be pleased to see you. It's this way.'

I followed her down the wide hallway and into a large room where around twenty little girls dressed in purple, blue, and pink princess gowns sat around a huge table. 'Wow this is amazing,' I said. 'Are they making their own crowns?'

A woman dressed as Elsa from Frozen looked up and smiled. 'Yes, they are.'

Was this the sort of thing we had to look forward to with Amelia? 'Didn't have parties like this in my day. And they're so quiet.'

'Yeah,' Katie said. 'It's worth booking these themed ones. Not cheap though but then Billy's mum and dad are paying.'

'Is this their house?'

'It is, but we live here too. It works. Lots of room for the girls and Billy's mum is always happy to help out with them. Did you bring what you found?'

'Nope, I didn't bother.' I tapped the carrier. 'I've got pressies for the girls though.'

'Aw, you didn't need to do that. Thanks, though.'

The twins darted towards me and each hugged my legs. 'Aunty Zara,' they said in unison.

I bent down towards them. 'Don't you look gorgeous.' I dug into my bag. 'Name badges are a great idea,' I said to Katie before turning back to the birthday girls. 'This one's for you, Emma, and this one's for you, Ella.' I passed the presents to each of them. 'Happy birthday.' I touched their crowns. 'And I love these.'

Elsa from Frozen came over. 'Sorry to interrupt but is it all right if I take the birthday girls?' She tossed the white plaited wig to the back of her head. 'Only it's singsong time.'

'Mummy?' The girls waited.

'I tell you what,' Katie said. 'You can open your presents once all your friends have gone home. Aunty Zara will still be here.'

'Thanks, Mummy,' they rattled in unison before running towards the circle and dropping to the floor with the other children.

'Sorry about that.' Elsa held the turquoise dress away from her ankles as she joined the girls.

'You will still be here, won't you?' Katie asked me.

I shrugged. 'Er, I suppose so.' I was wishing I'd never agreed to come because I felt out of place.

Katie took my hand. 'Tell you what, let's go and have a drink and chat. They'll be singing for a while so we won't be missed.' She led me into the kitchen. 'Do sit down. Prosecco? Or are you driving?'

'Prosecco sounds good. I don't actually drive.' I sank into one of the grey velvet dining chairs.

Her eyes widened. 'How did you get here then?'

'Taxi.'

'That must've cost you.' The wine fizzed as she poured it into goblets.

I gave a half smile. 'Just a bit.'

She passed me a glass and took a seat next to me. 'I'll drive you home.'

'You don't have to.' I sipped the drink. 'Mmm, nice.'

'Now, what did you find out?'

'It doesn't really matter because my psychiatrist said there was an explanation for it all. It appears I was delusional after all.'

'I don't believe that. Let me just get my laptop.' She hurried out of the room and was back before I knew it, took a seat next to me and opened the computer. 'Bridge View Hall, wasn't it?'

I nodded. 'But...'

'Please, humour me.' She typed in Edward Pendleton. She moved closer to the screen. 'This article here is about Edward. My god he was hanged.'

'I know. I almost threw up when I first found out.'

'Yeah, awful, isn't it? Mind you. Only what the murdering monster deserved, I suppose.'

'Maybe.'

'It says here he was charged at the Old Bailey and sent to Pentonville Prison. Well you were right about that. How would you have known that he was arrested unless you were there?'

'Craig said I must've seen it on the internet sometime and stored it in my subconscious.'

'I suppose so, but hey, what about this photograph. Look, that's clearly you.'

'At first glance it appears to be me but if you look closer. Zoom in.'

'Oh okay, maybe not quite you, but that still doesn't mean you weren't there. Trust your instincts, Zara. So your psychiatrist reckons all of this was in a memory but how does he explain that the dress is just like you described.'

'He says I must've seen it, but, honestly, Katie, it wasn't there when I did my early research. Or from the file that Scott gave me. It's not in any of my paperwork. Surely, I'd have printed it off if it was.'

'I think Craig's wrong. Okay, that might not be you' – she pointed to the photo – 'but that doesn't mean you weren't there. Surely you must've appeared as Rebecca, otherwise the others would've thought you were an imposter.'

'Mmm, you're right. So I wasn't delusional then?'

'I don't think so, but it might be better to not push it to everyone else. They won't believe you, but I do.'

My eyes filled. 'Thanks, Katie.'

'Hang on.' She continued to scroll. 'Look here, this one is of Rebecca and Richard in their forties. 'Don't they look happy?'

'Yes, but I can see that's not me.'

'But you see what it means?'

'No.'

'That you completed your mission successfully. Because of you, Edward wasn't able to hurt them so they were able to live happily ever after.'

I took her hand. 'Thanks, Katie.'

She continued to read on. 'They had four children. Oh this is sad, one of them, a girl, didn't survive. Rebecca lived until she was eighty-five, and Richard, died three months later of a broken heart.' She smiled. 'What a wonderful love story.'

'I'm never going to get back there, am I?'

'Probably not, but to travel back in time once was amazing. Don't be sad, Zara. Instead, go into work Monday morning and tell your boss that you're ready to start writing stories.'

Emma and Ella ripped open their gifts and afterwards clung either side of me. 'Thank you, Aunty Zara.'

'You're welcome. Maybe once you've created your own unicorn night lights, Mummy will let me come back here and take a look.'

'Can she, Mummy?' The girls jumped up and down.

'She can. Now you girls go with Grannie to have your baths. It's been a long day for you.' Katie topped up our Proseccos.

It looked like I'd be getting that taxi after all.

'The boys are just finishing off clearing up but have asked if you can pop the kettle on.' Billy's mum led the girls out.

'See what I mean.' Katie filled the kettle and flicked the switch.

'Yes. My mum's a bit like that with Amelia.'

Katie took two mugs from the cupboard. 'Jack said he'll drop you off home when he goes, if you like.'

'Jack?'

'Billy's brother. You'll like him, he's really nice.'

Was she trying to matchmake? It made me think of Caroline back at Bridge View Hall when Rebecca had done exactly that.

Heavy footsteps came through the door. 'Well that's all done, love.' A blond-haired man who must've been Billy kissed Katie on the lips. 'Dad's asleep in the chair. He's exhausted.'

'Come and meet my friend Zara,' she said.

Billy came over and shook my hand. 'We've heard a lot about you.'

'All good, I hope.'

'Where's Jack?' Katie put the two steaming coffees on the table.

'Jack's here,' a man resembling Billy said as he strode in.

I looked up. 'Goodness, you can see that you two are brothers. Almost like twins. Which one's sweet, Katie, and which one's the rascal?' I laughed at our private joke.

'I'm the sweet one.' Jack winked. 'I hear I'm giving you a ride home.'

Butterflies fluttered in my tummy at this handsome bloke. He was definitely the better looking out of the two of them. 'Er, if you're sure you don't mind?'

'Not at all. It's on my way.'

He didn't live at home. Was he married?

'I have my own flat in case you're wondering.' He gave a gorgeous smile making his light blue eyes twinkle. Katie tells us you're a writer for that women's magazine in town.'

'Well more of an editor but I've dabbled in writing.'

'Cool.' He took a gulp of the coffee.

'What is it you do?' I caught Katie winking at Billy. This was a set up.

'I'm a software engineer.'

'That sounds interesting.' I glanced at my watch.

'What time would you like to leave?' Jack asked.

'I wouldn't mind going soon, but only if that's okay. I'm happy to call a cab.'

'No way. I drive almost past your door.'

Jack pulled up the black Fiesta outside my flat.

'Thanks for the lift.' I opened the door.

He rested his palm on my wrist. 'Before you go, I wonder...'

'What?'

'Did Katie mention it's her birthday next week?'

'No, she didn't.'

'It's her twenty-first and Billy's throwing her a surprise party. How do you fancy being my plus one?'

It would be lovely to go to Katie's party but I wasn't ready to step into another relationship. 'Thanks, but I'm not ready to start dating yet as I've only just broken up with my boyfriend.'

Jack shook his head. 'Blimey, Zara, I'm not asking you to marry me. For god's sake, I'm only just out of a messy divorce.'

'I'm sorry to hear that. How long were you married for?'

'Five years. Like my brother I got married young. Shotgun wedding. Two kids and I thought we were happy until I discovered she'd been having an affair with my best mate.'

'That's awful.'

'Yeah, it is rather. So you see there's no way I'm ready to move into a new relationship either. I just thought that you'd like to be there for Katie, and make up the numbers but...'

'Sorry for jumping to conclusions. I'd love to come. Thanks for asking me.'

'Great. I'll pick you up Saturday evening, shall we say sevenish?'

Chapter Thirty-Four

My new teal dress fitted perfectly. I swayed from side to side in the mirror making sure the hugged waist showed no tummy bulges. The burnout velvet had a gorgeous luxurious feel against my skin and the off the shoulder cut was flattering.

Holly tapped on my door. 'Okay if I come in?'

'Sure.'

'Wow, who are you trying to impress?'

'Too much?'

'No. You look fab. What's his name again?'

'Jack, but we're just friends. Neither of us are ready for anything else.' I stroked my throat. 'I could do with something here. What do you think?'

She held up a finger. 'Hang on. I've got just the thing.' She left the room and was back in a couple of minutes. 'What do you think?'

'It's lovely. Thanks. Will you put it on for me?' I took a seat at the dressing table and Holly fastened the silver choker around my neck.

'Did you mention Jack to Scott?' she asked.

'No, why should I?'

'I just think if you're seeing other blokes it would be the right thing to do.' She peered out of the window. 'I think that's your ride now. A black Fiesta?'

'Yep, that's him. I'll see you tomorrow as I imagine it'll be late when I get home.' I hurried out of my bedroom, grabbed my wool blend shacket from the hook, knowing that the blue checked design accentuated my eyes.

Jack drove the Fiesta into the Round Tavern car park and pulled into a space close to the front. 'We're early,' he said. 'I imagine this will be packed later. Come on, this way.' He led me by the hand.

I hadn't been in this pub before as it was the other side of town. It was open plan with cosy seating on the left side of the area, and on the right a couple of lads played pool, and a woman sat on a high stool operating a fruit machine.

'This way.' Jack guided me through another door and upstairs. 'It's in a private function room.'

'Great.' I followed him up the steep stairs into a large area with a low panelled ceiling. An arch made up from rose gold balloons dominated the back wall with a Happy Birthday Katie banner, and *21* shaped silver balloons hung from the light fittings. 'This is nice,' I said.

'Yeah. Billy sorted it.'

I glimpsed at the tables set up with board games and immediately felt uncomfortable at my choice of outfit. 'I thought it would be a dance.' I pulled my shacket closer to hide my cocktail dress.

'Oh sorry, I should've said, but do twenty-one year olds like that sort of thing these days?'

I shrugged. Chloe would, that was for sure. There was no way she'd want a games' party. I imagined being back in Bridge View Hall wearing an azure lurex gown with a tight bodice pulling my waist smaller and Richard gliding me around the room. *Stop it.* I had to accept that while I now acknowledged it had happened, I was unlikely to ever be sent back. Richard wasn't mine and I had been there to fulfil a mission, that was all.

'Hey, don't cry.' Jack put his arm around my shoulder. 'You look lovely. In fact you look proper sexy.' He kissed me on the cheek. 'That's Mum and Dad over there. Let's go and say hi, and you can meet Katie's parents.' He led me by the hand across the room to where his mum and dad were chatting to another couple most likely in their late thirties.

'Mum, Dad' – Jack smiled – 'you remember Zara?'

'Of course.' His mum turned towards me. 'How are you, dear?'

'I'm fine thanks, although I'm feeling a little overdressed.'

'Nonsense. Katie and the other young women will be wearing something similar, you'll see.' She caught the attention of the couple next to them. 'Angela and Lee,' she said, 'this is Katie's new friend, Zara. Zara works for the local magazine in town.'

'How do you do?' I said, wishing that Katie would arrive soon. 'Is there anything you'd like me to do?' I asked.

'No, you're all right, love,' Lee answered. 'Jack get Zara a drink.'

'Of course. What do you fancy?'

'Surprise me.'

'Okay.' He headed up to a window-like opening where a bar had been set up in the kitchen area.

'So how did you meet our Katie?' Angela asked.

'In the park at the duck pond.' I tittered.

'Hmm. And how long have you known each other? I haven't heard Katie mention a Zara.'

'Last year. We just kind of connected. Like we've known each other for years.'

'I see.' Angela gave me a disapproving look. It was obvious she'd taken an instant dislike to me. I didn't belong here. I wished I hadn't come.

'Here you go, Zara.' Jack passed me a ruby-toned drink garnished with an orange wedge.

I took a sip and coughed. 'Crikey, what is it?'

'See if you can guess. Taste it.'

'I've no idea.' I took another sip. 'It's a little bitter. What's it called?'

'A Negroni. Not up to it?'

'I didn't say that.'

Angela glared at me.

I turned away to face Jack. 'So what's in it then.'

'Hmm let me see. Gin, Campari, and sweet Vermouth. It's the Campari that gives it the bitter taste. Want to sit down?'

'Yes, please. I feel a little out of place just standing here.'

'Over there.' He signalled to a table at the other side of the room.

Once seated I said, 'I don't think Katie's mum likes me.'

'Don't worry about it. She's like that with everyone. Why do you think Katie and Billy live with my parents and not hers?'

I shrugged.

'Because her mother has too many airs and graces. You wouldn't believe she grew up in a council house. She married money and became someone she's not. Katie gets so irritated with her. She was relieved when they couldn't make the twins' party in the end.'

'Well I'm glad it's not just me.' I glanced across the room at the young couple who'd just come in, pleased to see that the woman was in party gear. 'Are many coming tonight?'

'Of course.' He turned towards the door. 'Look, they're all starting to come in now. And check out the girls' dresses. You'll fit right in.'

'Thanks.'

'The oldies are here to supervise the set up and then don't worry, they'll be gone.'

I breathed a sigh of relief. Jack's mum and dad seemed nice enough but that Angela. Angela seemed to be a nasty piece of work.

As the room filled up with more guests, I slipped off my jacket, no longer feeling out of place.

Jack ran his fingers down my arm making me shiver. 'I'll be the envy of the room tonight with you as my date.' His mobile bleeped. 'Hang on, that's Billy.' He stood up. 'Right peeps, turn the lights down low and hide.'

We all got down. Someone dimmed the lights just before the door opened. Everyone jumped out and shouted. 'Surprise.'

Katie put her hands to her face. 'Oh my God.' She playfully hit Billy. 'Why didn't you tell me?' She spotted me. 'Zara.' She ran across and hugged me. 'And you were in on it too.'

'Happy birthday.' I passed her my small gift.

Once Angela had left, I immersed into the game world and surprised myself by having a good time. It was a struggle keeping up with the different strategies but at least it stopped me thinking about Richard and Scott. Katie on one side of me and Jack the other kept me relaxed throughout the evening.

The games were packed away and everyone congregated to the kitchen for the buffet. Caterers had put on a wonderful vegetarian and vegan spread. I piled my plate with a couple of

Quorn sausage rolls, vegetable samosas, carrot sticks, humous, plum tomatoes, cucumber slices, mushroom pate and a butterbean salad.

I followed Jack to a table in the corner of the room where we joined Katie and Billy.

'Are you having a good time?' Katie asked me.

'Yes, I am, but more to the point, it's your party, are you having a good time?'

'Loving it.' She nibbled on a cracker. 'I can't believe you didn't even give me a hint at the girls' party.'

'I didn't know then.' I turned to Jack and squeezed his fingers. 'Your brother-in-law here asked me when dropping me off.' Jack and Billy were good company, just like Katie. I'd been reluctant to come but was glad now that I had. 'Probably just as well I didn't know,' I added, 'as I may have struggled to keep it a secret.' I chuckled.

A couple headed our way. The female seemed familiar. She glared at me and moved closer. 'I know you,' she said, 'you're Scott's fiancé, or at least you were' – she snarled – 'until you dumped him after he took you on holiday.'

'Hey.' Jack put his finger up. 'That's enough. This is Katie's party.'

'You don't want to get caught up with the likes of her.' The young woman dug her fingers into my shoulder.

'Ow. Get off me.'

'She's a manipulative bitch,' she continued. 'Got my cousin to put a deposit on a place down by the sea for when they got married. And look at her now, dressed up like a tart and ready to offer herself to the next idiot who'll have her.'

'How dare you?' I sensed my eyes filling up. 'For your information, I was never engaged to Scott, not that it's any of your business, and further more, I haven't moved on.' I couldn't cope with this, and what lies had Scott been telling his family?

Feeling self conscious of my outfit, I covered my shoulders with the shacket.

'Don't.' Jack eased my jacket away. 'You look lovely, and don't let that cow tell you otherwise.'

Katie shot up. Her face reddened. 'Get your girlfriend out of here, Liam. This is my party and I won't have her speaking to my best friend like that.'

'I'm sorry, Katie.' He pulled on the girl's hand. 'Charlie, you're making a scene. I'm sorry,' he said again, as he dragged the female away.

'I need to go.' I rose from the chair. 'I'm sorry your party got spoilt, Katie.'

'You don't need to go.' Katie hugged me. 'Stay, please.'

'I can't.' I dabbed my hanky under my eyes.

'You're shaking. At least have a cup of tea first.'

'I'd rather just go but we can meet up again soon.'

'If you're sure, but...'

'Don't worry, Katie' – Jack was standing by my side – 'I'll see that she gets home okay.'

Jack pulled up outside my flat. 'Don't let that witch get to you. She's an immature little girl.'

'But' – I sniffled – 'what has Scott been saying to his family? I never agreed to marry him, not once. He asked but I always said no.' I sobbed.

'Shh' – he put his arms around me – 'I imagine she got hold of the wrong end of the stick. He likely said he'd asked you. You've done nothing wrong. Can I see you again?'

'You mean you want to?'

'Yeah. Like I said, I'm just looking for a bit of female company, nothing more.' He kissed me softly on the lips.

I pulled away.

'Sorry. I didn't mean anything by it. It just seemed the right moment.'

'Not for me. Sorry. I just can't do this right now.'

'Sorry, my mistake.'

I got out of the car, and leaned back in. 'But yes, if you still want to hang, then yes, I'll see you again.'

'Great. I'll text you.'

After stepping out of the Fiesta I watched him drive away. It was a shame the way the evening had ended as for the first time in ages I'd had a good time. Richard and Scott had occupied my mind long enough. Time to move forward, but romance wasn't on the agenda yet.

Chapter Thirty-Five

Scott pulled up the Porsche into a car parking space. I waited for him to get out and then approached him.

'What gives you the right to go telling your family that we were engaged?'

'Calm down, Zara,' he said. 'I don't know what you're on about.'

'Yes you do.' I raised my voice even louder. 'Your dear cousin gave me a right mouthful on Saturday evening. Totally humiliated me while I was at my friend's party.'

'Ah.' He nodded. 'It all makes sense now. Charlie.'

'Yes, Charlie. Why did you tell her that?'

He rested his hand on the top of my arm. 'I didn't. I promise you, but she did happen to mention that you'd moved on.' He shrugged. 'Not that's any of my business. I just want you to be happy. The last thing I'd ever want to do is hurt you.' He stared at me. 'Surely you must know that?'

'Sorry. But why would she say that? And she called me some awful names?'

'Who knows? It was common knowledge in the family that I always hoped we'd marry and that we'd look at moving to the coast but I promise you, Zara, I never said we were engaged.'

'Good. FYI though, I've not moved on. Jack's just a friend. I'm not interested in anything else right now. It's too soon after you and me.'

'Sure. Just remember I'm here for you whether that's as a partner or a friend. I'll have words with Charlie and put her straight.'

I knocked on Annabel's office door.

'Come in.'

'Thanks for seeing me.'

'That's all right. Sit down, pour yourself a coffee.'

'Thanks. Did you want one?' I poured an Americano.

'I have one already.' She took a sip from her drink. 'Now, what is it you wanted to see me about?'

I sat across her spick-and-span desk. 'Well you know you've been at me to write fiction for the mag?'

'You're ready?'

I smiled. 'I think I am.'

'And how are things with you and Scott now?'

'Fine.'

'Are you sure? Only I witnessed something that looked rather like an altercation in the car park earlier.'

Oh god, she must've seen us from her window. 'A little misunderstanding but we're okay now.'

'You sure? Because I'd like Scott to mentor you as he's an experienced writer. Is that going to be a problem?'

'It won't be a problem. I promise, and I don't think it'll be for Scott either.'

'That's good to hear. I suggest you start with a few short stories. Warm yourself up before another serial. Let's get Scott in now.' She picked up her mobile from the desk and tapped in a message. In minutes there was a knock on her door. 'That'll be Scott now.'

He stared at me on entering. 'Sorry, I didn't know you were in a meeting. I must've misunderstood the message.'

'No, you didn't. Come on in. Pour yourself a coffee if you want one.'

'I'm okay thanks.' He looked at me again before taking the seat by my side. 'How can I help?' he asked Annabel.

'Zara feels she's ready to start writing stories again.'

He nodded. 'And where do I come in?'

'I'd like you to mentor her. Are you able to put your personal life aside and work with her?'

'Yes, yes of course. If you think I'm the right person for the job.'

'I do, but this means you'll be working together in close proximity as I'd like Zara to move into your office.'

'What?' I said.

Annabel looked across at me. 'Is this going to be a problem?'

I glanced at Scott. He shrugged. 'No, no that's fine,' I said, 'but why do I need to move out of my office?'

'Because you're on the writers' team now. This means I'll need to get someone else in to help Megan with the editing.'

That made sense, although I couldn't help thinking that Annabel was testing me, or perhaps she thought by throwing us together that we'd rekindle our relationship. Scott would be a good teacher, I was sure of that, and after our conversation outside work this morning, I didn't see why we shouldn't be able to move on and work together. 'I understand. Thank you for allowing me this opportunity and I know I'll learn a lot from Scott.'

'Good. Right then I'll expect your first story by the end of the week. Three thousand words will suffice.'

'That won't be a problem,' Scott said. 'I'll make sure Zara has it ready. If you have time in your diary' – he turned to me – 'we can meet later after lunch, say two, and we'll brainstorm an idea.'

'Excellent.' Annabel stood up. 'Now that you two are sorted, you'll have to excuse me as I've a client to meet.'

Holly was chopping an onion when I got in from work. 'Are you feeling better today?' She looked at me with watery eyes.

'What do you mean?'

'Well, Saturday night, you marched into the flat and slammed your bedroom door without even speaking.'

'What you making?'

'Spag bol. Enough for us both if you're in?'

'Yeah, I'm not going anywhere. Did you stay at Adam's yesterday?'

'Yep. We'd been to a christening and then back to his but we both had a bit too much to drink so I stayed over. Were you okay?'

I nodded.

She threw the onions into a grill pan, along with garlic, diced courgettes and sliced mushrooms. 'You've still not told me what was up. How was the party?'

'Spoilt.'

'Oh?' She stirred in stock and added herbs. 'Did you have a row with the new boyfriend?'

I slammed my hand onto the kitchen table. 'He's not my boyfriend. We're just friends. Okay?'

'Sorry. I obviously touched a raw nerve.' She added chopped tomatoes, left the pan on simmer and sat down next to me. 'Hey, what's up. Tell me what happened.' She clasped her hand in mine.

'If you must know, I was having a great time at the party. We played games and I learned some new ones and then afterwards this girl came over and started shouting at me that I looked like a tart and how I'd dumped her cousin after he'd put down a deposit on a place near the sea for when we were married.' I shook my head.

'Scott's cousin?'

'Yes. Did I look like a tart in that dress?'

'What? You've got to be kidding. You looked gorgeous. I hope you put her right.'

'Sort of but to be honest I was just so humiliated. Then poor Scott got it today. He said he'd never said any of those things and he hoped I'd be happy, but Jack and me, we're just friends. Although...'

'Although?'

'He did try to kiss me when he dropped me off but I wasn't in the mood.'

'Hang on.' She got up and gave the sauce a stir. 'Are you seeing him again?'

'I will do, yes.'

'Do you think there's any chance that you and Scott may reconcile?'

'None. I must admit I miss the intimacy we shared but it wasn't fair on him. He wants marriage and kids and I don't feel like that about him.'

'Shame. I'd have laid odds you and he were meant to be together.'

'Hmm, that seems to be Annabel's way of thinking too. She's making me move into his office and he's to be my mentor.'

'Mentor. Why? You've been doing that job for years. Why do you suddenly need a mentor?'

I grinned. 'Because I'm now officially part of the writers' team.'

'Wow.' Holly sat back down next to me. 'That's huge. Are you going to write another serial?'

'Not yet. Short stories to start.'

'That's brill, although...'

'What?'

'You don't think you'll get delusional again, do you?'

I wanted to shout that I hadn't been delusional, that it had really happened. Katie believed me so why couldn't Holly? But instead I smiled and said, 'No, I shan't get delusional. I'm ready for this.'

Working with Scott wasn't as bad as I thought. In fact, he was a brilliant critique partner. My first story was a romance where the narrator fell in love with a ghost. When Scott first read it he looked carefully at me and said, 'This is just a story now, Zara, isn't it?'

'Of course,' I said. 'As if I would believe that someone could have a relationship with a ghost.'

'As long as you're sure.' He held his gaze. 'Do you need to start seeing Craig again?'

'No, Scott, I don't. This is my imagination writing a story like writers do.'

'Sorry, babe, I had to ask. In that case we'll get this over to Annabel for her okay before going to press.' His eyes lit up. 'Your readers are going to love it. They'll be begging for more.'

'Thanks. That means a lot.' And it did.

Chapter Thirty-Six

I threw on a pair of denim jeans and a blue T-shirt. Blue had become my favourite colour since I'd been Rebecca.

'Zara, are you in?' Holly slammed the front door.

I waltzed into the hallway. 'Yep, but not for long as I'm off out shortly.'

'Oh? I was hoping we'd get time together this afternoon.'

'Sorry, I've made arrangements.'

'Again? You're always out. If it's not with Katie then it's with Jack.'

'Sorry. That's where I'm going now.' I took the loaf out of the breadbin. 'Want some toast?'

'Yeah, go on.' She slumped down on one of the kitchen chairs. 'I miss us.'

'You can't blame it all on me as you were out last night with Adam.'

She chewed her lip. 'Suppose. It's just these days we seem to be like ships in the night. Why don't you and Jack come out with Adam and me sometime?'

'Coffee?'

'Ta.'

I pushed the button on the coffee machine. 'Don't think that would work. Me and Jack, we're not like that. That's why it works when we meet up with Katie and Billy. Katie's mum's having the twins for her this afternoon and so I'm going round Katie's. Jack's picking me up in half an hour.' The toast popped up. I took the Sunflower marg from the fridge and spread the four slices, passing a couple on a plate to Holly, along with her drink.

'How about tomorrow then? We could play a game or watch a DVD or something on Netflix?'

'Yeah, okay. There's a new game I'd like to teach you. I'll ask Katie if I can borrow it.'

'I'll text Adam and see if he can make today instead of tomorrow.'

'Great.' I chewed on the piece of toast.

Katie's mum beeped the horn.

'Get your coats, girls,' Katie said to the twins.

They came running in with their coats. 'Can't we stay and see Zara?' one of them said.

'Zara will be here when you get back. Nanny's waiting for you.'

'Oh all right,' said the other.

I'd never get the hang of telling the difference between them. 'Come here,' I said, 'and I'll help you put on your coats.' One at a time I helped them into their identical toffee pink padded jackets. These girls were such cuties. 'Give me a kiss then.'

At the same time, either side of me, two little pairs of lips planted a kiss on my face.

'Come on then.' Katie took their hands.

Jack packed away the tiles with a huge smile on his face.

'I can't believe Billy won, yet again.' I passed Jack the cards.

'Hmm, he's too quick at working things out, that's our problem.' Jack closed up the box of Splendor.

Katie carried in a tray of coffee and biscuits. 'Jack, Billy wants you to have a peep at his PC. Something to do with a software update.'

'Sure.' Jack helped himself to a custard cream and took a bite on his way out of the room.

Katie sighed. 'At last. I've been waiting for us to have a private natter. Now, tell me, have you managed to go back in time again?' She passed me a coffee.

I wrapped my hands around the mug. 'Nah, nothing. To be honest, I think they were right. It was in my imagination.'

She frowned. 'No, remember we worked it out that you must've been there because you knew too much.'

I shrugged. 'Yeah, and like Craig said, I most likely found them on the internet at some point and it remained in my subconscious. It was ludicrous of me to think I travelled in time. I mean' – I gave a little laugh – 'like my dad said, "who did I think I was? Dr Who." His exact words.' I shook my head. 'Nope, I have to resign myself to the fact that it wasn't real.'

'You're wrong, I'm sure of it. It read too real. You had to have been there.'

I rested my fingers on hers. 'You're a good friend.'

The door slammed. The twins hurried into the kitchen and darted into my arms. 'Aunty Zara.'

'They love you.' Katie smiled.

'Mummy, mummy, can Zara stay to tea?'

'Hmm, I'm not sure. Zara?'

Katie's mum glared at me.

'Yeah, sure.' I hugged the girls in turn. 'Long as Uncle Jack can take me home.'

The girls ran out of the kitchen and upstairs shouting, 'Uncle Jack, Uncle Jack.'

⋆

Billy clapped his hands. 'Right, girls, bedtime.'

'Don't want to,' said one of them.

'I want Grandpop to read us a story,' the other one said.

'Now you know that Granny and Grandpop are on holiday. They'll be back tomorrow.'

Their little lips dropped. 'Can Aunty Zara read us the story then?' one asked.

'Yes, yes.' The other one jumped and grabbed my hands. 'Please, Zara.'

I glanced at Katie. 'I don't mind.'

'If you're sure. Just a small one though, girls, as Uncle Jack's waiting to go home.'

The twins dragged me hand-in-hand upstairs. 'In here,' one of them said.

'Wow. This is nice,' I said on entering their room which was decorated in purple and pink. A little white bedside cabinet separated the matching single beds that were covered in a rose bedspread. Identical cupboards with lamps stood at the other side of each bed and the light shone under pictures on the wall. 'What lucky girls you are. Whose bed is whose?'

The twins darted to the relevant bed and I could at least then tell which one was Emma and which was Ella.

'Okay, Emma, do you want to choose the book?'

She hurried over to the bookcase. Ella followed and pushed her. 'No, not that one. This one.'

'All right,' Emma said, 'you can choose.'

Ella pushed the book into my hands. 'This one.'

'All right,' I said, 'but you know it's not nice to push and snatch, don't you?'

She nodded. 'Sorry, Emma.' She gave her sister a hug.

I sat on the bed with the girls either side of me and opened the book. '*The Fox who Stole the Moon.*'

Jack stood at the bottom of the banister. 'You ready for the off?'

'Yep. That Ella's a little pickle, isn't she?'

Katie sighed. 'Has she been up to her old tricks again?'

'Afraid so.' I slipped my arms into the sleeves of my coat. 'Katie, what's your mum got against me?'

She squinted. 'What do you mean?'

'She obviously doesn't like me. What I don't know, is why?'

'I told you before,' Jack said, 'she's like that with everyone.'

'No. It's more than that. It's like she hates me. She gave me daggers earlier.'

'Look' – Katie licked her upper lip – 'you're not imagining things. She's jealous of you because the girls adore you, well they never stop going on about you. And Mum's nose has been put out.'

'Seems petty to me.'

'Yeah I agree. And she can be. That's why I don't like her having the girls but with Billy's parents being away we don't get a break otherwise. Don't worry about it, though, Zara. She's really not worth it. By the way,' she whispered, 'I'm not, you know? It was a false alarm.'

Chapter Thirty-Seven

The weeks ticked on and I was enjoying losing myself in the stories. I'd written the ghost romance, the girl next door, and a vampire story with a romantic element. I thought all had gone down well with Annabel so therefore I was confused when I got an urgent message to go to her office.

I knocked on the glass door and walked in as it was open. Scott was sitting opposite Annabel. What was this?

'Ah, good you're here, Zara. Take a seat.'

I looked to her and to Scott as I took the chair next to him. 'Have I done something wrong?'

'No, on the contrary. Scott came to see me earlier to say that he thinks you're ready to fly solo.'

'Really?'

'Yes, really, and following the feedback from our readers, I'm inclined to agree.'

'Thanks, Scott.' I grinned. 'Does that mean I get my own office?'

'Nice try' – Annabel laughed – 'but like I told you when Megan first joined, we don't have any spare.'

'I may not need to be your mentor anymore,' Scott said, 'but we'll still work as a team.'

'You mean you still want to check my work?'

'Not check, but offer feedback, and I'd like you to do the same for my stories.'

'Like equals?'

'Yes, like equals.' Annabel scribbled something down in her notepad. 'The main reason we called you in though is...'

'Yes?'

'Scott and I have been talking and we think you're ready to start a new serial.'

'I'm not sure.'

Scott squeezed my fingers. 'You're ready, Zara. You can do this.'

'Do you mean together?'

'No, the project is solely yours.' Annabel pushed a handful of letters across to me. 'Our readers want to know when they can expect a new serial from Zara Wiseman. Check them if you don't believe me, and like I've told you before, that's not counting the numerous emails that land in my inbox each day. Have a think, talk it over with Scott, and get back to me with a synopsis by the end of the month.'

'The end of the month?' Gosh I'd no idea what to write. It was one thing coming up with these short stories after Scott and I had brainstormed together but now they wanted me to come up with a longer length of work and all on my own. 'I'm not sure I'm up to it.'

Annabel flicked her long wavy hair behind an ear. 'Yes, you are.'

Scott nodded in agreement. 'You're ready.'

'Is it okay if I leave early this evening only...'

'Of course. We hadn't forgotten it's your birthday.' Annabel grinned. 'Drinks and a buffet have been organised for lunch. All the staff have been invited.'

My face heated up. 'I wasn't hinting.'

'I know that. This was already booked. You'd better act surprised though.' She popped her glasses on. 'Right, I'd better get cracking if I'm going to get this issue sorted on time, and, Zara, I look forward to seeing what you come up with. Make it a romance. That's what our readers want.' She peered up from her computer. 'By the way, if you're looking for inspiration, don't forget there are stacks of old newspapers in the attic dating right back to pre eighteen hundreds. That should help your muse.'

A pink *Happy 25th Birthday* banner was pinned on the back wall in reception. Underneath a trestle table laden with a cold buffet of sandwiches, mushroom tartlets, a large asparagus tart, mixed salads and various dips, were neatly presented on a white cloth, along with ten glasses of sparkling wine served in champagne flutes.

The staff congregated around the food, loading up their plates, and each taking a glass. I helped myself to a cheese and cucumber sandwich on brown, a slice of the asparagus tart, a spoonful of mixed salad and a couple of teaspoonfuls of dip. This was so kind of Annabel to organise this, although I was a tad embarrassed being the centre of attention.

Annabel clapped her hands. The room went silent. 'Make sure you each have a glass,' she said, 'and let's toast Zara on reaching a quarter of a century. And don't worry, the wine is non-alcoholic so you'll be able to continue working this afternoon.' She chuckled and everyone joined in. 'Happy birthday, Zara.' Annabel raised her glass.

'Happy birthday,' my colleagues said in unison, raising their glasses and each taking a sip.

'Thank you, everyone, but a particular thank you to Annabel for arranging' – I waved my hand – 'all of this.'

'You're welcome.' She smiled. 'Make sure you do something nice to celebrate. Now everyone, eat up, as it's back to work' – she lifted a wrist to check her watch – 'at one o'clock. We have a deadline to meet.'

My colleagues headed back to the table and refilled their plates. Scott came up to me. 'Happy birthday.' He kissed me on the side of my face.

'Thanks.'

His eyes twinkled. 'Can I have a word?'

'Er yes, let's sit down?' I made my way to the comfy seating in the corner. 'Here okay?'

'This is fine.' He sat close to me. 'How are you really doing, Zara?'

'Good, thanks. No signs of delusion, I promise.' I chuckled.

'That's good to hear.' Scott took my hand. 'Look, I wanted to let you know that I've started seeing someone.'

'Really.' I rested my fingers on his hand. 'I'm pleased for you.'

'Ta. It's Charlie's mate, so she's a bit younger than me. Thankfully she doesn't have the same mouth on her as my cousin.'

'I'm happy for you, Scott.' Part of me felt a sadness at what we'd shared and was now gone but I knew I'd made the right decision. Even though I'd never get back to Richard, Scott and I were never meant to go the long road. 'Was it really your idea to stop mentoring me?'

'Yes. I think you're ready. Are you still seeing that guy that Charlie saw you with?'

'Yes, but like I told you weeks ago, we're just friends. I'm not looking for a relationship with anyone right now. Instead, I'm concentrating on staying well and working on becoming a great writer.'

I unwrapped the rose quartz crystal tree from Holly and Adam. 'Wow, this is lovely. Thanks. You will thank Adam for me, won't you?'

'Of course. It's a shame we're not spending this evening with you.'

'Sorry, I'd already agreed to spend it with Jack, but perhaps we can do something tomorrow evening? I'll keep it free.'

'Sure. I miss you though, Zara. We used to be so close but now you always seem to be with your new best friend.'

'Katie gets me. It doesn't mean that I don't still love you. You'll always be my best friend.' I took Holly into a hug.

She sniffled. 'Doesn't feel that way but anyway, it's your special birthday so I'm not going to spoil things. The crystals are healing but also help with creativity so they might help you with your new story.' She checked her watch. 'I'd better get on as Adam will be here any minute. What time's Jack picking you up?'

'He's not. I'm meeting him at that new Italian in town.'

She grinned. 'A romantic meal for two?'

I laughed. 'You never give up, do you? No, Katie and Billy are joining us. Jack and Billy's mum and dad are looking after the girls. Katie didn't want to ask her mum as she's a piece of work. She doesn't like me at all and keeps telling Katie not to have anything to do with me. Katie says it's jealousy because the twins are always talking about me.'

'She sounds nasty.'

A car tooted outside.

'Right' – she kissed me on the cheek – 'that sounds like Adam, and you'd better get in that shower. I'll see you in the morning as I'm staying over at Adam's. Have a lovely time.'

※

After a quick shower I stepped into my new dress and gazed into the mirror. It was attractive without showing off too much. That Charlie had made me self conscious about what I wore. This was a high necked navy lace so not too revealing but at the same time sexy. I traced my fingertip across my lips. It had been a long time since I'd had a proper kiss. No wonder I couldn't come up with inspiration. How did I expect to write romance when I hadn't had any intimacy for months now.

Hmm, maybe if tonight had the right vibes I'd invite Jack back for coffee and maybe have a bit of a kiss and cuddle. It didn't have to mean anything. After all, he didn't want anything serious either so I wouldn't be using him as he had no inclinations that way, unlike Scott had. Yes, I'd see how I felt at the end of the evening.

I slipped into a pair of black cross-strap sandals, and headed out of the front door, down the path, and along the road into Bridge View village. The sun was still warm with a gorgeous blue sky.

※

The Italian restaurant was quaint with high wicker chairs, pictures on the walls, white cloths, and candles on the table. I spotted Katie waving at the back of the restaurant and made my way to join her, Billy and Jack.

'Happy birthday,' they said in unison. Katie stood up and hugged me and Jack followed.

'Wow.' He kissed me on the cheek. 'You look hot, and I mean that in a sexy way. Here' – he pulled out a chair – 'sit next to me.'

'Thanks.' The vibes were good. 'It's nice in here. Kind of feel like I'm stepping back into the seventies or something.'

'Yeah, it does have that feel,' Billy said. 'Mum and Dad came last week. They recommended it.'

I picked up the menu. 'What's everyone else having?'

Jack pointed on the card. 'I rather fancy the baked cranberry Camembert for starters.'

'Yes, that looks good. I think I'll have that too. What about you two?' I asked.

Katie and Billy agreed to have the same and we all chose vegetable pasta, with a mixed salad, green olives, and garlic bread to share for the main course. The waiter took down our order along with a jug of water, a bottle of Prosecco and a couple of beers for the boys.

'It's been a scorcher today.' Katie blew her nose. 'I took the girls to the park. I hope I'm not getting a cold.'

'Most likely hay fever,' I said. 'Mine's been bad.'

'You're probably right. Ella was coughing today too.'

Our small talk was interrupted by the waiter bringing the drinks. He poured sparkling wine into glasses for Katie and me, leaving the remainder in an ice bucket, and settled the beers in front of the men.

Jack raised his glass. 'Happy birthday, Zara.'

The others joined in.

'Thanks.' I took a sip and the bubbles went up my nose.

In no time at all we had plates of delicious hot food in front of us. As the evening progressed we chatted about the girls, Jack and Billy's jobs, while Katie and I managed to polish off the

Prosecco and order another bottle. During the conversation I smiled at Jack. Tonight I'd put my imaginary husband Richard out of my mind and clear out Scott too. I slipped my hand under the table and ran my fingers across Jack's thigh. His eyes twinkled. I sensed he was feeling the chemistry too.

Katie broke my X-rated thoughts. 'How's work going?'

'All right. Annabel wants me to start a new serial.'

'That's good, isn't it?'

'Hmm, not sure. I need to come up with an idea by the end of next week. She says the readers want romance.'

Jack winked at me. 'I'm sure you'll come up with something.'

My head spun a little and I wasn't sure whether it was from the Prosecco or the strong attraction to a fit bloke. Jack had walked me home. I put my arms around his neck and kissed him. He responded. 'Want to come in for coffee?' I asked.

'You sure?'

'Yeah, thought you could help with my research.' I brushed a fingertip across his lips.

He rested his hand on mine. 'You sure? I don't want to take advantage of you when you've had a fair amount to drink.'

'I trust you.' I turned the key in the lock and pushed open the door. 'Welcome to my abode.'

He strode in and peered around. 'Looks like a nice gaff.'

'Thanks.' I kissed him again, only harder this time.

'Let's get that coffee,' he said. 'Which way to the kitchen?'

'That way.' I pointed straight ahead.

I followed him into the kitchen and slid my arms around his waist.

He checked the water level on the kettle before flicking the switch. 'Mugs?'

'Up there.' I giggled.

He took a mug from the cupboard.

I kissed the back of his neck.

After adding a spoonful of Gold Blend from the canister marked *coffee* he turned towards me. 'You've no idea how hard you're making this for me, sweetie.'

I kissed him hard on the lips.

'No, Zara.' He backed away from me. 'Not like this.' He poured boiling water into the mug. 'Drink.'

'Thanks.' I fluttered my eyelashes.

'Zara, you've had too much to drink and you don't know what you're doing. Therefore, I'm going to go, because I can't trust myself to keep saying *no*.' He gave me a peck on the side of my face. 'You'll thank me in the morning.'

The following morning I headed off to the station, this time not to try to get back to Bridge View Hall but I felt an urgent need to see Chloe. After purchasing my ticket I made for platform 2 and within no time at all the train snaked in.

The carriage was quiet with only two other passengers there, giving me time with my thoughts about last night. I'd been wanton. How was I ever going to face Jack again? Thank goodness he'd been gentleman enough not to take advantage of me.

Where did I start for that serial though? I sighed. Annabel wanted romance, not sex. I had no idea where to begin. Perhaps Monday morning I'd go up to the attic and sift through those old newspapers. Annabel seemed confident that I'd find a gem.

The train pulled into Sandypoint. That was my stop. I stepped out of the carriage. Supposing Chloe was out. I hadn't thought to give her a ring. Oh well, if she was I'd just spend the time on the beach. It was another scorcher. The weatherman reckoned the next week would bring a heatwave. The wide brim cap and sunglasses should help prevent me getting sunstroke.

The sea was the most perfect aquamarine. I could almost imagine I was at the Seychelles rather than this little sea resort in Sussex. Seagulls squawked as they swooped down on the sand and rocks. I checked my watch. It was gone two. They should've had their lunch by now. I headed up the footpath and was greeted by wonderful shades of purple, reds, and pinks in the front garden from the geraniums, peonies and poppies. Chloe must've inherited Dad's green fingers, unless Matt was the gardener.

I rang the bell and waited. I rang the bell again. Footsteps padded closer. Matt opened the door in blue mules. His eyes widened. 'Zara, were we expecting you?'

'Nope. Sorry to just turn up but I had this urge to see Chloe.'

'Is everything okay? Your mum, Dad?'

I smiled. 'Everything's fine. It was an impulse thing. Is she in?'

'Who is it, Matt?' Chloe called from inside.

'It's your sister.'

Chloe hurried to the hallway as I stepped inside. 'Zara, what's up?'

'Nothing.' I hugged her. 'Just woke up needing to see you. How's Amelia?'

'She's sleeping.'

'Any chance of a stroll on the beach?'

Chloe turned to Matt. 'Is it okay if I pop out for an hour?'

'Of course. Take as long as you like.'

'Thanks, darling.' She kissed him on the lips. 'Won't be too long.' She slipped on a pair of flip flops, opened the door, and I followed her out.

'Your garden's pretty.'

'Matt's work. Look, Zara, I love seeing you but this isn't like you. You never just turn up. What's wrong?'

'Nothing.' I hooked my arm in hers as we strolled down to the front.

'It's not happening again, is it?'

'What?'

'You thinking that you're time travelling.'

'No, not at all. The opposite in fact. I now know that it was all in my imagination.'

'You've said that before.'

'This time I mean it. I tried to seduce Jack last night.'

'What?'

'I know. I'd had far too much to drink and I wasn't myself.'

'Are you and him an item now?'

I threw a pebble into the waves. 'Nope.'

'But you tried to sleep with him?'

'Yeah, I did. I behaved like a hussy.'

'So you're sleeping around now. That's hardly normal now, is it?'

'I'm not sleeping around. For goodness sake I'm twenty-five years old and Scott's the only guy I've slept with. How does that make me someone who sleeps around?'

'But you're not an item and you tried to.' She nudged me. 'Supposing he'd taken you up on it.'

'I know. I was lucky. I'll make sure it doesn't happen again.'

'Make sure it doesn't.' She shook her head. 'You should be thinking of settling down and having kids before you get too old.' Smiling, she held her stomach. 'We're expecting again but it's early days so keep it to yourself. No one else knows yet.'

Another child and she wasn't even twenty. 'That's wonderful news for you,' I lied, 'but I'm not in a rush to have babies. Guess what though?'

'What?'

'I'm officially part of the writers' team at work and Annabel has asked me to write a new serial.'

'That's great news, but no delusions, please.'

'No delusions, I promise. I've no idea what I'll write, or even if I'm up to the job, but...'

'What?'

'I'm sure something will come to me.'

Scott tapped away on the keyboard while I peered into space hoping something would springboard a new story. Why did I ever agree to this? If Bridge View Hall had been my imagination then why wasn't a new idea forming? Was I thinking too hard?

Scott looked up from his PC. 'You okay there, Zara? Only you've been sitting there staring into that screen for the last half hour and not written a word.'

I sighed. 'To be honest, I've no idea where to start. Annabel's put me under too much pressure giving me such a short deadline. I'm not up to this.'

He got up from his chair, came around to mine and put an arm around my shoulder. 'Hey, you're absolutely up to this.'

'I'm not. Perhaps I should go back to editing.'

'No. You're ready for this. A challenge is what makes this extra fun. Look, would it help if I brainstormed with you for a bit?'

'Maybe.'

'Or...'

'What?'

'Remember Annabel mentioned those archived newspapers in the attic?'

'Yeah.'

'Why not pop up there now and have a look through? See if anything bounces back from them? And then if you still need to brainstorm we'll at least have something to work on.'

'That's a good idea.' I'd never been in the attic. 'I'll go now.'

'You'll need to get the key from Annabel first as she keeps it locked. It's not something she offers to everyone. I've not even been in there.'

My muse kicked into action. A locked attic with hidden secrets. 'Thanks, Scott.' I got up from my desk and headed straight to Annabel's office, knocked on the door and entered. 'Morning.'

'Zara, come in.' The rose and white twirl skirt rested just below her knees when she crossed her legs. 'What can I do for you? Sit down.'

'It's okay. I've just come to collect the key for the attic.'

'Good girl.' She opened the top drawer of her desk. 'Guard it with your life. Apart from myself, only one other person has ever been up there since my grandfather died.'

I shivered. 'Is it haunted?'

'You'll have to decide that for yourself. Imagine it's a secret chamber. Have fun and let your imagination run free.' She passed me a brass key on a small silver chain.

'Thanks.' I headed out of her office and along the corridor until I reached an old wooden door. I pushed it open, flicked the light switch on the right, and trekked up the narrow, steep stairway with my pulse pounding. What was I going to find up there? On reaching the platform at the top there was another entrance. This one arched. I inserted the key into the lock and turned. A flutter echoed throughout but when I pushed the door open the room was still. I hovered around. Boxes of old newspapers were piled high. I brushed my fingers across an antique typewriter's keys, stroked the glass of a cheval mirror. The area had an eerie sensation but I couldn't work out what it was from. My heartbeat was going wild. 'Stop it,' I told myself. I was letting my imagination run riot, but then wasn't that what I wanted?

I bent over one of the boxes. A waft of scents reached my nose. Almond? Vanilla? Floral? Rather like the smell of an old book. I pulled out a wad of newspapers and filtered through the batch. What was this? *Bridge View Chronicle* 3rd July 1925 with HELP ME as a headline. That was today except just under a hundred years ago.

The newspaper rustled and a flash appeared before my eyes. I peered up in front at the cheval mirror. Had it become a doorway? I took a step towards it. Where did it lead? To the past like my last adventure? Or even to the future? I stared into the glass but the blinding light prevented me from seeing where it led.

My friend, Katie, had been right. My timeslips to Bridge View Hall had been real.

I looked at the headline again. It glared back at me. The newspaper was sending me a message. Someone needed my help. How could I ignore this plea? But was I brave enough to enter? What of my health? Would I end up in a coma again? What of my parents and my sister, Chloe? Supposing I didn't come back. But I'd always returned when I transported back to 1910 and became Lady Rebecca.

Somehow I'd deal with the after-effects. I dropped the newspaper to the floor, stood up straight, and made my way to the flashing portal. Putting my trust in fate, I stepped forward ready for my next mission, wondering whose life I'd step into.

Acknowledgements

Special thanks to my friend Maureen Cullen. Not only for her perceptive and thoughtful editing of *The Girl in the Ticket Office Window* but for her continuous support, encouragement and faith in me.

A big thank you to my fabulous beta readers for their invaluable feedback, and to Andy Keylock for the cover design.

Finally, a big thank you to my husband, children, family and friends for their continued support and faith in me.

About the author

Patricia M Osborne was born in Liverpool but now lives in West Sussex. She is married with grown-up children and grandchildren. In 2019 she graduated with an MA in Creative Writing. She is a published novelist, poet and short fiction writer. Her debut poetry pamphlet, *Taxus Baccata,* was nominated for the Michael Marks Pamphlet Award.

Patricia has a successful blog at Whitewingsbooks.com featuring other writers. When Patricia isn't working on her own writing, she enjoys sharing her knowledge, acting as a mentor to fellow writers.

You can find out more about Patricia by visiting her website, whitewingsbooks.com.

Also by Patricia M Osborne

House of Grace Family Saga Trilogy:

House of Grace (Book 1)

The Coal Miner's Son (Book 2)

The Granville Legacy (Book 3)

The Oath (A Victorian era saga)

The Woodhaerst Family Drama Trilogy:

The Woodhaerst Triangle (Book 1)

The Woodhaerst Reunion (Book 2)

The Woodhaerst Women (Book 3)

Poetry Pamphlets Published by The Hedgehog Poetry Press

The Montefiore Bride

Taxus Baccata

Sherry & Sparkly

Symbiosis

Spirit Mother: Experience the Myth

Stickleback

Nature's Bookends

The Treepoets: A Life of Sand

www.ingramcontent.com/pod-product-compliance
Lightning Source LLC
Chambersburg PA
CBHW020356080526
44584CB00014B/1042